IRAQ AND THE SECOND GULF WAR

State Building and Regime Security

Mohammad-Mahmoud Mohamedou

IRAQ AND THE SECOND GULF WAR

State Building and Regime Security

Mohammad-Mahmoud Mohamedou

Austin & Winfield, Publishers
San Francisco - London - Bethesda
1998

Library of Congress Cataloging-in-Publication Data

Mohamedou, Mohammad-Mahmoud
   Iraq and the second Gulf War : state building and regime security
   / Mohammad-Mahmoud Mohamedou.
      p. cm.
   Includes bibliographical references and index.
   ISBN 1-57292-097-1 (hc : alk. paper). -- ISBN 1-57292-096-3 (pbk.
   : alk. paper)
   1. Iraq—Foreign relations—Kuwait. 2. Kuwait—Foreign relations-
   -Iraq. 3. Persian Gulf War, 1991. I. Title.
   JZ1682.A57K9   1997
   327.56705367—dc21   97-33151
                                                                CIP

Editorial Inquiries:
Austin & Winfield, Publishers
7831 Woodmont Avenue, #345
Bethesda, MD 20814
(301) 654-7335

To Order: (800) 99-AUSTIN

To My Father,
State-Builder and Master Diplomat

La résolution finale d'une équation aussi complexe qu'une guerre n'est jamais dans l'évidence de la guerre. Il s'agit d'en saisir, sans illusion prophétique, la logique de déroulement.

— Jean Baudrillard, *La Guerre du Golfe n'a pas eu Lieu*.

CONTENTS

TABLES AND FIGURES

ABBREVIATIONS

ACC	Arab Cooperation Council
CIA	Central Intelligence Agency (US)
CNN	Cable News Network
DIA	Defense Intelligence Agency (US)
EC	European Community
FGW	First Gulf War
GCC	Gulf Cooperation Council
IAEA	International Atomic Energy Agency
ICP	Iraqi Communist Party
IFF	Identification Friend-or-Foe
IKF	Iraqi Kurdistan Front
IMF	International Monetary Fund
IP	Independence Party
IPC	Iraqi Petroleum Company
KDP	Kurdish Democratic Party
KTO	Kuwaiti Theatre of Operations
MIMI	Ministry of Industry and Military Industrialization (Iraq)
NBC	Nuclear Biological Chemical
NCRC	National Council of Revolutionary Command
NDP	National Democratic Party
NPF	National Progressive Front
OAPEC	Organization of Arab Petroleum Exporting Countries

OPEC	Organization of Petroleum Exporting Countries
PLO	Palestine Liberation Organization
PNF	Progressive National Front
PUK	Patriotic Union of Kurdistan
RCC	Revolutionary Command Council
SCFO	Supreme Committee of the Free Officers
SGW	Second Gulf War
UAE	United Arab Emirates
UAR	United Arab Republic
UMA	*Union du Maghreb Arabe* (Arab Maghreb Union)
UN	United Nations
UNIKOM	United Nations Iraq Kuwait Observation Mission
UNSCOM	United Nations Special Commission
US	United States of America
WMD	Weapons of Mass Destruction

GLOSSARY

'asabiya	group consciousness / tribal solidarity
al-turath	historical heritage
dawla	state
ghalaba	domination
iltiham	coalescence
majliss	assembly
mukhabarat	intelligence services
thawra	revolution
qa'immaqam	governor
qawmiya	nationalism
qiyada	leadership
vilayet	district
wataniya	patriotism

Foreword

As the lengthy Cold War competition between the United States and the Soviet Union came to an end, United States President George Bush proclaimed "a new world order" while leading a broad coalition against Iraq compelling that country to withdraw from Kuwait, which it had invaded on August 2, 1990. In the course of the confrontation, Bush demonized Saddam Hussayn, Iraq's leader, conferring on the episode a personalized interpretation of Iraq's behavior that has affected most accounts of the invasion and its aftermath. Moreover, in writing about the phenomena, analysts discuss most of Iraq's actions in 1990-1991 and subsequent years almost entirely from the viewpoint of western countries. Inasmuch as a number of actions by Iraq appear merely defiant or perplexing, this dominant view remains inadequate, for it presents commonplace anomalies or conjectures about Iraq's behavior without any search for deeper explanation.

If one shifts his viewpoint from the West to Iraq itself and inquires into the national interests at stake, a very different perspective appears. Instead of regarding the Iraqi leadership as either madmen or gross miscalculators, one holds out the possibility that rational judgment may have guided decision making during the incidents in 1990-1991, while still acknowledging that mistakes were made. Whereas a victorious coalition perspective tends to treat the events as relatively isolated and short-term, an approach that focuses on Iraq's position and behavior may offer a long-term view that connects with regional history, national experience, economic circumstances, and dissatisfaction with territorial arrangements that emerged from the colonial period. Rather than imposing rigid categories on messy facts, one may seek to discover a complex reality. It requires only brief reflection to perceive the need for an analysis of Iraq's requirements and interests in the war between Iraq and the United States-led coalition that reversed the former's military takeover of Kuwait. The coalition's domination does not provide an excuse for a failure to understand how Iraq came to its critical decisions to invade Kuwait and then resolutely to resist the overwhelming military force brought to bear against it.

The scholarly and policy-making communities are fortunate that Dr. Mohammad-Mahmoud Mohamedou has addressed this need in a particularly effective way in his study of Iraqi foreign policy during the Gulf War. He shows how Iraq's national interests were expressed through its state-building activities that had been continuous since 1921, across four ruling regimes. Dr. Mohamedou clearly explains the critical decisions in 1990 and early 1991 in terms of the needs of the state and the regime in the circumstances of domestic politics in Iraq as well as in the context of the international political system.

Not only does this study narrate the unfolding of circumstances but also it provides a rich conceptual framework for understanding Iraq's actions. Dr. Mohamedou brings together three analytical literatures to give theoretical foundation to the insights that he draws from his investigation of Iraqi foreign policy. First, he draws on the tradition of foreign policy decision making to identify the critical choice points for Iraq and to analyze the processes by which options were selected. Second, the study employs state formation literature, especially that part which handles the process by which states are built over time and explains how these political units – specifically, in this case, Iraq – exist in a condition of becoming. Finally, Dr. Mohamedou writes in the historical tradition of Ibn Khaldun, the great fourteenth century North African scholar who sought to find patterns and causes in history. Like Ibn Khaldun, Mohamedou discusses a concrete state in rich detail, examines the identity of the state and its regime, and appreciates the cyclical processes of building and decay that occur in state formation. As the reader will see, this three-legged intellectual apparatus affords rich insight into the topic at hand. And, unlike much academic writing, this study has an engrossing quality that allows the reader to move easily through the material.

To explore the Iraqi understanding of its aims and actions regarding the takeover of Kuwait, Dr. Mohamedou consulted the available, official documentation, and he interviewed government officials both in New York and Baghdad. From both the secretive nature of the regime and the circumstances of ongoing conflict, it is clear that these sources remain quite limited. Still, the resourcefulness that sought and gathered the materials has paid off with additional insight and sense of reality that could hardly have been gained by any other means.

The resulting study, *Iraq and the Second Gulf War - State and Regime in History*, offers a very high quality analysis. This significant treatment of a poorly understood case adds importantly to the literature of foreign policy analysis and to the interpretation of a critical episode in history. Its review of the theoretical literature, too, provides a very useful addition to scholarly thought about the *problematique* of foreign policy analysis.

The reader gains from Dr. Mohamedou's highly intelligent, exceptionally industrious, persevering, and imaginative approach to his research. One who peruses this work also benefits from the extraordinary range of a young scholar who has standing in three intellectual communities, English, French, and Arabic.

—Howard H. Lentner
Graduate School of the City University of New York
June 1997

Preface

Iraq and the Second Gulf War provides policy-makers, social scientists, and students with a different perspective on the Gulf conflict. The purpose of this study is to reevaluate the foreign policy-making process of the Iraqi leadership during the events of 1990 and 1991. The logic of the argument presented here is that this process is not as one-dimensional and misguided as it has often been regarded.

The academic discourse on the Second Gulf War (a conflict that has alternatively been known as "Gulf War," "Iraq War," "Gulf Conflict," "Persian Gulf War," and "Iraq-Kuwait Crisis") has been incomplete from the very beginning. The media's ultra-sensationalist and erroneous reporting has colored knowledge about this event. Instant literature on the topic has equally undermined production of serious works. Uncertainty and ambiguity still prevail as regards what actually transpired in the Gulf in 1990 and 1991. Every year brings its share of revelations, some major some trivial. This state of affairs has two main consequences. First, acceptance of the "official story" is difficult. Studies based on the major premises of the account as it is provided by the actors themselves are necessarily incomplete. Indeed, besides military reports and officials memoirs, little in the way of evidence is available to the researcher to build on. Second, any alternative interpretation, such as the one I endeavor to offer here, is limited by the conspicuous absence of actual undisputed evidence. Oftentimes, it proceeds on intuitive analysis. A misstep to be certain. Furthermore, the lack of an unquestioned body of facts, renders any theoretical construct dependent on an accompanying investigative task that distracts from the theory *per se*.

We all have "memories" of the Gulf War when we ought to command knowledge about it. Published estimates of Iraqi deaths range from 1,500 to 500,000. One analyst argues that George Bush opted for an all-out war on January 18, 1991, and an official writes that the American President did so on August 9, 1990. In the face of these and many other contradictory versions, how are we to adequately understand the events? As time passes, it becomes harder and harder to establish what exactly happened at Ras al-Khafji? What do we really know about the clashes between US forces and the Republican Guard, not those engagements with the hapless, mostly aging conscripts left in the dark about their leadership's decisions? Questions abound. Did Iraq lose the war? Why didn't the Iraqis withdraw before the deadline? Why didn't they use all their weapons? Why did they free the hostages? There is a sense of frustration as regards information about this war. We want to know and we want to understand. One might then ask Which way should the political scientist turn his attention in the face of such widely diverging uses of information? Clearly, there are no simple answers, and the 1990-1991 Second Gulf War remains a mystery.

What is more, many an observer remain puzzled by the aftermath of the conflict for it further emerged that there was nothing secure in the partial victory over Iraq. A cursory glance at the title of some works attests to this uncertainty: *Desert Mirage, Illusions of Triumph, Triumph Without Victory, The Gulf War Did Not Happen, Hollow Victory, Adventures in the Politics of Illusion,* and so on. For all practical purposes, several accounts have been proven wrong in record time. Witness the demise of the Patriot missile myth. It is no small paradox that the first conflict to be globally televised live is also the one about which there have been so many disputes about what took place.

Surprisingly, the profusion of logics on the part of the actors is counterbalanced by unanimity on the part of the analysts. To be certain, the illusion of a perfectly conducted US operation is the effect of a neutralization of questioning. Most scholars have not been able to depart from the popular view of

Saddam-the-brutal-dictator-invading-its-democratic-neighbor-before-being-kicked-out-by-the-US-after-taking-stupid-decisions. At best, this is a shorthand for complex phenomena. At worst, it is a loaded proposition. Still, all three schools on the war – political psychology studies, military reports, and diplomatic accounts – provide elements of analysis that, one way or another, have this notion as sheet-anchor. More generally, a regurgitation of US and Iraqi propaganda by the expert academic is a poor substitute for appropriate scholarly analysis of an important international crisis. Nevertheless, focusing on diplomatic issues and beginning with the invasion of Kuwait, there has been a manifest trend towards isolating the events of 1990 and 1991 from their historical context. It is, however, relatively difficult to substantiate in empirical terms that the behavior of the Iraqi leadership was not affected by long-standing historical dynamics and their evolution over time. To dramatize the extent and the *ad hoc* nature of the invasion is to ignore a welter of reports as to the persistent aspect of the Kuwaiti matter.

Having already received the imprimatur of media reports, a tale is therefore being codified through scholarship. Marked by heavy emphasis on the military aspect, knowledge about the Second Gulf War continues to be marred with non-specific and random uses of sketchy historical references. The commentaries of military analysts and orientalists have largely dominated the study of this conflict. They are indeed becoming the yardstick for accounting for the 1990-1991 events. As a result, the Second Gulf War has not received much attention in international relations and foreign policy analysis. By virtue of being the first conflict of the post-Cold War period – indeed the first war of the "End of History," a "Clash of Civilizations" involving "Pivotal States" – the Gulf conflict (an all-out inter-state war between the United States and a country with NBC and WMD capabilities) demands a theory. The uniqueness of the Second Gulf War has not yet been fully addressed.

In reaction, this book tries to explain. To be sure, we will have to await further investigation to substantiate the real character of this conflict. In the meantime, this work in all its modesty constitutes an attempt at understanding the Iraqi side. It also tries to cast a new analytical light on the process of foreign policy formulation by offering a state-centric framework. My intention is to demonstrate that the Iraqi regime did not act erratically during the Second Gulf War. The Ba'thists' decision-making process was historically-determined, dynamic and, contrary to the commonly-held view, flexible. That being as it may, both its domestic requirements and its external articulation were limited in terms of what was actually feasible. Here and there, there were actions that this regime could not and would not take.

Most of this book was written between November 1994 and November 1995. It emanates from a doctoral dissertation that I embarked upon in July of 1994 and which was defended in November of 1995 before the political science department of the City University of New York Graduate School. I wish to extend my gratitude to Dr. Howard Henry Lentner – with whom I began the entire endeavor – for the ongoing support of my work. His interest and support were instrumental in bringing this project to fruition. The excellent comments and suggestions of Dr. Wentworth Ofuatey-Kodjoe, Dr. Jacqueline Braveboy-Wagner, Dr. Kenneth Erickson, and Dr. Evand Abrahamian on the original draft helped enormously, as did the meticulous reading of my dear friend John Kenney.

I am grateful to Dr. Robert West, my editor at Austin & Winfield, for providing me with the opportunity to publish this analysis in its full form and for deciding to bring the work out as quickly as possible. Insights and difficult-to-come-by documentation were offered by several officials who will remain unnamed. I would like to thank them as well. I have benefited greatly from the perceptive advice of several international colleagues, in particular Dr. Sa'doun Jabbar al-Zubaydi in Baghdad; Ambassador 'Abdullah Salah, Dr. Musa Buraizat, and Dr. Mustapha Hamarneh in Amman; Faleh 'Abd al-Jabbar in London; Anthony Pazzanita in Cambridge; Nubar Hovsepian, Tom Kono, and Dr. Sa'id Hasan in New York.

Additional research for the revised draft was conducted in the winter and spring of 1997 while I was a Visiting Scholar at the Center for Middle Eastern Studies of Harvard University. I express my gratitude for administrative support to CMES Director Dr. Roger Owen and to Susan Miller. At the Ralph Bunche Institute on the United Nations in New York, I wish to extend a sincere thanks to the Director, Dr. Benjamin Rivlin, who has been especially supportive, and to Associate Director Nancy T. Okada for her cooperation and assistance. Finally, it is to the members of my family – who unfailingly demonstrated confidence and enthusiasm in my projects – that I owe the greatest thanks.

I expect that many will disagree with my interpretation of the Gulf war. Needless to say, the responsibility of what follows is mine alone.

—*Mohammad-Mahmoud Ould Mohamedou*

Introduction

This book seeks to address the issues of state-building and regime security as key variables affecting and determining a foreign policy-making process during an international crisis and a confrontation. I proceed from the notion that decisionmakers' dispositions matter – worldview, ideology, beliefs, and axioms – as does their societal, regional, and international historical operational environment. The case this study is concerned with is the Second Gulf War (SGW), which was initiated on August 2, 1990, with the Iraqi invasion of Kuwait, and which came to an end on February 28, 1991, after a 44-day military confrontation between Iraq and an international coalition of twenty-eight countries led by the United States of America.[1]

The design is (i) to explain the Iraqi decisions during the Second Gulf War and (ii) to assess the quality of the foreign policy-making process in and of itself. Within a historical perspective, the analysis is grounded in the axiom that state-building structures constrain the choices made by a political regime in the enactment of its foreign policy.

The object of the study is to demonstrate how, in the aftermath of its conflict with Iran, the specific mind-set, goals, calculations, and behavior of the Iraqi Ba'thi regime – as exemplified by its principal decision-taking organ, *Majliss Qiyadat al-Thawra*, the Revolutionary Command Council (RCC) – worked in conjunction with a preexisting and continuing process of building of the Iraqi state. That conjunction, I propose, is best suited to account for the immediate and remote causes of the August 2, 1990, decision to invade Kuwait and the subsequent related Iraqi moves. Hence, the discussion focuses on four defining decisions taken by the Iraqi government in 1990 and 1991:

(i) the decision to invade Kuwait on August 2, 1990;

(ii) the decision to internationalize the conflict starting August 12, 1990;

(iii) the decision to reject the January 15, 1991, deadline to withdraw from Kuwait that was set by the United States-led United Nations coalition; and

(iv) the decision not to abide by the February 23, 1991, ultimatum to remove its troops from Kuwait within the following 25 hours.

By ascertaining the configurations of these decisions and by fitting the pieces of the puzzle into a synthesis that accommodates internal and external dynamics, I attempt to identify the Iraqi leadership's foreign policy process and its relationship to its society. The understanding to be gained from this examination connects with the larger Iraqi polity, enabling us to see the decisionmaking process of the Ba'thi leadership during the SGW not as an isolated unit – i.e., an *ad hoc* episode of territorial expansion – but as a set of interrelated dynamics reflecting the social, cultural, historical, political, and strategic realities of a continuing state-building process in which the particular requirements of the regime's broad security needs were embedded. As such, the Iraqi leadership's foreign policy making during the Second Gulf War was a historically conditioned and domestically oriented aborted attempt at redistribution of power in the international system.

The argument presented here, as it relates to this concept of state-building, is that the designs over the integration of Kuwait into Iraq were a prime example of a concern continuously shared, but differently dealt with, by the four regimes that have come into existence in Iraq: the Hashemite monarchy (1921-1958), the militaro-Communist republic of 'Abdelkarim Qassem (1958-1963), the nationalistic period of the 'Aref brothers (1963-1968), and the Ba'thi regime (1968-present). This particular

2

Iraqi concern over Kuwait – the object of our study as it was revived in 1990 – is articulated in tandem with domestic, regional, and international state-building issues.

Domestically, all four Iraqi regimes have historically sought to build a strong state. This effort was essentially meant as a necessary response to the multidimensional polarization of Iraqi society. Religiously, the country is divided between Sunna and Shi'a. Ethnically, there is an opposition between an Arab majority and a Kurdish minority. And geographically, the north is Kurd-dominated; the central part is the hub of Arab Sunnis; and the southern region is inhabited by Arab Shiites. These multi-layered divisions have historically created the conditions for the need for the emergence of a strong state whose immediate and continuous task was primarily the building of social cohesion.

Similarly, historically, the Iraqi state has had to struggle continuously to survive within the regional polities of the Middle East. The arrival of a Hashemite monarch from the Hejaz (Arabia) in 1921, Faysal ibn Hussayn, combined with the emerging local nationalistic class of former Ottoman officers, created a formula of instability springing from the tension between two sources of power: one traditional, religious, and civilian; the other revolutionary, secular, and military. The kinship ties between Faysal and his brother 'Abdallah in Transjordan, on the one hand, and indigenous demands of the Mesopotamians, on the other, created further power-sharing struggles which also led to the need for developing a strong central state. That necessity was, in addition, reinforced by the legacy of a rigid Ottoman administration.

The establishment of a strong state as a requirement of the nation's perennation became ever more pronounced with the subsequent praetorian and nationalistic regimes that existed between 1958 and 1968. Thus, there developed a tradition of need of strong state-building (underscored by a highly salient political role for the military), which the Ba'thi regime came to inherit when it took power in 1968.

Regionally, the process was similar, as tensions have existed with each of Iraq's neighboring countries. In the north, Turkey has since the 1918 Mudros armistice regarded some of Iraqi Kurdistan as having historical ties to it. In the East, Iraq has

3

been formally challenged by Iran over the Shatt-al-'Arab territory since the mid-1930s. The legal dispute eventually led to the 1980-1988 First Gulf War (FGW) between the two countries. In the south, Iraq has never totally accepted the creation of a Kuwaiti state which it always considered as part of its territory. And in the West, a federation with the Kingdom of Jordan has periodically been discussed by the two countries, particularly in the mid-1950s and early 1970s.

This overall situation of uncertainty as to its borders also justified the formation of a strong Iraqi state as an internal counterbalance to external threats. In addition, (i) a decades-old dispute with Ba'thi Syria, (ii) a long contest with Egypt over Arab leadership (that was decisively at play during the 1990-1991 Second Gulf War), and, since 1948, (iii) a struggle with Israel as to which would be the most powerful state in the region (beyond the Palestinian issue) created an inherently conflictual environment that conditioned the strong nature of the Iraqi state in general and its most recent particular incarnation, the Ba'thi regime.

Method of Analysis

The project's hypotheses are three. First, the invasion of Kuwait was an attempt by the Iraqi leadership to incorporate Kuwait's territory and to enhance Iraq's regional standing. A state-building concern – the historical issue of Kuwait as Iraqi territory – was revived. Second, this pre-existing situation was dusted off and tied to the particular and immediate financial and material needs of the regime for Iraq's reconstruction in the wake of the 1980-1988 war with Iran. Finally, the attempt to annex Kuwait was prompted by the serious and pressing need to give a mission to the Iraqi army (which came to number one million men in 1990, one-third of whom were the highly professional eight Republican Guard divisions) and keep it away from urban centers, where it was poised, upon its return from the Iranian front, to engender socioeconomic problems of re-integration and political concerns about the regime's security. The theoretical background of the hypotheses is, then, the following:

(i) state-building and regime security influence foreign policy-making processes as far as perception, choices, strategies, and goals are concerned – the Iraqi leadership's foreign policy process during the SGW simultaneously resulted from the regime's attendance to its own security needs as well as those of the continuing Iraqi state;

(ii) the combined influence of state-building and regime security as a dual decisional set largely defined Iraqi behavior during the SGW – it constituted the primary consideration ensemble for the Ba'thi regime all along the conflict.

The independent variables are state-building and regime security. The dependent variable is the actual Iraqi decisionmaking process that was displayed during the crisis and subsequent conflict, as represented by the four defining decisions to (i) invade, (ii) internationalize the conflict, and reject the (iii) January 15 and (iv) February 23, 1991, ultimata. The unit of analysis is the Iraqi political leadership as embodied in President Saddam Hussayn and the Revolutionary Command Council.

Insofar as I start from the postulate that there is a causal relationship between Iraqi state-building, the Ba'thi regime's security, and the process underlying policy-making during the SGW – wherein policy-making is the consequence of the influence of immediate regime needs and remote state considerations – the sequence will consist of a twofold construction: (i) investigating and laying down the elements pertinent to the Iraqi state-building process (institution-building, maintenance of national consensus and domestic cohesion, and sovereignty) and the Ba'thi regime's particular post-First Gulf War security requirements (economic reconstruction, power consolidation, external and internal threat diffusion, as well as legitimacy renewal); (ii) identifying and appraising the impact of these elements during the Second Gulf War.

5

In addition to existing scholarly sources and public documents, I rely, in my analysis, on interviews of Iraqi officials I met in New York, Amman, and Baghdad between March 1992 and June 1997. In spite of my attempts to get specific responses and in spite of the candor of some answers, the unfinished nature of the events I set out to study as well as ongoing episodes of hostility between Iraq and the United Nations and the United States made it difficult to obtain definitive and explicit data. In this regard, it is important to note that as Jerrold Green pointed out:

> Special access to usually reticent political élites is accompanied by certain risks. To ask Iraqi leaders to evaluate their own performance or to explain their political motives or agendas is unlikely to be especially productive. Indeed, other than providing a cachet of authenticity that is an important part of policy research, interviews with Saddam Hussein and his colleagues do not accomplish very much; they reveal little that is not already known to scholars of the Middle East.[2]

The remark is a valid and accurate one. Two caveats are, nonetheless, in order. First, I have attempted to treat the information gathered from my visit to Iraq with the same scholarly standards that I applied to other research, subjecting it to political contextualization. Secondly, primary data – even if relayed by politicians – remain just that: primary data. Their value, or "authenticity," as Green writes, lie in their unmediated quality to the researcher. In this case, I met with high-ranking Iraqi officials at difficult and most sensitive junctures for both their regime and for the Iraqi state as a whole. Combining the information gathered from such research with historical material and current scholarship and applying it to the analysis of a conflict whose study has so far been overwhelmingly dominated by journalistic accounts, military memoranda, and diplomatic chronicles is what I set out to do here.

Bringing the data into the analysis determined by the state-building and regime security parameters essentially consists in three exercises. The first two are associated with the regime security dimension and consist in (i) the identification of the Iraqi security objectives during the SGW and (ii) the description of the interaction amongst these goals. The third exercise concerns state-building and consists in the unveiling of

6

the issues that have come to dominate Iraqi state-building in general and its aspects vis-à-vis the Kuwaiti question in particular.

Organization of the Study

Chapter One reviews the studies on foreign policy analysis. The so-called deadlock of foreign policy analysis is discussed, in particular with regard to the traditional neglect of the state as a foreign policy concern. Sections are devoted to the foreign policy of Arab states and studies about the Gulf conflict, noting a general descriptive and reductionist tendency with regard to the former, and the need for more focused works for the latter. Chapter Two outlines the proposed state-centered framework on the basis of a Hegelian reading of the concept of state and its role in foreign policy-making. The two principal concepts introduced, state-building and regime security, are defined and identified and the components of each determined. Chapter Three reviews the history of the Iraqi state. It chronicles the country's endemic instability, the different regimes' successive dealings with continuing sociopolitical problems besetting the Iraqi state and society, and the recurrence of the Kuwait question. Chapter Four is devoted to the articulation of the framework in conjunction with a case-study of the Iraqi leadership's decisionmaking process during the 1990-1991 crisis and conflict. Through a chronological review of the different actions engaged in (or not engaged in) by the Iraqi authorities, it is maintained that most of their decisions came under the general umbrella of both state-building and regime security, and that other actions were engendered primarily by regime security requirements. Overall, to explain the Second Gulf War, both causal constellations have to necessarily be analytically accommodated.

Chapter Five deals with the evaluation of the dimensions of the Iraqi foreign policy-making process during the SGW. I look at how the process stands with regard to (i) what it initially set out to accomplish and (ii) what it improvised during the seven months that the crisis and confrontation with the coalition lasted. I assess the failures

7

and successes for the state of Iraq and for the Ba'thi regime and consider the consequences, looking at the Iraqi polity (regime-society relationships) and, beyond, at the effects of the SGW on intra-Arab relations and regional conditions. Finally, Chapter Six summarizes the findings and tries to put the ensuing developments – in particular the UN inspections campaign, the January 1992, June 1993, October 1994, August 1995, and September 1996 renewed clashes and tensions, as well as the embargo question – in perspective, noting how they are defined by previous episodes and how, in turn, they illuminate them.

NOTES

[1] Insofar as the 1980-1988 conflict between Iraq and Iran was also known as the Gulf War, it is more appropriate and less confusing to refer to the Iraqi invasion of Kuwait and subsequent related developments as the Second Gulf War (SGW).

[2] Jerrold D. Green, "Are Arab Politics Still Arab?," *World Politics* 38, 4 (July 1986), p. 622.

1

Foreign Policy Analysis Literature Review

This chapter reviews theoretical contributions to foreign policy analysis. In examining the literature, I make the argument that the traditional focus on components, structures, and processes of decisionmaking has obscured the understanding of the role of the state in foreign policy-making. In addition, I look at the analyses which have been put forth about the foreign policies of Arab states in general, and that of Iraq in particular. In that respect, it is noted that descriptive and reductionist approaches have initially dominated, only to be replaced by perspectives overemphasizing the nature of the current Ba'thi regime and its leader, President Saddam Hussayn. In conclusion, I argue for a state-centered approach to foreign policy that would bring to light neglected phenomena such as the state's need to maintain position and perpetuate its existence in the international arena.

General Approaches

Significant theoretical advance in the field of foreign policy analysis was first made with the publication of a monograph in 1954 authored by Richard C. Snyder, H.W. Bruck, and Burton Sapin. Departing from the classic power school approach and the descriptive approach it engendered in foreign policy analysis, as best exemplified by Macridis (1958) and Black and Thompson (1963),[1] Snyder and his colleagues presented a systematic scheme for the study of foreign policy making. Their postulate was that an understanding of all states is to be founded on an understanding of any one state through the use of a scheme that could permit the analytical construction of properties of action that will be shared in common by all specific states. Against this fictional state background, the scheme revolves around the study of foreign policy as (i) a process of decisionmaking constituted of (ii) crucial variables clusters. Together, the process and the variables constitute a system of action.

Decisionmaking is defined as "a process which results in the selection from a socially defined, limited number of problematical, alternative projects of one project intended to bring about the particular future state of affairs envisaged by the decisionmakers." This process is affected by a basic set of interrelated variables with differential impacts. In other words, foreign policy-makers are seen as functioning at the intersection of several basic pressures or forces. The operational environments are overlapping as the decisionmaker simultaneously holds four types of memberships (in a culture and society; in noninstitutional social groupings; in a total institutional structure; and in a decisional unit).

Identified, thus, as multidimensional decisional units, foreign policy makers are presented as being influenced by three major determinants of action: (i) social structure; (ii) internal setting; and (iii) external setting. The decisionmaking system is itself conditioned by three stimuli:

1. spheres of *competence*, that is, the explicitly prescribed and conventionalized activities that decisionmakers engage in in the course of achieving national goals;[2]

2. *communication* and *information*, that is, communicative activity between decisionmakers,[3] and a net of information of varying types and varying significance which flows through prescribed (and deviant) channels;

3. *motivation;* that is, the personality and the psychological state of the decisionmaker, which create a disposition to certain actions or reactions –

10

in turn, setting a motivational pattern.

In sum, Snyder *et al.* presented a framework in which the actions of a state in the international system – i.e., its foreign policy – are understood as being primarily the actions of the state's decisionmakers. In addition, the actions of these decisionmakers are seen as essentially taking the form of definition of a situation through a process of decisionmaking. As members of a decisional unit, state actors operate within an internal and external setting that mediates an organizational behavior influenced by stimuli from three main sources: spheres of competence, communication and information, and motivation.

Besides bringing the human dimension into the foreign policy process more effectively (Jensen, 1982), Snyder *et al.*'s work advanced foreign policy analysis in at least three respects. First, it introduced a systematic approach to the study of the foreign policy of any given state by relying on identifiable categories which could be used for taxonomic and comparative efforts. Secondly, it recognized the role of the decisionmaker and the decisionmaking unit as primary movers of state actions in the international sphere. Thirdly, it offered a blend of psychological and sociological insights to understand the many stimuli and influences on the process of decisionmaking. Snyder's framework was later criticized for putting out an overwhelming and analytically unmanageable quantity of variables and for dismissing the role of the operational environment in affecting the outcome of decisions, in particular with regard to feedback consequences for future choices.

Although the approach did provide a more precise and systematized conception of how to look at foreign policy problems, it, in effect, required an amount of information which was excessive and empirically almost impossible to obtain. More importantly, it reduced the process of foreign policy-making to a set of tasks enacted by a decisionmaking unit. Thus doing, it obstructed the identification of (i) the historical role of the state as a builder through foreign policies, and (ii) the introduction of this continuing state-building process in the decisional background of any given

11

present regime or administration. Another proponent of the decision-making approach, Frankel (1963) offers a similar analysis to that of Snyder *et al.*, although he retains the state as main decisionmaking unit. He specifically notes that:

> The adoption of this [decisionmakers-for-persons] focus does not mean that foreign policy is considered as ultimately reducible to a series of identifiable decisions made by identifiable individuals and groups. The making of decisions is only one of many aspects of international relations.

Nonetheless, Frankel understands the nature of the state primarily through the actions of individuals or group of individuals; "foreign policy consists of decisions....[and]....decisions take place in the decisionmaker's mind." For him, the state is ultimately conceived in terms of decisionmaking power, not of formal governmental authority (Brecher *et al.*, 1969). He thus prods researchers to consider the variables influencing the decisionmaking unit regardless of the historical governance context.

James Rosenau (1966) attempted to produce a "pre-theory"[4] of foreign policy analysis. Arguing that foreign policy studies are fundamentally short on causal propositions, Rosenau proceeds to outline a model based on "if-then" hypotheses which would serve as a basis for comparative examination of the foreign policy and behavior of different countries in given situations. The idea is to progress towards a general theory of foreign policy analysis by devising generalizations that treat societies as actors subject to stimuli that produce external responses.

Rosenau identifies five ingredients (individual, role, governmental, societal, systemic) and attaches to them causal priorities using three distinction criteria (actor, situation, penetration). His scheme is driven by the belief that the explanatory power lies essentially in the ranking of the variable clusters as potential influences of foreign policy. As he puts it:

> To be theoretical in nature, the rankings would have to specify *how much* more potent each set of variables is than those below it on each scale, and the variables themselves would have to be causally linked to specific forms

of external behavior. (Original emphasis.)

Two main problems lie in this approach. First, the variables put forth are not clearly enough identified, and the outline of their interconnections is overlapping and misleading (Hanrieder, 1968; Brecher *et al.*, 1969; Weinstein 1972). Secondly, and more importantly, the attempt to rank variables in terms of their relative potency is an exercise in futility, for it is a fact that foreign policy making emanates simultaneously from the different variables (Ofuatey-Kodjoe, 1993).

Also, the categories presented by Rosenau are static rather than dynamic. They hardly account for changes in both internal and external polities – which more often than not affect the formulation and implementation of foreign policy behavior. This shortcoming is particularly highlighted with regard to developing nations (see McGowan, 1968; and Korany, 1974).

Rosenau offers a rationale for constructing a pre-theory of foreign policy analysis, but this rationale – i.e., a ranking logic – merely yields a taxonomy wherein basic information about countries is compartmentalized and then compared, given the presence of particular types of societies and issues.[5] The result is the reductionist identification of a dominant causal variable. Here, also, the perpetuation of the state through foreign policy and its historically-determined nature and patterns escapes the analysis.

Rosenau's contribution has led to the development of a number of research agendas most of which have tended essentially to (i) identify a list of variables believed to influence foreign policy behavior and (ii) outline the scheme of interrelationships between these variables (Wilkinson, 1969; McGowan and Shapiro, 1973; Shapiro and Bonham, 1973; Andriole, Wilkenfeld, and Hopple, 1975).

Shapiro and Bonham (1973) focus on the cognitive process and offer a perspective which holds that the beliefs of the foreign policy decisionmakers are central to the study of decision outputs and probably account for more of the variance than any other single factor. In addition, "affective" and "cognitive" concepts are seen as informing the beliefs of the decisionmaker by representing a map. Andriole, Wilkenfeld, and Hopple (1975) are concerned with the variance within decision situations that can be attributed to recurrent patterns or nonidiographic factors. To grasp this variance, any evaluative design, they argue, should meet four criteria: (i) comprehensiveness, (ii) comparability, (iii) operationalizability, and (iv) public policy relevance. Against these conceptual requirements, Andriole *et al.* offer five independent variables, (i) psychological (psychodynamics, personality traits, belief system, perceptions), (ii) political (bureaucracy, interest groups, domestic pressures, descriptor variables), (iii) societal (national culture, domestic conflict, social structure, descriptor variables), (iv) inter-state (alliance ties, bloc memberships, trade agreements, policy inputs), and (v) global (systemic attributes, status rank, subsystemic phenomena, textural phenomena), and three intervening variables, (i) structural (economic) dimension, (ii) structural (governmental) dimension, and (iii) power (capability) dimension, coded in relation to five dependent variable dimensions, spatial, relational, behavioral, situational, and substantial. In short, they offer three interrelated sets of variables to account for what they present as multidimensional foreign policy events. Yet both Shapiro and Bonham and Andriole *et al.*'s framework neglect the role of inputs into the decisionmaking process as well as the larger historical polity of statehood which particular decisionmakers come to affect (that is, perpetuate, alter, or discontinue).

In reaction to frameworks which were merely expanding Snyder et *al.*'s initial three influences into many cross-cutting variable clusters, attention shifted in the early 1970s to the analysis of foreign policy behavior through case-studies concerned with a single predominant factor: structure or process. Jervis (1970) looked at the way states can affect the "images" others have of them and how these images can supplement the more usual forms of power and are indispensable for reaching certain goals. Arguing that states rely on the image they have of another state to predict behavior, Jervis demonstrates that the formulation of images, their perception, and ultimately their effect on interstate relations are an integral part of foreign policy making. Allison

14

(1971) studied the Cuban missile crisis of 1962 through the rational actor model and two alternatives, the bureaucratic politics model, and the organizational process model. Janis (1972) looked at foreign policy fiascoes and offered the explanation that the occurrence of these debacles can be attributed to the presence amongst the decisionmaking group of a negative psychological phenomenon which he terms "groupthink." Excessive strivings for unanimity, unrealistic optimism about the group's actions, underestimation of the opponent's capabilities, illusions of invulnerability, and disregard of ethical issues are some of the main psychodynamics characteristic of groupthink and symptomatic of defective decisionmaking. The process ultimately yields a low probability of a successful outcome. Janis' work is important in at least two respects: (i) its intricate blend of small-group dynamics and political decisionmaking, and (ii) its clear distinction between quality of process and quality of outcomes. Rosenau developed research proposals about issue-areas (1967) – which were already part of his pre-theories – and linkage politics (1969). And Steinbrunner (1974) adopted a cybernetic perspective on decisionmaking. In contradistinction to previous works, studies of this wave did not aim for comprehensiveness (as did explicitly Andriole *et al.*, 1975), but rather focused on a few elements or aspects of the foreign policy-making and attempted to investigate their causal potential with respect to the decisionmaking output.

Departing from the decisionmaking-oriented and psychological perspectives, Brecher, Steinberg, and Stein (1969) and Lentner (1974) offer different, more all-encompassing approaches. Both describe a greater role for the state. Brecher *et al.*'s framework rests on the identification of (i) pressures on (ii) the state, which is operating within (iii) a multidimensional environment. They postulate that "the core unit of analysis is the state as it functions within an international system at any point in time and space." Brecher and his colleagues look at foreign policy as being a system of dynamic and continuous flow immersed in a dual environment (operational and psychological) composed of a network of structures and institutions from which it receives inputs continually conversed and channeled as policy. The reality beamed by the external and internal operational environment, on the one hand, and the evaluation and interpretation of it operated by the decisionmaker(s), on the other, are the two major determinants of foreign policy making.

The core of the argument lies in its recognition of an objective operational environment – which is composed of internal (military capability, economic capability, political structure, interest groups, competing élites) and external (global, subordinate, subordinate other, bilateral, dominant bilateral) variables – subject to an active interpretation operated within the societal/personality psychological environment of the decisionmaker(s) on the basis of an attitudinal prism (ideology, historical legacy, personality predispositions) and élite images (competing élites' advocacy and pressure potential).

The merit of the approach lies in the analytical space it provides for the factors that are *initially* potential influences on the decisionmaking process – be they objective/structural or subjective/conjunctural. Brecher and his colleagues also recognize historical factors as part of both psychological and operational environment.[6]

Retaining a narrow-gauge definition of the foreign policy-making élite as more appropriate for comparative research, Brecher *et al.* nonetheless give the decisionmakers ascendance over the state. Their framework has been criticized for observing and attributing causal significance to possible factors of foreign policy, but failing to indicate which of those are appropriately relevant to the process through which policy is made. This work managed, notwithstanding, to strike a delicate balance between macro- and meso-level international and regional structures and micro-level decisionmaker-centered processes which Brecher (1972) later applied to the foreign policy system of Israel.

Lentner (1974) comes closer to an understanding of the role of the state in foreign policy-making. Arguing that the decisionmaking approach – whatever its merits – is fundamentally incomplete because it does not account for (i) implementation of policy and (ii) mobilization of resources, he maintains that these two actions, along with (iii) the statement of objectives, constitute policy. Against this background,

Lentner posits foreign policy as being that policy which is directed towards or that responds to the environment of a territorial state and its government, referred to as an actor. The state's external environment is understood through the role of (i) the international system (i.e., a pattern of interaction amongst states within a structure), and (ii) situations (i.e., limited patterns of interaction). In addition, foreign policy is seen as the result of the active interaction between domestic and international influences. The framework leads to a classification according to which states, through the enactment of their foreign policy, may be (i) insulated, (ii) engaged, or (iii) expanded. Therefore, for Lentner, foreign policy is an exercise conducted by *states* embedded in *situations* within the *international system*.

According to Andriole *et al.* (1975), Lentner accounts for virtually all of the variables important in the understanding of foreign policy formulation and implementation. But the approach has been criticized for failing to distinguish with precision between a comprehensive set of potential foreign policy factors and those factors that actually influence the process as sources of constraints and opportunities. The introduction of the concept of "situation" is also the subject of criticism by Ofuatey-Kodjoe (1993), who regrets the absence of a full articulation of the notion, and Andriole *et al.* (1977) who argue that Lentner ignores important "situational" dimensions, such as threat, decision, time, and awareness.[7]

The merit of Lentner's approach lies in its recognition of the state's primary role as foreign policy actor – which it assesses through a combination of a larger and permanent environment (the nature and structure of the international system) and more immediate concerns (articulated through situations). In addition, the perspective is dynamic rather than static, giving central roles to the concepts of "adjustment," "adaptation," "transformation," and time itself as a relevant foreign policy analysis consideration. Lentner admits, for instance, the presence of constant short-term adjustments in the foreign policy of a given country. (Those, it might be argued, resulting from the idiosyncratic orientations of any current regime or administration.) But he also points out that

> Broadly speaking, countries have *continuing and constant policies for given situations.* The process of change is normally slow for most countries with respect to most situations most of the time. Although adjustments are continuously made in situations, they tend to persist in their essential qualities and characteristics. (Emphasis added.)

Jensen (1982) seeks to ascertain why states behave as they do in the international system. He identifies six determinants, acting, he argues, in combination. These are: (i) the human dimension (common and idiosyncratic factors influencing the decision); (ii) the societal dimension (effect of membership in a social group); (iii) the ideological dimension (effect of religious, historical, and mythical beliefs); (iv) the political structure dimension (influence of the type of system and its actors); (v) the economic and power dimension (impact of economic resources and power patterns and channels); and (vi) the inter-state dimension (role of the behavior of other states). These determinants are posited as being in the permanent background of foreign policy-making and their particular arrangement is dependent upon the situation and the actor. Nonetheless, in spite of recognizing the combined effect of these foreign policy determinants, Jensen is preoccupied by the assessment of their relative potency. Such a concern brings him back to the ranking logic initiated by Rosenau. He, then, isolates *perception* as the overarching foreign policy variable. By ranking the perceptual propensities of the decisionmaker(s) over the other decisional parameters, and although he emphasizes the role of political structures as well as power, Jensen reduces the latitude of the impact of statehood processes as continuous foreign policy determinants – innate in the political "background." Nevertheless, Jensen makes an important contribution by drawing attention to the importance of power in the analysis of foreign policy. Power capabilities, he points out, define the range of options available to a state and whether that state can play a significant role in the international system. Yet pursuit of this interesting line of inquiry, it would seem, lies more in the investigation of attributes of the state, namely, organization of the power apparatus, nature and role of the military, economic strength (which Jensen considers), control over the social body, security requirements, and the state's historically dominant foreign concerns – which more often than not are tied to domestic affairs.

Hermann, Kegley, and Rosenau (1987) attempt to assess and provide new directions to the analysis of foreign policy. The study they present, composed of twenty-two contributions, recognizes the profusion of logics of inquiry in the field – resulting, according to Rosenau, from the multiple meanings and explanations that underlie even the simplest of foreign policy actions. The findings are that foreign policy analysis has departed from its initial concern: the search for a paradigm. There exists now in the field many theories cohabitating. This potentially negative situation, and the many viewpoints it houses, is regarded by the authors as an acceptable state of affairs implicitly creative of a body of knowledge. For, it seems, there only remains a common concern, namely the plans and actions of national governments oriented towards the external world, approached from an increasing number of analytical points. Dismissing the inventory approach best exemplified by the propositional inquiry of McGowan and Shapiro (1973) for gathering empirical rather than theoretical findings – and thus yielding exceedingly little knowledge about foreign policy problems to date – Hermann and Peacock (1987) argue in favor of the cumulation and juxtaposition of competing theories as a way to expand theoretical knowledge.

The trend advocated by Hermann *et al.* is towards the recognition of the value of (i) middle-range theories rather than all-encompassing frameworks, and (ii) single-country studies. This, they argue, will pave the way for the emergence of a global theory through cumulation. Yet concern about the role of the continuous processes of statehood and their repercussions in the foreign policy behavior of a given government is again scant in these research proposals. Although Rosenau mentions "the reinforcement of a historical tradition" as one possible foreign policy causal layer, we are left to guess whether that reinforcement process could have any meaning without the presence of a permanent structure around which it would develop; namely, the state. By the same token, any "reinforcement" instance speaks, it would appear, to a

19

building logic. Rosenau, nonetheless, emerges as one of the few foreign policy analysts – along with Lentner and Moon – explicitly calling for exploration of the role of the state. As he puts it:

> [F]or several decades [students of foreign policy] have not been inclined to treat the state as a substantive concept, preferring instead to equate it with the actions of governmental decision-makers and thus to bypass the questions of its role, competence, and autonomy. For better or for worse, such an inclination is no longer tenable.

More explicit is Moon (1987), who offers a theoretical treatment of the role of the state in his presentation of a political economy approach to foreign policy analysis. In sketching such a perspective, Moon offers three guiding principles: (i) policies arise from states lodged within a political economy that shapes their behavior; (ii) the environment shaping the character and behavior of states is to be grasped globally and with regard to economic as well as political phenomena; and (iii) the crux of most countries' foreign policies lies in the sphere of economic relations and domestically-determined distribution patterns. Although it primarily confines the defining mission of the state and the locus of its activity to the economy, not security,[8] Moon's foreign policy framework is inherently state-centric.

A significant novelty in this approach is that foreign policy is no longer the dependent variable in the analysis but an independent one. Rather, political economy conceptions of the state and its primary objectives suggest economic policy as the centerpiece from which the remaining elements of foreign policy flow. It is, nonetheless, possible to ask where the logic ultimately leads. For if, as Moon emphasizes, the backbone of the approach is the growing interdependence of public policy, comparative politics, and international relations theory (each endowed with its own research questions), focusing heavily on the economic bases, structures, and processes of national power reflected only secondarily in foreign affairs, we risk losing sight of the initial query of foreign policy analysis – more simply formulated by Jensen

20

(1982) as, "Why do states behave the way they do?" In the end, Moon's laudable effort boosts political economy analysis, not foreign policy analysis.

Another approach, offered by Papadakis and Starr (1987), also suggests that one of the weaknesses in the study of foreign policy has been an insufficient conceptualization of the state. In particular, these authors argue that to comprehend the nature of foreign policy it is necessary to understand the relationship between the state and its environment. Foreign policy is posited as resulting from the state's action with regard to all aspects of its environment and its capacity to make use of particular opportunities. Papadakis and Starr add texture to Lentner (1974), who also viewed the action of the state with regard to its environment as the key component of foreign policy. In the model they offer, the state (i.e., institutions and structures) is the central actor, whose choices (based on its willingness) affect both the output (i.e., the decision) and the outcome of foreign policy behavior. The effects of this process are reverberated in different levels of the domestic and international environment, providing, in turn, opportunities and constraints for the state to act and react. The centrality of the relationship between the state and the environment stems from the fact that the latter – in both its tangible and relational aspects – establishes the range of possibilities for the former's action.

Nonetheless, both Lentner (1974) and Papadakis and Starr (1987) formulate a rather static vision of the relationship between the state and its environment matrix, failing in particular to accommodate the historical environment.[9] For if the state, on the one hand, and the environment, on the other, are permanent structures, and given their ongoing set of relationships, foreign policy becomes then a repetitive exercise. That being as it may, the foreign policy behavior of a given regime or administration can better be comprehended as part of a global pattern of its state's historical foreign policy. More precisely, the use of specific opportunities (Starr and Papadakis) or situations (Lentner) – such as the 1990-1991 Iraqi annexation of Kuwait – is seen as answering to the logic of both the state's foreign policy *telos* and a (Ba'thi) regime's own disposition.

21

In addition to the historical environment of the state, a state-building approach to foreign policy analysis should investigate the dividing line between the state and the regime or administration identifying the concerns of each[10] – as well as the regime leaders' understanding and use of their state's history. Looking at the linkages between domestic politics and the decisions to go to war, Hagan (1994) demonstrates that the interests and the beliefs that a regime holds and shares with its support network (interest groups, party, military) are an important motivational basis for the general orientation of a state's foreign policy. Pointing to connections between international environment, state, regime, and domestic structure, he notes that

> It is assumed that who governs matters because it is normally a small élite who makes choices related to going to war. Nonetheless, the ability of these leaders to carry out their preferred policies is conditioned by ongoing domestic constraints. These domestic political pressures are of sufficient magnitude that they can significantly modify the constraints of an anarchic international system. With these assumptions as a backdrop, it is possible to identify two basic approaches to linking domestic political systems to war proneness – a 'regime structure' approach, and a 'statist' approach.

The presumption that foreign policy is made by government officials and that it is in terms of the interests of these officials that the analysis of interests begins is increasingly giving way to a growing concern about the role of the state and its institutional structures, and the way these features are causal to foreign policy behavior. A state-centric approach to foreign policy analysis also makes it possible to discern the role of the effect of a given regime's norms. It is such a combination that this study seeks to apply to the foreign policy-making of the Iraqi republic during the 1990-1991 Gulf War.

22

Approaches to Foreign Policy-Making the Arab World

Summarizing the trends in the study of Arab foreign policies, Korany and Dessouki (1984) noted that "the underdeveloped study of underdeveloped countries is nowhere more clearly demonstrated than in the analysis of Arab foreign policy," and recognized three traditional approaches leading to syncretistic accounts: (i) the psychologistic approach, (ii) the great powers approach, and (iii) the reductionist approach.

The first school, they argue, views foreign policy as a result of impulses, desires, and idiosyncrasies of a single leader. Relying on a static, paradigmatic understanding of Arab leaders – for instance, Saddam Hussayn as heir of Gamal 'Abd al-Nasser[11] – this school errs by overemphasizing the individual choice as primary determinant of foreign policy. Moreover, it ignores the context (domestic, regional, and global) within which the foreign policy-making process occurs. This school has long dominated and has often been relayed by journalistic accounts and, recently, political psychology formulations. The particularist dialectic of this approach is an impediment to systemic aggregations.

Derivative of realist political thinking, the great powers approach sees the foreign policy of Arab nations as a function of the international bipolarity of the Cold War. The foreign dynamics of these countries, it is argued, cannot be but ones of reaction to external political and economic stimuli. The main criticism leveled against this school is that it neglects domestic factors. Focusing on the East-West conflict and not taking into account the internal variables as well as the relevant regional geo-strategic interplay is another shortcoming of the approach. In addition, the end of the Cold War and other changes in the international during the past decade scene render the explanatory power of this approach limited if not obsolete.

A proponent of the great powers approach is Safran (1985),[12] who argues that the determinative role of the external powers is both crucial and constant. Specifically, he notes that:

The involvement of rival outside powers has been at the heart of the Middle East problem....for some two centuries. During the period, the specific geographic focus of the problem often shifted, the particular configurations of domestic and regional weakness changed, the identity of the rival outside powers and the nature of their interests altered, but *the matrix that made up the problem remained constant*. It always involved the extension into the Middle East arena of big-power struggles involving external interests and wider power configurations. (Emphasis added.)

Safran places the outside powers "matrix" at the heart of Middle Eastern foreign policy causal connections. Thus, the great powers dimension, and the American-Soviet rivalry in particular, is the narrative of the history's region. Domestic developments are secondary. Its effects, Safran continues, are reflected back in all facets of foreign policy – internal politics, regional politics, and conflict situations. Hudson (1976) also adopted that approach – focusing on the occurrence of conflicts and the role of external powers – although he recognized that the interrelationship of regional and foreign powers has become more complex than in previous decades. Noting that the relationship is one of "mutual exploitation," he argued that it is conflicts (Arab vs. Israeli, Arab vs. Persian, and Arab vs. Arab) that form the matrix of the system – providing springboards for influence. Domestic stimuli of foreign policy as well as the role of the state are absent from his discussion, as they are from Safran's.

The reductionist or model-builders approach explains the foreign policies of Arab countries through the use of the same factors as for developed nations. The variations in terms of resources and capabilities provide the framework for comparison. Postulating unchanging rational actor behaviors and similar foreign policy rationales, this approach fails in particular to account for institutional specificities and differing behavioral motivations.

Rosenau's linkage politics (1969) is a case in point of reductionist approach when applied to the Arab world. An off-shoot of his "penetrated political system," linkage politics are a sub-type defined as:

The recurrent sequences of behavior that originate on one side of the boundary between the two types of systems and that become linked to phenomena on the other side in the process of unfolding [or]....as any recurrent sequence of behavior that originates in one system and is reacted to in another.

When applied to Arab political systems, the concept proves to be problematic. Indeed, as Kienle (1990) points out, the sub-type of linkage processes actually depends on a dichotomy between internal and external politics – as no linkage would exist if the two systems were to coincide. Yet in Arab foreign policies the frontier between the interior (domestic) and exterior (other Arab States) is razor-thin – pointing to an overarching Arab polity encompassing in various ways the several Arab states. In sum, inasmuch as Arab states' foreign policy-making processes are largely affected by the notion of the Arab region as a segmentary society, Rosenau's linkage politics concept – as an example of model-building approach – loses much of its explanatory power. To determine the degree of fusion between the internal and external Arab affairs, one need only look at the Syrian-Lebanese, Egyptian-Libyan, Saudi-Yemeni, Moroccan-Mauritanian, or Jordanian-Palestinian relations, all characterized by a high level of policy interference and multi-layered interrelatedness.

The three traditional approaches, identified by Korany and Dessouki, hence, lack sound explanatory power. Focusing on an often arbitrary set of idiosyncrasies, they have tended to account for isolated features of Middle Eastern and North African Arab states. This has resulted in the development of a body of theory too scanty to be useful for the foreign policy analyst. The need is for more substantive and systematic frameworks.

Korany and Dessouki offered their own framework in which the foreign policy output is conceptualized as role. The role category is broken down into role conception (the actor's objectives and strategies) and role performance (the actual behavior). This duality is meant to enable the analyst to identify the conformity, or lack thereof, between conception and performance. Against this background, four categories are offered to understand (Arab) foreign policy: domestic environment (geography, population and social structure, economic and military capabilities, political structure); (ii) foreign policy orientation; (iii) decisionmaking process; and (iv) foreign policy behavior. In sum, conditioned by its domestic conditions, a foreign policy output is the sequential result of an orientation, a decision, and an action.

Korany and Dessouki's recourse to role theory is useful in having the process of foreign policy analysis start from the actor's perspective. As a reaction to great powers approaches, where the level of analysis was beyond the subordinate nation, it is particularly appropriate. The framework is undoubtedly a seminal contribution to the study of Arab foreign policies and a welcomed departure from the three classical schools. It provides the first systematic scheme and comprehensive design to study the foreign policies of these countries. Yet it is faced with at least two problems. First, little information is conveyed about the actor(s) conducting foreign policy. In effect, although Korany and Dessouki correctly note that the process of foreign policy-making takes place in a specific social and institutional context, the interaction between the presidency (as head unit of a regime) and the state (permanent all-encompassing institutional unit), and its effects on foreign policy, are not given attention. Second, although the four categories of information seem qualified, their interconnections, if any, are not articulated and they lack a historical perspective. Notwithstanding, the work of Korany and Dessouki inspired a certain type of studies of Arab foreign policies more analytically focused and using concepts as varied as ideology (El-Warfally, 1988; Deeb, 1991), the operational code (Rashdan 1989), revolution (Halliday, 1989), cognition (Layachi, 1990), legitimacy (Dawisha, 1990), and nationalism (Tueller, 1992). This wave of new studies share a common emphasis on the interplay between domestic sources of foreign policy-making and international environment. In effect, internal constraints and external influences are understood as the determinative patterns of Arab foreign policies.

Rashdan (1989), for instance, analyzed Jordanian foreign policy by looking at the role of King Hussayn. He used the operational code method (Leites, 1951; George,

26

1969; and Holsti, 1971) to assess the king's beliefs, his policy orientations, and his choices. His study reveals the centrality of the king in the policy process in the absence of major domestic structural constraints, and the direct repercussion of the king's operational code on Jordan's foreign policy behavior. Tueller (1992) looks at the role of Arab nationalism in the foreign policies of Egypt, Libya, and Syria. In appraising the interactions between the three countries, she determines the presence or absence of Arab nationalism as an ideological concern in their foreign policies. Her conclusion that different domestic factors – beyond nationalism – are involved in relations between the three nations suggests that it is more fruitful to examine the inter-relations of Arab countries on a bilateral level than to treat all Arab states as one (Tueller, 1992). Kienle (1990) is another proponent of such an approach. He looks at several issues which have determined Syro-Iraqi relations and have, in turn, affected their foreign policies at large and domestically in the period between 1968 and 1989. Having analyzed the changing dynamics of this Ba'thi-Ba'thi relationship and its successive phases (roughly from party quarrels to state consolidation conflict to competition for regional influence – with an intervening period of rapprochement in 1978-1979), Kienle concludes that "inter-Arab relations are characterized by a blurred distinction between internal and external affairs." More explicit in their use of domestic dimensions are Ismael and Ismael (1986), who adopt the examination of the patterns of variation in domestic environments as a way of accounting for Arab foreign policies and their fluctuation. Their argument is that domestic socioeconomic issues (such as the challenge of national development) and ideological concerns (primarily religious ones along with the attitude towards the West) affect the foreign policy process of Arab states.

Yet most of these research agendas still reserve a disproportionate role to external linkages. "Domestic circumstance and international posture" (Ismael and Ismael, 1986) and "the primacy of constraints" (Korany and Dessouki, 1984) are the overriding and all-encompassing categories. Their interplay supersedes the state's multi-layered and continuous attempts at maintaining legitimacy and authority through foreign policy behavior. Despite the renewed interest in the effect of domestic politics on foreign policy making, the state as a focal point remains largely absent from the reflection. The (Arab) state is, notwithstanding, the actor of domestic foreign policy where internal politics formulate regional and international designs for their country which the state is supposed to enact. On the other hand, the state's control over the nation's economic resources also provides it with an opportunity to pursue through foreign policy its own structural agenda of building, with regard, in particular, to sovereignty notions. Both these dimensions point to the need to go beyond the interplay of domestic and international environments, first identified by Korany and Dessouki and followed by other writers. The state deserves more analytical attention as both a catalyst and an initiator of foreign policy.

The Foreign Policy of Iraq

Pre-Second Gulf War studies of the foreign policy of Iraq generally emphasize the issue of national political development and the authoritarian nature of the Ba'thi system. McLaurin, Mughisuddin, and Wagner (1977) offer a detailed and often accurate account of Iraq's ethnic and religious cleavages (Arab vs. Kurd, and Shi'a vs. Sunna), the Iraqi policy environment and the forces it houses (the Ba'th party, the Communist party, and the Kurdish groups). They equally and correctly list a number of major issue areas with which Iraq has been concerned (the Shatt-al-'Arab boundary problem with Iran, the Kuwait question, the Palestinian issue, and economic development). On the basis of these categories – in which a substantial amount of information is stored – they assert that, since the 1958 revolution, Iraqi foreign policy has pursued seven goals:

[i] to maintain [Iraq's] political independence and territorial integrity;
[ii] to develop a sense of national unity among the diverse ethnic,
religious, [and]... regional groups;
[iii] to participate in Arab unity efforts;

28

[iv] to maintain cordial relations with regional powers, especially Turkey;

[v] to accelerate the country's economic and industrial development;

[vi] to maintain good relations with at least one superpower;

[vii] to assert Iraq's leadership in the eastern Arab world.

Apart from providing us with information about each bin and offering general policy objectives, McLaurin and his colleagues tell us little about the dynamics at play between the various influences on the policy process, as well as the way these influences are worked out in the policy behavior. Specifically, we are told about domestic schisms, political aspirations of different factions, confessional conflicts, and internal dissension, but we are left in the dark about the cardinal principles of domestic and foreign policies interaction.

More importantly, McLaurin *et al.* note that there has been a striking continuity in Iraqi foreign policy – with successive regimes working around the same set of problems – but they fail to identify the causal locus of continuity, namely, the state itself. As they write:

> Since its independence, Iraq has had a series of monarchist and revolutionary governments whose domestic and foreign policy goals have not differed radically. Since all these governments were confronted by practically the same set of problems, the goals they pursued did not differ substantially; *only in the formulation and implementation of their policies might they be considered different.* (Emphasis added.)

The identification of the issues is only a first step. But if we need to understand "the formulation and implementation" of these Iraqi policies, we have to ask, What is it in the nature of these issues that makes them persist? How do the processes of statehood promote such continuity? And, finally, how are these problems played in the foreign policy behavior of each regime?

29

McLaurin, Peretz, and Snider (1982) offer an updated version of McLaurin *et al.*'s 1977 chapter. As such, it is plagued by essentially the same shortcomings. The Tikriti clan – named after city of Tikrit, the birthplace of President Saddam Hussayn – and its growing influence on party, army, and governmental apparatuses is added to the policy environment as a most decisive unit. The Progressive National Front (PNF) – a Ba'thi-dominated coalition also including the Iraqi Communist party, the Independent Democrats (of Nasserite obedience), and the several Kurdish parties – is introduced as an additional variable in the policy environment whose primary (domestic) role – the minimization of political rivalry – is without major effect on foreign policy-making. As the First Gulf War was in its second year, the contest with Iran is added to the issue areas dominating Iraqi foreign policy.

Dawisha (1983) sees Iraqi foreign policy as being (i) the domain of the Chief Executive, and (ii) characterized by a minimal emphasis on religion. His focus is narrower than McLaurin *et al.*'s sweeping categorizations. Emphasizing the central role of President Saddam Hussayn in the foreign policy sphere and documenting – through content-analysis of the Iraqi President's speeches – the predominance of Arabist ideology over Islamist overtones, Dawisha does not address the larger structural issues of policy-making. He does, nonetheless, point to the fact that, having broadened his personal support base in the party and the government, President Hussayn's foreign policy action is "enhanced by the party's perceived legitimacy and its organizational responsibilities within the country, and the party's control is aided by the population's acceptance of presidential authority." But this interplay between institutions (as well as vis-à-vis the societal body) is not explored further, and Dawisha confines himself to the confirmation of the thesis that Iraq, under Hussayn, has been following a secularist foreign policy which was decisively at play during the war with Iran.

In a brief discussion in her general study about Iraq, Helms (1984) isolates three prime considerations in the formulation of the country's foreign policy: (i) strategic vulnerability, (ii) authority, and (iii) statehood. Regrettably, this last concern is not discussed at length. Mention must also be made of the respective chapters in Majid Khadduri's trilogy on Iraq (1960, 1969, and 1978) which provide a descriptive but very detailed narrative of the foreign policies of Iraq between 1932 and 1977.

A more incisive analysis of Iraq's foreign policy-making is provided by Ahmad (1984). Applying Korany and Dessouki's framework, Ahmad offers two theses: (i) domestic influences are the primary foreign policy stimuli, and (ii) Iraq suffers from an unfulfilled leadership role. Of the two propositions, the second is the most interesting, although it is less articulated. Ahmad points, in effect, to geographical constraints – the most important of which are the lack of access to the sea and the absence of natural defenses against invasion – underpopulation, and the cleavages in the Iraqi social fabric which prevent a satisfactory exploitation of the ingredients of national power (oil wealth, strong agricultural and industrial sectors). This situation, heightened by the presence of the largest and most experienced Arab army, sets the stage for a dynamic of frustration.

Like Dawisha, Ahmad places Saddam Hussayn at the center of the foreign policy decisionmaking process.[13] But he wisely warns against overemphasizing his influential role. As he writes:

> Although Saddam Hussein may be relatively free from institutional
> constraints, he is subject to a variety of internal constraints, determined
> by geography and population structure, that severely limit his freedom of
> action.

By and large, Ahmad's essay is one of the most insightful studies of Iraqi foreign policy.[14] It correctly identifies the role of domestic structures, the perception of a frustrated leadership role, and the centrality of the presidency in policy-making. Ahmad does not, however, do two things. First, he does not differentiate between the continuing objectives of the Iraqi state and those of the Ba'thi leadership – which President Hussayn and the Revolutionary Command Council may have been pushing. Secondly, while he notes the gap between possibility and performance in Iraq's

31

development and leadership designs, he fails to look for the dynamics of this building process.

Studies on the Second Gulf War

Academic literature on the Second Gulf War is at a very early stage. There is a serious need to sharpen research and analysis of Iraq's role in this conflict. As an instance of post-Cold War international dynamics with wide-ranging regional consequences, the importance of the issue is only the more reinforced.

Over the six years since the conflict ended, and putting aside the numerous military and journalistic accounts (see table 1.1), there have been two main avenues of research on the issue.[15] A first one originates in political psychology (Karsh and Rautsi, 1991; Post, 1991; George, 1992; Renshon, 1993; Karsh 1993) and is essentially concerned with notions of personality and "good" decisionmaking, i.e., the analysis and assessment of the quality of the decisions taken by the actors of the crisis. Both focuses share a primary concern with the individuals, rather than governments or regimes, as units of analysis – thus perpetuating the psychologistic school criticized by Korany and Dessouki.

Post (1991, 1993) is the best example of the tendency to locate Iraqi foreign policy-making in the mind of its President. His approach holds that the perceptions, calculations, actions, and style of Saddam Hussayn are the main parameters of the Iraqi invasion of Kuwait and what followed. This analysis errs primarily because it uses inaccurate evidence. In effect, Post gives an account of the childhood of Hussayn – which he later offers as determinative to his political career – based on no cited sources. He makes detailed references[16] to founding episodes concerning his relationship with his family without distinguishing from governmental propaganda and myth-making and serious biographical literature. In particular he asserts that Hussayn's paternal uncle, 'Adnan Khayrallah, indoctrinated him in Arab nationalism and anti-

32

Semitism – equalling, in the process, the two. The result, as Post would have it, is that "Saddam has been consumed by dreams of glory since his earliest days." That may very well be. But neither the nexus between Hussayn's childhood and contemporary Iraqi policy-making nor the relevance of it is established. Similarly, Post blames – as do even more explicitly Karsh and Rautsi (1991) – the failure of the October 7, 1959, Ba'thi assassination attempt against President 'Abdelkarim Qassem on "a crucial error in judgment by Saddam." If, indeed, Hussayn participated in the preparation of the coup and was reportedly wounded, his role was at best peripheral.[17] The mid-1960s split inside the Ba'th party – which initially originated as result of a dispute in the Syro-Iraqi National Command – is attributed to Hussayn, and the 1968 Ba'thi revolution is reduced to a coup mounted by him. In sum, the policies of Iraq acquire meaning, according to Post, only from the impulses of Saddam Hussayn. This lays the ground for Post's analysis of the Second Gulf War, which, he notes, was personalized by the President of Iraq: "He will continue to attempt to cast the conflict as a struggle between Iraq and the United States, and even more personally between the gladiators – Saddam Hussein versus George Bush." The fact, however, is that the Iraqis explicitly avoided that dimension, constantly calling for an examination of the issues *per se*. Commenting on the question, Deputy-Prime Minister Tariq 'Aziz declared: "There is nothing personal, at least on our side, between President Saddam Hussayn and the American President George Bush....These kinds of questions, maybe, can arise within Arab conflicts and between Arab heads of states."[18] Post's analysis overstresses Saddam Hussayn's role[19] and its logic of inquiry is essentially anecdotal.

Renshon (1992, 1993) is also interested in using the Second Gulf War as a test of good judgment insofar as this political crisis "provides us....with a set of sharply etched circumstances....within a sharply bracketed time frame." Adopting such a perspective, Renshon narrows his understanding of the SGW to the whims of one individual during a seven month period. In addition, as with Post, most of the literature that constitutes his factual reference material is misleading, as is some of the public information relied upon. Algosaibi (1993) and Bahbah (1991) also present the role of

33

Saddam Hussayn's psychology as a prime factor in their analyses of Iraq's invasion of Kuwait. Algosaibi sees the SGW as the result of Hussayn's "adventurism" and his "gambler" cavalier attitude. In broader terms, Algosaibi also extends this vision to all Arabs, arguing that they tend to rationalize international crises in terms of foreign conspiracies. Bahbah, for his part, emphasizes Hussayn's "miscalculations" and "misperceptions."[20]

By focusing almost exclusively on the psychological make-up of President Saddam Hussayn, the analyses of Algosaibi, Bahbah, Karsh, Post, and Renshon obscure the determinative role that the historical context plays in informing both the social and political categories in which the decisionmaker is immersed. As Snyder *et al.* have noted in their 1962 monograph:

> What is required....is a sociological conception of personality....[A] scheme that places the individual decision-maker (actor) in a special kind of social organization. Therefore, we must think of a social person whose 'personality' is shaped by his interactions with other actors and by his place in the system. This does not mean that we reject the influence of ego-related needs and tensions but only that the behavior of the decision-making actor be explained *first* in terms of personality factors relevant to his membership and participation in a decision-making system. In this way, we can isolate what area of behavior must be accounted for in terms of idiosyncratic factors, that is, self-oriented needs not prompted by the system. (Original emphasis.)

The difficulties in assessing the determinative role of personality or context arise, Snyder and his colleagues further argued, because:

> We are still confronted by the empirical puzzle of the extent to which an individual policy-maker (such as a particular foreign minister or head of state) influences policy outcomes and the extent to which impersonal forces (such as historical movement, ideologies, and governmental systems) also determine actions.

The psychological analyses of the Second Gulf War – as represented by Post, Renshon, Algosaibi, Bahbah, and Karsh – fail to balance macro and micro dimensions of foreign

34

policy making, in such a way as to place the idiosyncrasies of the Iraqi President *within* a historically defined space (the Iraqi state) and an equally ongoing issue (Kuwait as part of Iraq). The result is extreme reduction of the conflict and magnification of Hussayn.[21]

A second wave of literature on the Second Gulf War is of a politico-diplomatic tone (Salinger, 1991; Freedman and Karsh, 1993; Danchev and Keohane, 1994; Khadduri and Ghareeb, 1997). In this school, it is the diplomatic chronicle, international law, economic and strategic – even ecological – questions of the conflict which are emphasized (Terzian, 1991; Halliday, 1991; Watson *et al.*, 1991; Danspeckgruber and Tripp, 1996). Because of the chronicle aspect – and although they are certainly informative from a purely historical point of view – the insights we get from this perspective have tended to be more descriptive than analytical. Essentially, the study is a narrative, an observation of sequential events. From the annotated collection of legal documents (Lauterpacht, 1991, 1992; Stern *et al.*, 1993) to the thematic recording of events (Smith, 1992), these studies share a lack of contextualization of the events, which they do not illuminate but simply document. Although less psychoanalytically pinpointed, Saddam Hussayn's personality and "miscalculations" are here also the explanatory background. Ibrahim *et al.*'s (1992) thorough study epitomizes this approach. Ibrahim and his colleagues emphasize the economic dimensions of the conflict, looking at the oil factor, the consequences on OPEC, and the business opportunities in the aftermath of the hostilities. They devote a section to the various international parties – the United States, the Soviet Union, China, the United Nations, Israel, Turkey, the Gulf Cooperation Council – summarizing each party's position and concern. Yet the principal actor, the Iraqi state, is almost secondary to this array of economic and geopolitical considerations. Only Ibrahim's essay briefly considers the historical origins of the crisis. Danchev and Keohane (1994) adopt a similar perspective, as do Freedman (1993) and Freedman and Karsh (1993) within a rigorous chronological narrative. The conduct of diplomacy – "successful" in the case of President George Bush and "failed" in the case of his Iraqi counterpart – is the unit of analysis. (Foreign) policy-making is, here, the province of diplomatic maneuvering and the chronicle is the technique of analysis. Thus the approach – and in particular its reliance on official documentation – could be likened to what one commentator said of another Orientalist school:

> It would appear that these trained historians, in order to compensate for the deficiency arising from the poverty of documentation in conventional history, depend almost solely on documents and archival material, endeavoring to substitute documents for history, owing to the fact that the majority in general lack theoretical and conceptual tools, which are the keys to unlock the riddle of the events with which the documents in their hands abound.[22]

Some studies have attempted to break out of the psychological and historico-diplomatic confinement. Hybel (1993) looks at the prevalence of power over rationality during the conflict, but his demonstration focuses primarily on the American side.[23] Ali (1993) argues that the crisis is inextricably linked to the history of the area and that the conflict between Iraq and Kuwait was mostly economic.

Crawford (1992) sees Iraqi foreign policy-making during the SGW as being determined by Iraq's force-proneness, which, she offers, is driven by the country's domestic instability and its regional aspirations. For her, Iraq's invasion of Kuwait was a rational response (in an instrumental and tactical sense) to the perceived threat by the Ba'thi regime of an increasingly difficult political future. Musallam (1996) uses Kenneth Waltz's framework of the three images of the causes of war to examine the conflict. Evaluating the roles of (i) President Saddam Hussayn, (ii) the state of Iraq, and (iii) the international system in the wake of the end of the cold war, he argues that the collective use of these three referents demonstrate that the causes of war are indeed complex and multivariate.

Matthews (1993) makes an insightful contribution, attempting to produce a "reasonably analytical examination of the crisis even at this relatively early stage after the actual events." His stance is that a combination of historical and structural factors

36

presents a series of propensities within which individuals have a freedom of action. In circumstances that he terms "structural flux," there may be scope for individual actions and decisions actually to change the structure or influence the structural change that is taking place. Against this conceptual background, Matthews separates the sources of Iraqi antagonism to Kuwait into four different groups: (i) the "cultural" differences between "northern" Arabs and "southern" Arabs; (ii) economic factors; (iii) Iraqi strategic aspirations; and (iv) Iraqi regional political aspirations. Building on Russett (1974), he then classifies the cultural cause as remote background cause, Iraqi strategic and regional hegemony as proximate cause, and the economic factor as immediate cause. Matthews does not, however, offer a paramount conclusion. His main contribution lies more in his recognition that:

> [To explain] events like crises and wars entails an investigation of the immediate context in which those decisions are made as well as some examination of the historical and structural context in which events take place. *Events are the product of contingent factors, historical factors, and structural factors.* (Emphasis added.)

In spite of the profusion of publications on the 1990-1991 Second Gulf War, the role of Iraq remains paradoxically understudied. Both a combined domination of militaristic, journalistic, and psychologistic perspectives, on the one hand, and a serious lack of value-free information – which would lead us to reassess some of the accepted myths of the conflict[24] – on the other, account for this insufficient attention to Iraq. As Aharon Klieman points, "To date....Gulf-related questions are being addressed by the military sciences more than the political or social sciences, giving an additional boost to security studies broadly defined at the expense of what traditionally fell under the purview of foreign and international affairs."[25] As the conflict between Iraq and the United States (and, to an increasingly lesser degree, between Iraq and the international community) persists with sporadic outbursts, it is surprising that foreign policy analysts have invested so little in seeking to understand the process of Iraqi policy-making during the

37

Table 1.1

A Classification of the Literature on the Second Gulf War

MILITARISTIC	DIPLOMATIC	PSYCHOLOGISTIC	JOURNALISTIC
Atkinson (1993)	Baker (1995)	Algosaibi (1993)	Bennett (1994)
Bergot and Gandy	Baram (1994)	George (1993)	Bennis and
(1991)	Bulloch and Morris	Glad (1991)	Moushabeck (1991)
Billière (1992)	(1991)	Karsh and Rautsi	Brown (1991)
Black (1991)	Danchev and Keohane	(1991)	Heikal (1992)
Blackwell (1991)	(1994)	Karsh (1993)	Kelly (1993)
Brenner (1991)	Danspeckgruber and	Post (1991, 1993)	Laurent (1991)
Cordesman (1994)	Tripp (1996)	Renshon (1992, 1993)	MacArthur (1992)
Cordesman and	Freedman (1993)	White (1991)	Macy (1991)
Wagner (1996)	Freedman and Karsh		Miller and Mylroie
D'Athis and Croizé	(1993)		(1990)
(1991)	Gittings (1991)		Mowlana (1992)
Dorr (1991)	Gresh and Vidal		Salinger and Laurent
Dupuy (1991)	(1991)		(1990)
Friedman (1991)	Hiro (1992)		Sackur (1991)
Gordon and Trainor	Jentleson (1994)		Sciolino (1991)
(1995)	Khadduri and Ghareeb		Simon (1992)
Hallion (1992)	(1997)		Yant (1991)
Hilsman (1992)	Munro (1996)		
Mazarr, Snider, and	Nefzaoui (1991)		
Blackwell, Jr. (1992)	Powell (1995)		
Record (1993)	Sifry (1991)		
Scales, Jr. (1994)	Smith (1992)		
Smallwood (1993)	Stern (1993)		
Smith (1991)			
Sultan (1995)			
Summers (1992)			
Watson (1991)			

decisive 1990-1991 events and what shaped it. The "Saddam Mind" as all-purpose explanatory device is evidently no longer viable – if it ever was – for the understanding of a territorial, regional, and ideological issue spanning seven decades. Nor is, for that matter, the acceptance of diplomatic memoirs as comprehensive works on the subject. If for no other reason than its persistent recurrence, the Kuwait question goes beyond the political agenda of President Saddam Hussayn. This study adopts the position that only a historical look at the Iraqi state's ever-increasing need to acquire substance can appropriately shed light on the Ba'thi adventures in Kuwait during the 1990s.

Summary

The objective of this chapter has been threefold: (i) to point out that most of the preexisting foreign policy literature has overemphasized the centrality of the decisionmaking process, thus neglecting the overriding and continuous role of the state; (ii) to indicate that the study of Arab foreign policy has been largely descriptive and reductionist and, more recently, overly concerned with the dynamics of domestic and external environments at the expense of statehood development processes; and (iii) to chart a course for the possible study of a foreign policy instance – the 1990-1991 Iraqi invasion of Kuwait and related developments – through a state-centric approach.

After forty years of existence, foreign policy analysis has proved to be strong on description but relatively weak on explanation. One reason for this is the overemphasis on decisionmaking processes in most research agendas. Ever since Snyder, Bruck, and Sapin (1962) identified the perception, choice, and expectations of leaders as the main notions to be investigated, the process of foreign policy analysis has been dominated by decisionmaking-oriented frameworks. The notion of decisionmaking was always the primary focus of foreign policy analysis. This confinement obstructs understanding of the major problems of international relations. Foreign policy is indeed about short-term decisionmaking, but that is not all. There is a

39

broader, more long-term concern. How a decision originates from a historically-determined reality and how it fits in societal, regional, and international patterns of politics is eventually more significant than how it is made.

An alternative way to study comparative foreign policy lies in the state-building approach. Bringing the state back into the analysis of foreign policy can yield improvements in the quality of findings in the field. The postulate in research agendas based on the role of the state is that there is a need to look beyond the idiosyncrasies of a decision process. To limit the analysis to the understanding of decisionmaking confines foreign policy making to *ad hoc* hypothesizing. In contradistinction, the theoretical assumptions of a state-building approach reach to the twofold nature of foreign policy: (i) state-building as a continuous process (the state as becoming); and (ii) state-building as maintenance of the state's position in the international system, i.e., state survival (Lentner, 1993).

Both notions are inscribed in a competitive continuum. As such, they are indistinguishable from a historical understanding of the country's position with regard to its regional and global environment. Therefore, using the state as the unit of analysis and working within the parameters of the two theoretical assumptions aforementioned, an analysis of foreign policy can be constructed on the explanatory logic that states seek to survive within a competitive and anarchical environment, and that their essential and immediate concern is to gather economic and political resources.

"It is inadvisable to personify states and to attribute decisions directly to them," wrote Frankel (1962), stressing that "personification implies continuous and constant units." Yet continuity and constancy are indeed appropriate characteristics of the state. My view holds that the abstractness of the state, not the psychological make-up of its leaders, is the locus of foreign policy. The process of policy-making is an aggregate and continuous one, and it is inherently linked to the position of the state within a global system. Beyond Weberian and juridical approaches to the state, a normative Hegelian understanding of the state's need to achieve (as a collectivity) becomes a tool to grasp the nature of a country's foreign policy. The rationale behind the approach is that there

40

should be a symbiotic relationship between foreign policy analysis and international relations. This, I submit, can be achieved through the statist prism.

NOTES

[1] Roy C. Macridis, ed., *Foreign Policy in World Politics*, Englewood Cliffs, New Jersey: Prentice-Hall, 1958; and Joseph E. Black and Kenneth W. Thompson, eds., *Foreign Policies in a World of Change*, New York, New York: Harper and Row, 1963.

[2] Snyder *et al.* make it clear that this first determinant has both an objective and a subjective dimension. The structural components (norms, rules of behavior, formal dispositions of the organization) are enacted along with the decisionmaker's interpretation of his competence, which is also informed by the social structure in which he operates.

[3] With regard to the context in which the communication is taking place, Snyder and his colleagues put emphasis on the idea that the actors are assumed to have a large number of shared similar experiences in order to communicate meaningfully about the world they interact with.

[4] Rosenau defines a pre-theory as "an early step toward explanation of specific empirical events and a general orientation toward all events, a point of view or philosophy about the way the world is" (1966: 41). According to Mennis (1969), this effort of pre-theory construction is geared towards providing the foundation for fruitful theoretical speculation and empirical investigation initially with an examination of internal properties, i.e., approaches, concepts, and methods.

[5] Brecher *et al.* argue that Rosenau's model has merit because it goes beyond a taxonomy to explore relationships among the variables (1969:79). There is, however, no evidence that this "exploration of relationships among the variables" is an advance in itself, since it could be maintained that any new information is of necessity replaced in one of the bins to bolster or infirm the relative influence of one of the sets of variables.

[6] In his analysis of the foreign policy of Israel, Brecher correctly categorizes a foreign policy decision – the proclaiming of Jerusalem as Jewish capital – as a response to a historical desire, namely the continuity of Zion (1972: 19)

[7] In point of fact, Lentner does include time in his conceptual construction. He specifically maintains that "time has an impact on foreign policy....[and] is an important consideration in the analysis of foreign policy....[affecting] the kinds of support that are necessary domestically for implementation of the policy" (p.9).

[8] Whereas, it may be maintained, economic and security considerations are complementary concerns.

[9] Papadakis and Starr list six levels of environment (international system, international relations, societal, governmental, role, and individual) that combine to create opportunity or constraints for the state. Adding a historical dimension could have been an improvement. Nevertheless, Papadakis and Starr's levels are homogenous, for they are spatial categories, whereas the proposed historical dimension is temporal. Yet if foreign policy is – as has often been argued – a spatio-temporal activity, then a combination of the seven levels is possible. In addition, if, as Papadakis and Starr maintain, some characteristics of the environment will be consistently more important than

others, the history of the state can in certain instances gain greater explanatory force with regard to the foreign policy behavior. Lentner, for his part, recognizes that using a concept of the state in foreign policy analysis, and emphasizing longer term considerations, brings in historical developments in a theoretical context (1994: 9).

[10] As particular and temporally-limited incarnations of a state, regimes and administrations are synonymous. The main difference is that the term "regime" is traditionally used for developing countries – where regimes can last for only months, sometimes days – whereas "administration" is reserved for democracies where the alternation of power is usually more peaceful and institutionally stable.

[11] This particular thesis was, for example, offered by Peter Mansfield in "Saddam Husain's Political Thinking: The Comparison with Nasser," in Tim Niblock, ed., *Iraq: The Contemporary State*, New York, New York: St. Martin's Press, 1982, pp. 62-73. For a counter-thesis that proposes Nasser as a universal paradigm, see Saad Eddin Ibrahim, "A Socio-Cultural Paradigm of Pan Arab Leadership: The Case of Nasser," in Fuad I. Khuri, ed., *Leadership and Development in Arab Society*, Beirut: American University of Beirut, 1981, pp. 30-61.

[12] Safran's essay, included in the sixth edition of Macridis' *Foreign Policy in World Politics*, is supposedly devoted to the foreign policies of Middle Eastern countries. Yet its very title – "Dimensions of the Middle East Problem" – announces that it is providing a modern formulation of the so-called "Eastern Question."

[13] Also see Adeed Dawisha, "The Politics of War: Presidential Centrality, Party Power, Political Opposition," in Frederick W. Axelgard, ed., *Iraq in Transition*, Boulder, Colorado: Westview Press, 1986.

[14] El-Behairy maintains that "several conclusions are reached without adequate support or substantiation." *The American Political Science Review* 79, 4 (December 1985), p. 1247.

[15] This review is concerned with Western studies of the conflict. For a summary of the different trends present in Arab works, see Mireille Paris, "La Crise et la Guerre du Golfe à Travers la Production en Langue Arabe - Bibliographie Sélective," *Annuaire de l'Afrique du Nord* 31 (1992), pp. 317-343. Besides military publications and those on the role of the media, Paris distinguishes (i) a "polemical" literature, vehemently anti-Saddam Hussayn and anti-Iraq (Sid'Ahmad, 1990; Amin, 1991; Badawi, 1990; Bahgat, 1990; Hussayn, 1990; al-'Abbassi, 1990; al-'Uthman, 1991; al-Naqib, 1991); (ii) a debate on the question of historical and juridical validity of Iraqi claims over Kuwait (Barrada, 1991; al-Rashidi, 1991; Raqibi, 1991; al-'Atri, 1991; al-Qassem, 1991; Mahfoudh. 1991); and (iii) a discussion on the regional and international implications of the crisis for the Arabs (Ahmad, 1991; Ibn Hussayn, 1990; al-Bazri, 1991; al-Bassam, 1991; al-Baqush, 1991; Gayit, 1991; Hafez, 1991; al-Zaghl, 1991; al-Sayed, 1992; Sha'rawi, 1992; al-Farmawi, 1991; al-Filali, 1991; al-Kenz, 1991; Huwaidi, al-Mashat, and al-'Alawi, 1992; al-Shukri, 1991; 'Usfur, 1991; and Ghalioun, 1991).

[16] Such as "[Saddam Hussayn] left his home in the middle of the night" (1991:280), or "Saddam's mother....may have attempted suicide" (1993:50).

[17] Saddam Hussayn's name is not once mentioned in the extensive account that Uriel Dann gives of the incident in his *Iraq Under Qassem: A Political History*, 1958-1963, New York, New York: Praeger, 1969, pp. 253-264. Dann writes: "An executive committee [to carry out the assassination plan] was formed composed of Fuad al-Rikabi, 'Abdallah al-Rikabi; Ayad Sa'id

42

Thabit, and Khalid al-Dulaymi, all members of the Ba'th regional command. The operational responsibility was in the hands of Thabit" (p. 253). In an equally detailed account, Khadduri (1969: 126-132), makes vague mention of one "Sudam Tikriti" who was present.

[18] Press conference held in Baghdad in October 1991, broadcast by the Arab-American Television in Detroit (AATD). Translation from Arabic. Jean Edward Smith noted the opposite perception: "The fact is, Bush personalized the confrontation up to the very end" (1992: 233).

[19] This is not to assert that the chief executive of Iraq is not central to the policy-making process of that country. Both the government's style of leadership and the political machinery of the Ba'th party have, since 1979, become increasingly dominated by him (see Dawisha, 1983). Nonetheless, this study takes the position that overemphasis of this aspect of Iraqi politics is inherently reductionist as it obscures historical and macro dimensions of state behavior.

[20] Bishara A. Bahbah, "The Crisis in the Gulf: Why Iraq Invaded Kuwait," in Phyllis Bennis and Michel Moushabeck, eds., Beyond the Storm - A Gulf Crisis Reader, New York, New York: Olive Branch Press, 1991, pp. 50-54.

[21] Najib Ghadban, "Some Remarks on the Distorting Literature about Saddam Hussein," Political Psychology 13, 4 (1992), p. 787. The roots of the psychologistic school as it is applied to the Arab world can be traced back to works such as Joel Carmichael, The Shaping of the Arabs - A Study in Ethnic Identity, New York, New York: MacMillan Company, 1967; Raphael Patai, The Arab Mind, New York, New York: Charles Scribner's Sons, 1973; and L. Carl Brown and Norman Itzkowitz, eds., Psychological Dimensions of Near Eastern Studies, Princeton, New Jersey: The Darwin Press, 1977.

[22] Khaldoun Hasan al-Naqeeb, Society and State in the Gulf and the Arab Peninsula: A Different Perspective, New York, New York: Routledge, 1990, p. 2.

[23] On the prosecution of the war from the American side, also see Jean Edward Smith, George Bush's War, New York, New York: Henry Holt Company, 1992; Stephen R. Graubard, Mr. Bush's War - Adventures in the Politics of Illusion, New York, New York: Hill and Wang, 1992; Bob Woodward, The Commanders, New York, New York: Simon and Schuster, 1991; and Michael R. Gordon and Bernard E. Trainor, The Generals' War - The Inside Story of the Conflict in the Gulf, Boston, Massachusetts: Little, Brown and Company, 1995.

[24] What in fact transpired during the conflict - even the occurrence of the war itself - is still very much debated. See, for instance, Martin Yant, Desert Mirage - The True Story of the Gulf War, Buffalo, New York: Prometheus Books, 1991; Jean Baudrillard, La Guerre du Golfe n'a pas Eu Lieu, Paris: Galilée, 1991; U.S. News and World Report Staff, Triumph Without Victory - The Unreported History of the Persian Gulf War, New York, New York: Random House, 1992; John R. MacArthur, Second Front - Censorship and Propaganda in the Gulf War, New York, New York: Hill and Wang, 1992; Reporters Sans Frontières, Les Mensonges du Golfe, Paris: Arléa, 1992; and Michael R. Gordon and Bernard E. Trainor, The Generals' War - The Inside Story of the Conflict in the Gulf, Boston, Massachusetts: Little, Brown, and Company, 1995.

[25] Aharon Klieman, "Lost in the Shuffle: The Threatened Marginality of the Gulf Crisis for International Relations Enquiry," in Gad Barzilai et al., The Gulf Crisis and its Global Aftermath, New York, New York: Routledge, 1993, p. 10. For a survey of the military debates

see, Earl H. Tilford, Jr., "The Meaning of Victory in Operation Desert Storm: A Review Essay," *Political Science Quarterly* 108, 2 (1993), pp. 327-331.

2

State-Building and Regime Security: A Framework of Analysis

In this chapter, I sketch the framework of analysis I apply to study Iraqi foreign policy-making during the 1990-1991 Gulf conflict. Adopting a Hegelian perspective on the state as an authoritative idea, I define and locate the respective properties of state-building and regime security, the two principal parameters of the design. The overall guiding principle of the framework is that the state is an abstract, continuous, survival-seeking, resource-gathering entity, and foreign policy is the process which follows from its very existence.

The Concept of State

The notion of state is not evident. As Philip Abrams pointed out, "We have come to take the state for granted as an object of political practice and political analysis while remaining quite spectacularly unclear as to what the state is."[1] To one degree or another, in most of American social sciences, the concept of state has in fact historically been equated with government and political system.[2] In contradistinction, the European tradition, in particular German and French[3] works, has been more concerned with a precise idea of the state *per se* – often positing the state as the natural subject and method of political science.[4] Max Weber and Otto Hintze are, in many ways, the pioneers of statism in the modern era.

For Weber, the state is an organization that enjoys the prerogative of maintaining order and a monopoly on the legitimate exercise of violence over a fixed territory and a circumscribed population. Sovereignty, territory, population, and international recognition are the four prime characteristics of the state. In the might-, power- and domination-oriented Weberian argument, the state is considered more than the government because of the continuous structuring role it plays vis-à-vis society (Stepan, 1978). Weber's take on the state points to the *prima facie* importance of (i) the structure (i.e., territory and population) and (ii) the activity (i.e., legitimate coercive monopoly) of the state. That being as it may, states express themselves not only in their own territories through domestic policy but also externally through foreign policy. Hence it appears that, as one commentator put it, "Weber's work....emphasi[zes] how the very nature of the state crystallizes at the intersection of international and national conditions and pressures,"[5] although Weber tilts the action of his state more inwardly than externally. In effect, the Weberian state comes into existence only after it brings preexisting modes of domination (patriarchy and feudalism) to an end. The birth of the state marks the end of patrimonialism as the state becomes a distinct institution within society (Badie and Birnbaum, 1983). Because it seems to assume an ideologically neutral state only concerned with a legal order, i.e., "the increasing subordination of individual behavior to a bureaucratic imperative brought about by the ever increasing rationalization of society," Weber's analysis has been criticized for being taxonomic rather than explanatory. Control of the state and the issues therein contained take precedence over the ideological factors that characterize the emergence, formation, and continuity of the state (Davis, 1991).[6]

Otto Hintze, for his part, brought to the fore the historical (changing) dynamics that affect the state and all of its environment. The state is presented as being part of an internal and external system that cuts both ways. As he noted, "The state is seen in isolation, exclusive in itself, without raising the question whether its peculiar character is co-determined by its relation to its surroundings."[7] Adhering to Leopold Von Ranke's emphasis on the primacy of foreign policy as the crucial element shaping the constitution of states, Hintze then argues that all efforts and activities of the state ought to be outwardly oriented in order to strengthen the state against its rivals and maintain its posture. He also points to the state, rather than economic forces, as providing impetus and direction to the political process (Gilbert, 1975). In that respect, he demonstrates the role that war and conflict in general can play in the building of a state noting that

> states are created by war, colonization, conquest and peaceful settlement
> through amalgamation of different parts and through their separating
> from each other; and all this is bound up with an alternating process of
> intermingling and separation of races and civilizations, tribes and languages.

And, in another essay, he writes:

> The form and spirit of the state's organization will not be determined
> solely by economic and social relations and clashes of interests, but
> primarily by the necessities of defense and offense, that is, by the
> organization of the army and warfare.

Hintze's work suggests, then, that there is a permanent collaboration between domestic and foreign fields, that war is often a shaping and delineating factor in the constitution of states, and that historical changes underlie and affect all processes of state development. Hintze in effect broadens the Weberian juridical perception of the state by placing emphasis on three other determinative factors ignored by Weber: foreign policy, conflict, and history.[8] He specifically states:

> I do not conceive of the 'organization of state' in the narrow,
> constitutional, and juridical sense that deals only with the distribution of
> the state's functions and powers among its various executive agents.[9]

47

During the first half of the twentieth century, the state's preeminence was by and large de-emphasized in most political science studies – and particularly so in foreign policy analysis, which emerged only late as a sub-field of international relations. The reappearance of the state in political science literature was initiated in the mid-1960s. This reemergence signified, in general, a divorce from a dominant society-oriented tradition in comparative politics and, to a lesser degree, in international relations. In a seminal article, J.P. Nettl (1968) denounced the absence of adequate conceptualization of the state with regard to modern theory or analysis, and noted that the state essentially stands as a concretization of structures which can be studied as such. That is, putting aside the area concerns of state activity – stemming primarily from its defining Weberian coercive nature – it is possible to look at the state *tel quel*, i.e., as "a collectivity that summates a set of functions and structures in order to generalize their applicability." An important distinction made by Nettl is the recognition of the state as a distinct sector in which a high societal generality is summated. For the state indeed stands apart because it benefits from aggregate yet exclusive qualities: primarily the legitimate exercise of power over a societal body located in a delimited territory. These qualities allow for both its preeminence and perennation.[10]

The notion of "bringing the state back" also originated with Samuel Huntington (1968). Addressing the political problems of modernizing nations, Huntingon made the argument that a fundamental political notion is stability. For the state to be effective in coping with the rapid social and economic changes that accompany modernization, he argues, it needs to get back and stand at the center of the societal process. This means control and regulation of the political process by constraining new groups from entering into politics and limiting the mobilization of the masses. At the heart of the argument stands the notion of political order (read state order) which depends, in large part, on the relation between the development of institutions and the mobilization of new forces into politics. The more complex and heterogeneous the society is, points out Huntington, the more achievement and maintenance of political community become dependent upon the workings of political

48

institutions. And this calls for a leading role for the state. Yet, as Huntington demonstrates, the development of the state has often lagged behind the evolution of society. In light of this, he points to the necessity of having the state (as an organization) refocus itself and perform its function adequately – that is, authoritatively. The payoff is that a society with highly institutionalized governing organizations and procedures (i.e., a state that is "back in") is more able to articulate and achieve its public interests. The way to do that, in Huntington's view, is centralization and rationalization of the political machinery of the state. Thus, according to Huntington, the full institutionalization of the political system requires state development (Badie and Birnbaum, 1983). And, as another proponent of the return to the state shows, a combination of factors makes it easy for the state to take that developmental action under the form of policy:

> The extranational orientations of states, the challenges they may face in maintaining domestic order, and the organizational resources that collectivities of state officials may be able to draw on and deploy – all of these features of the state as viewed from a Weberian-Hintzean perspective can help to explain autonomous state action (Skocpol, 1985).

Criticism of this neo-statism was provided by Gabriel A. Almond, who denounced the ambiguity of the term, as Sabine (1934) and Watkins (1968) had previously done.[11] For Almond, the state as it is perceived by neo-statists is a large and loose concept lacking clear specification and characterized by ambiguous phraseology. Agreeing with Easton (1981), he sees neo-statism as a phenomenon resulting from the revival in the 1970s of Marxism. Essentially, he argues that the new statist studies have not succeeding in articulating an operationalizable definition of the state, and that many of the concepts they employ in their demonstrations resemble those of the functionalist and pluralist traditions.

Yet "administration," "courts," "parties," "bureaucracy," "government," and other policy "agencies" are categories that any statist must use. The problem, it seems, does not lie in establishing another set of conceptual tools, but rather in identifying the complexity of statehood phenomena and pointing to the preeminence of the state as an organizing and organized idea which supersedes these categories. Responding to Almond, Eric Nordlinger (1988) does just that when he identifies the core of the statist perspective as being formed of (i) distinctive state internal variations; (ii) preferences patterned according to past and present strategies; and (iii) resistance to societal efforts to limit the state's institutional contours and activities. State-centric approaches are, thus, warranted because the state is the most consequential actor in both domestic and international polities.

A variety of definitions of the state have been offered. Benjamin and Duvall proposed a useful taxonomy identifying four types of definitions: the state as (i) government, (ii) administrative order, (iii) ruling class, or (iv) normative order.[12] A fifth definition, the state as a Hegelian abstraction, was added to this typology by Lentner (1984). Let us review them.[13]

The state as government. This school (Dahl 1961; Suleiman, 1974; Sklar, 1975; Lindblom 1977; Stepan, 1977; Krasner, 1978; Trimberger, 1978; Evans, 1979; Hamilton, 1982; Nordlinger 1981, 1987, and 1988) understands the state as a group of individuals fulfilling specific roles. Here, the act of governing, literally of holding office, defines and delimits the state, whose institutional structures – providing constraints, opportunities, and imperatives – are offered a secondary role. This approach is strongly influenced by behavioralist tenets and pluralism. Its take on leadership is, in Stephen Krasner's words, "heterogeneous and atomistic." Here, the state is a renewable temporary phenomenon as it is equated with individual atomistic actors – the state is "public officials writ large" (Nordlinger, 1987).

The state as a legal and administrative order. This perspective (Heclo, 1974; Panitch, 1977; Zysman, 1977; Katzenstein, 1978; Skowronek, 1982; Ashford, 1983; Krasner,

1984; Echeverri-Gent, 1993; Waterbury, 1993; Newberg, 1995) looks at the state as an apparatus of juridical institutions and infrastructures designed to establish and enforce societal codes of interaction. It is society-oriented in the sense that the state is seen as a reflection of the organizational requirements of the societal body – essentially, a large public sector dealt with by civil administrators (legislatures, bureaucracies, executives, agencies, courts, interest groups, political parties, media, and so on).

The state as ruling class. This is the Marxist and neo-Marxist (Miliband, 1969; Offe, 1971; Poulantzas, 1973; Anderson, 1974; Block, 1978; Therborn, 1978; Wright, 1978; Wallerstein, 1980; Skocpol, 1980) approach. It essentially focuses on the socioeconomic functions of the state. Here, also, the state is a temporary phenomenon as it is closely associated with the struggle and dynamics of social classes. This approach is also society-oriented, since the state is presented as being shaped by the outcome of these class struggles. In effect, the crucial question in all varieties of Marxism is the question of how much independence is actually enjoyed by the state in its relations with civil society formations (Abrams, 1988). In addition, the approach superimposes a microrationality (that of capital) over a macrorationality (that of the state). Miliband (1969) even disparages the state, seeing it as a non-entity. He holds that "[it] is not a thing,....it does not, as such, exist."

The state as normative order. This approach (Huntington, 1968; Geertz, 1981; Badie and Birnbaum, 1983) emphasizes the symbolic aspect of the state and the norms, practices, and customs dominant in a society. The state elicits patterns of political interaction that are characterized by stability and which, in time, become institutionalized. In sum, the state embodies, sustains, and perpetuates the existing polity because it corresponds to the bases of the prevailing social order. Attacks against the state are, for instance, posited as endangering that same polity and affecting the very societal community from which it springs. In this perspective, state and society are fused, mutually reinforcing, and follow an integrated evolution (Benjamin and Duvall, 1985).

The state as an abstraction. This is the Hegelian perspective. Advocates of this view (Bourdieu, 1970; Waltz, 1979; Lentner, 1984; Abrams, 1988; Mitchell, 1991)[14] stress the characteristics of continuity of existence and purpose of the state. The argument is that the abstractness of the state is a useful conceptual tool to understand and accept the reality surrounding it. The state is the actor of politics defined as rule. It has to deal with constraints of institutional nature, and it is endowed with a sense of history and consequently of continuity/discontinuity dimensions. Most importantly, the state embodies the social interest as it carries a public purpose and summarizes a variety of components.

Insofar as they de-emphasize state autonomy, liberal and Marxist interpretations of the state are restrictive (i.e., devaluative) of the concept of state. The Hegelian, for its part, is positive (i.e., promotive). The state is not viewed as a captive as in Marxist perspectives but rather as an arena, although not one of competing interests as in pluralism. Rather, it is understood as an autonomous arena. Skocpol (1979) argued that, for instance, such autonomy is reflected in the capacity of states to behave as actors to realize policy goals and have a direct impact on the formation of politics. For the purposes of this study, I retain the Hegelian definition of the state as a rational actuality which is mediated subjectively as an end product of activity: the state is an absolute end in itself. This choice echoes a concern with adequately assessing the state as first and foremost a historical project – one that I maintain resonates in foreign policy-making. For Hegel (1821), the state:

(a) Has immediate actuality and is the individual state as a self-dependent organism....(b) passes over into the relation of one state to other states....
(c) is the universal idea as a genus and as an absolute power over individual states.

Later in *The Philosophy of Right*, Hegel specifies the dimensions of the building of this idea of the state as external necessity and higher authority vis-à-vis the subaltern organized realms of family and civil society:

> The constitution of the state is, in the first place, the organization of the state and the self-related process of its organic life, a process whereby it differentiates its moments within itself and develops them to self- subsistence. Secondly, the state is an individual, unique, and exclusive, and therefore related to others. Thus it turns its differentiating activity outward and accordingly establishes within itself the ideality of its subsisting inward differentiations.

The state is apprehended as something that develops *actively* both domestically and on the foreign front. The Hegelian perspective is indeed useful for our purposes insofar as it accommodates history. Hegel's view is that the modern state is the culmination of historical development, whereas the liberal tradition refutes this, opting for the immediacy of the private sphere, and the Marxist perspective looks at history as something to be changed, as the object of an action rather than an objective category in which the state becomes. In effect:

> Hegelianism....add[s] emphasis on the community that pervades and cuts across individual and class interests, stressing the continuity of history as against the Marxist view of the disjuncture of history, and the importance of the state as the instrument for preserving the continuity of and formulating and executing community purposes (Lentner, 1984).

It is the elusiveness which is attached to the concept of state that so often makes it appear problematic; the couching of the concept in more metaphysical than substantive terms. And it is true that nowhere more than in the Hegelian formulation is that abstractness of the state more pronounced. However, it is equally true that "the imprecision that made the term unsuitable as an analytical tool was the source of its political strength as a mythic or ideological construct" (Mitchell, 1991). Similarly, Nettl spoke of its "skeletal, ghostly existence" (Nettl, 1968) that can be used positively. On that aspect of the state, Hegel remarks that:

> (i) The abstract actuality or the substantiality of the state consists in the fact that its end is the universal interest as such and the conservation therein of particular interests since the universal interest is the substance of these. (ii) But this substantiality of the state is also its *necessity*, since its substantiality is divided into the distinct spheres of its activity which correspond to the moment of its concept, and these spheres, owing to this substantiality, are thus actually fixed determinate characteristics of the state, i.e., its *powers*. (Original emphasis.)

Over and above being something intrinsic to it, the abstractness of the state infuses the notion with authority. As a focal point of action and reflection, the idea of the state becomes a common source from which all organization (i.e., institutions and other organized social dynamics) spring. As the state is built, all new and gradually all preexisting decision sites come to reflect part of the idea of the state.[15] "Stateness" becomes a quality to be developed (and surely maintained and even improved) by all agencies and processes. This is primarily done through policy-making. Machiavelli's *ragione de stato* is accommodated here as a most legitimate, because logical, dimension of state activity.[16] It is legitimate because, for Hegel, the universality of the state as something shared by the members of society is a sacred notion to be logically defended.[17]

Abrams demystifies such reification of the state. Calling for the abandonment of the state as a material object of study, he concludes that:

> The state is....in every sense of the term a triumph of concealment. It conceals the real history and relations of subjection behind an a-historical mask of legitimating illusion; contrives to deny the existence of connections and conflicts which would if recognized be incompatible with the claimed autonomy and integration of the state. The real official secret, however, is the secret of the non-existence of the state (Abrams, 1988: 77).

To be sure, the argument has merit. It is true that since the state has been a remarkably bemusing concept, then there is something of a "hidden reality" (Abrams' formula) masked by the unspecificity of the state. Nevertheless, what is left out here is that it is the very "non-existence of the state" which defines it. In other words because, as I suggest, there are constant efforts by the political actors to flesh out the state, the idea of state is perpetuated indefinitely. There is no need to reach further past that point where the "existence" of the state is established – beyond its actuality – for that would announce the obsolescence of policy (regarded as the act of "breathing" of the state)[18] and the end of the history of the state.[19]

All of this points to the notion that the state is first and foremost an idea, i.e., something that is divorced from the constitutive social relations and reified (Marsden, 1992). Recently, the notion of the state as idea was particularly articulated by Burdeau (1970) who pointed to the fact that the construction of the concept of state is not designed to account for a preexisting reality (of, say, a purely social concern) but, rather, it is aimed at the elaboration of an aggregate and superior order. As he notes:

> [L'État] n'est ni territoire, ni population, ni corps de règles obligatoires. Certes, toutes ces données sensibles ne lui sont pas étrangères, mais il les transcende. Son existence n'appartient pas à la phénomènologie tangible; elle est de l'ordre de l'esprit. L'État est, au sens plein du terme, une idée. N'ayant d'autre réalité que conceptuelle il n'existe que parce qu'il est pensé (1970).[20]

As such, the state becomes a justification for the relationships between the governed and their leaders – instead of a naked struggle for power. Ever tautological in this perspective, the state is, then, at once regulator of all societal activity and object of conquest. Thus, most of the value of the concept is generated definitionally. The state as an idea acquires significant political reality since it is constantly engaged in what Mitchell (1991) terms "the formation and expression of authoritative intentions." After Mitchell, I choose to identify these intentions as policy-making. The acceptance of the state *qua* idea allows us to explore the finality of such idea. How can the construct of the idea of the state be used in the elaboration of foreign policy?

In effect, from the "idea" flows an organization that seeks to build – literally to concretize – something around the notion of state. The dynamic of building the state becomes, thus, tautologically the action of the state.[21] Part of that building is reflected in the foreign policy behavior of any country, and it is even more so present in "statist" countries like Iraq.

The state is discernibly appropriate to the study of international relations because it constitutes the primary unit in the field. (The international environment in its modern form is in essence nothing but the result of the anarchical interaction of states within a systemic structure defining the positional relations of these states.) It is the one unit that can legitimately act internationally. There have traditionally been few challenges to both its sovereignty and autonomy in foreign affairs (Nettl, 1968), and its actions are authoritative and highly consequential (Nordlinger, 1988).

State-Building

I distinguish state-building from state-formation which, roughly, corresponds to what J.P. Nettl has called "the concretization of statehood in the historical experience of various countries." Although addressing similar needs on the part of the state, state-formation, as used by Malik Mufti (1992) for instance, essentially connotes a finality: the establishment of a modern state. (In the case of Iraq, the process of state-formation, it can be argued, was formally completed by 1968 when the Ba'thists came to power.) Mufti's state-formation refers to the story of the emergence and consolidation of the sovereign nation-state system in Iraq and Syria.

Nevertheless, it must be noted that state-building has often been used to refer to the same processes of nation-building[22] (i.e., the process by which national consciousness appears and becomes institutionalized in the structures of the society) and state-formation and consolidation. Thomson (1992, 1994) offered a different conceptualization of state-building in the context of the state's historical establishment as the defender of the legal order. Focusing on the demise of non-state violence, she uses the concept dynamically, seeing it as enabling a fundamentally modern function of the state – namely, the state's monopoly of external coercive capabilities. At the conclusion of her demonstration, she insightfully urges us to "abandon the notion that the state is the state is the state."[23]

In contradistinction, state-building in this study is explored as the promotion of state identity combined with the furtherance of particular regime needs in a given foreign policy exercise and its corresponding particular decisions. State-building is defined as *the permanent, continuous, and overarching historical becoming of the state.* State-building is simply the execution of the idea of state. It is permanent in the sense that it is not confined to the particular needs and aspirations of any one regime – as it is made up of the sum total of the contributions of all successive regimes. It is an exercise connected to the essence of the state (i.e., the reason of its functioning as historical project) and its inherent survival requirement.

State-building is not so much about the "managed construction of beliefs about the state" (Abrams, 1988) – that is more the task of political socialization. Rather, it is about the establishment of the idea of the state in and of itself. The former process has society as its object whereas the latter seeks to ascertain altogether an identity of the state. Again, state-building is the fleshing out of the idea of state. This is the actualization process of which Hegel speaks.

The idea is that the state responds primarily to its own needs. Yet attending to these needs – as well as defining them – depends essentially on the nature of the society and its history. State-building is an agenda that is largely aimed at what George Burdeau calls *la quête de la durée* (the quest for duration). Burdeau writes:

57

L'État ne meurt pas davantage. Indifférent à la succession des gouvernants, il assure la permanence de leurs actes dès lors que, réguliérement accomplis, ils peuvent lui être imputés (1970: 49).[24]

Moreover, it may be useful to establish that, at any given time, there is for the state extreme uncertainty in interactions with other states (Lentner, 1984). Therefore, the imperative quality its action is endowed with allows it to pursue the building action and present it as a sacred enterprise.[25] And, as Good (1962) points out, the demands of state-building are easily expressed in foreign policy behavior:

> [F]requently, foreign policy is recruited to the state-building task – or is intimately affected by the immensity of that task....The state's legitimacy is more easily asserted through its domestic policies, and it is more apparent when performing on the international than on the national stage. Domestic issues divide the nation....foreign issues unite the nation and mark it as a going concern.[26]

How, then, does the state-building process unfold? There are three elements characteristic of state-building: (i) the establishment of institutions, (ii) the pursuit and development of national consensus and domestic cohesion, and (iii) the maintenance of sovereignty. Underlying the pursuit of these three objectives is a rationale of exclusivity and maximization.

Institution-Development. The process of institutionalization leads to the concretization of the idea of state. As that idea becomes incorporated in a tangible institutionalized reality (a legislative body, an army, a police force, education structures, and a legal apparatus) – which it suffuses – it becomes available to the leaders of the state as a powerful representation. Yet as that representation takes a life of its own, it is no longer the exclusivity of the state. Duration of the state through institutions and irrespective of the regimes is primarily expressed within a general logic of political development. And development dynamics are more often geared towards the establishment of a state apparatus than they are aimed at reorganizing the texture of a

58

society. Indeed, the building process also reflects a modernization process and the state is the quintessential sociological phenomenon of modernity (Nettl, 1968). And, as Theda Skocpol remarks "'Political development'....end[s] up having more to do with concrete international and domestic struggles over state building than with any inherent general logic of socioeconomic 'differentiation'" (Skocpol, 1985). This means that without breaking its ties with certain social strata – with which it can come to be particularly connected in a multiplicity of ways – the state endowed with institutions rises beyond and towards the global interests of the community.

Finally, with time, as "the past [comes to] pattern the institutional present" (Nordlinger, 1988), the presence of institutions provides the state with empirical authority and the appearance of legality. In countries where the process is tilted more towards absolute respect of these institutions as guarantor of the state's continuity (and implicitly, beyond it, of the community) than towards their use as democratic means of civic regulation of political life, institutions can often become a means to an end – much like a policy tool – rather than an end in themselves. Under contemporaneous environmental conditions (globalization of patterns, limits to territoriality,[27] widening and intensification of the interdependencies of economies,..), it is becoming increasingly difficult to give coherent articulation to the institutional mission of the state without having to factor in external elements – although it is a fact that foreign impediments have been present since the Treaty of Westphalia established the principle of exclusive jurisdiction.

Maintenance of National Consensus and Domestic Cohesion. This aspect of state-building concerns the organization of common experience. For state-building to proceed, it is in effect necessary to have the community share a minimum of consensus about their political vision. A loose definition of the local general interest has to be attained in order to give meaning to the action of institutions and the orientation of policy. Seeking to establish unity in place of fragmentation, the leadership of the state will often rely, to that end, on inclusive nationalistic generalizations and historical metaphors. In nations involved in the creation of a modern state, the process has a particularly important role insofar as it establishes new founding myths. The action of the Ba'th party in Iraq is in that regard a case in point.

To provide coherence and consistency to the national consensus required to pursue state-building, a certain level of societal and political national cohesiveness has also to be maintained. This calls for the state to perpetuate continuously its control over developments in the societal body. After Burhan Ghalioun (1991), I understand this process of the state as its own expression of the organization of society and the reflection of the programs and interests of organized social forces: élites, social groups, and alliances. The state acquires coherence – and is thus built – as a result of convergence of interests springing from evolving power configurations. In ethnically, religiously, ideologically, racially, economically, and geographically segmented nations such as Iraq, these power configurations are the primary terrain upon which the building of the state takes place.

Nationalism, as it has pervaded the existence of most modern Arab countries, led to ambitious development projects. Underneath the authoritarian regimes and territorial concerns which it often determined, argues Ghalioun, there was a project of development of the state itself. This development, he points out, takes the form of one main function to which the state must attend: the political and material reproduction of society. Then the state becomes the pivot of societal and national construction. It is, hence, the expression of the ability, or lack thereof, to integrate the many dimensions of society that constitutes the *raison d'être* of the state. As I see it, as it exists continuously, this urge is one cement of state-building. Burhan Ghalioun speaks directly to this when he concludes that "the modern [Arab] state is itself in a perpetual quest for identity and legitimacy." Strengthened and confirmed in its role of guardian, the state can, then, use the concern about national cohesion as both a sacred foundational goal (to be "protected" when, for instance, putting down rebellions) and a basis for justifying policy choices and measures.

60

Continuation of Sovereignty. Finally, a global exercise of continuation of sovereignty encompasses the two previous components of state-building. The purely domestic aspects of institution-erection, national consensus, and maintenance of social cohesion provide the state with an internal reality to be externally collectively protected through the affirmation and preservation of its sovereignty. As Thomson (1994) reminds us, "Sovereignty is best seen as a set of institutionalized authority."

In countries that have historically lacked a strong tradition of state, the problem of establishing and maintaining sovereignty acquires particular importance. In the case of the Iraqi state, the integration of society, complicated by the survival of tribalism and the Ottoman legacy of three separate provinces in the north, center, and south, was from the inception coupled with a survival requirement. This combination, it is here argued, has always been a primary and immediate feature for which any Iraqi regime has had to account. The Hashemite monarchy (1921-1958), the militaro-Communist regime of 'Abdelkarim Qassem (1958-1963), the nationalist Republic of the 'Aref brothers (1963-1968), and the Ba'thi regime (1968-present) have successively been concerned with this element. A shared sense of urgency about the construction of their state (in order to ensure its continuity and external legitimacy) was, I posit, present as a companion to the concerns about their own regime survival needs.

In light of this, a sovereign Iraq always simultaneously meant control over domestic developments to prevent the resurgence of not-so-latent particularisms. It also meant aggressive pursuit of the "nationhood" of Iraq in order to counter any arguments about the artificiality of the country. And, finally, it also ensured the survival of the different regimes if they were to defend properly the state's sovereignty. To that end, a definition of the state's sovereignty through warfare falls under the category of the building mission of the state. Wars and conflict in general have often been resorted to by states as autonomy-enhancing acts.[28] As Hegel (1821) noted:

> The ideality which is in evidence in war, i.e., in an accidental relation of a state to a foreign state, is the same as the ideality in accordance with which the domestic powers of the state are organic moments in a whole.

61

This fact appears in history in various forms, e.g. successful wars have checked domestic unrest and consolidated the power of the state at home.

Through such operations, the acts of the rulers of the country (i.e., the state leaders) acquire new meaning as they are seen as part of the collectivity's becoming – not the immediate needs of the rulers. Nevertheless, sometimes these acts may be closely associated with those very needs.

In the final analysis, the dynamic of state-building is in the first place one of reproduction. It is also one of strengthening and replication. State-building is an open-ended and continuous exercise, and it can go astray leading to state-decay. The building process is continuous in the sense that it pervades the foreign policy behavior of all the different state regimes. Finally, state-building is overarching insofar as it encompasses all the foreign policy activities of the regimes. Specific instances of sub-activity – such as the attempt to invade Kuwait made by 'Abdelkarim Qassem in 1961 or the actual Ba'thi invasion of 1990-1991 – are engaged in by successive regimes.

Regime Security

The specific norms of a regime affect the general state-building process as much as they are conditioned by it. Regime security is *the idiosyncratic set of dispositions, orientations, and strategies of a particular regime as it seeks to maintain its physical presence, establish and perpetuate legitimacy, and further its permanent and ad hoc interests.* Regime security is evaluated against the background of state-building in which it is inscribed. A regime corresponds to a more modest historical unit than the state. It appears, describes a trajectory in time, and is extinguished (al-Azmeh, 1982). In the absolute, the regime is incidental to the history of the state. But because it comes to occupy its stage, the regime for a while *merges* with the state. In the case at hand, Ba'thi regime security is informed by the challenges and the fate met by its militaro-

62

nationalistic, Communist, and monarchical predecessors. Its main dynamic, thus, is one of constraint and confinement – although, as noted, there is a significant and defining margin of action for each regime. Tardanico (1982) remarks that "In examining state-building struggles, not to be overlooked is the possibility that regimes may act in their own organizational interests." Constricted by the parameters of state-building, regime security consists then of the use of the symbolic attributes of statehood to try to maximize the position of a regime. But the use of these attributes is primarily aimed at protecting the regime – through the use of the muscle of the state – and removing the conditions of its downfall. Its dynamic is thus also one of protection – underscoring Pascal's dictum that *le propre de la puissance est de protéger.*[29]

Discussing the primacy of the historical in the *Muqaddima* (1377) of Ibn Khaldoun, Aziz al-Azmeh (1982) indicates how the idiosyncrasy of a dynasty/regime/administration comes to be inscribed in the more general and superior idea of state:

> There is nothing that distinguishes any of these strains of historicity from another except for external factors: name and date. While these two elements are the very ones that define the specificity of an historical unit, the specificity in question is structurally and conceptually spurious. There is no difference of genus but only of sheer unspecific difference: *the fact that a state is that of the Fatimids or of the Hamdanids, for instance, is not pertinent in any way to the constitution of the state.* Both are structurally homologous in the strictest of senses: they consist of elements (sovereigns) in succession. In this structure, the name and date are contingent differences among structures that are, in essence, interchangeable. *The state is the succession of sections of duration,* each designated by the name of a sovereign, without reference to structures of the social, geographical, or even genealogical orders which, in fact, the state integrates. (Emphasis added.)

There are I offer four elements whereby regime security is realized: (i) power consolidation, (ii) economic viability, (iii) external and internal threat diffusion, and (iv) legitimacy renewal. It is important to understand that there will always be inherent unevenness in the pursuit of the various tasks that compose this securing imperative. Given the physically limited resources of a regime, simultaneous attendance to all four aspects of regime security is impossible. Regime security is fundamentally a disparate, across-the-board, exercise.

Power Consolidation. The most significant component of a regime's security concerns the effort to take control of the prevailing political situation and to structure state power around the core of the regime. Typically, this element appears immediately after the take-over (violent or not, legitimate or otherwise forced) of the state apparatus. The often volatile situation prevalent during the first phases of a regime's arrival to power makes it paramount for a regime to pay particular attention to the social and political developments that might reverse its newly-acquired leading status. Specifically, this translates into surveillance of real and potential adversaries' maneuvering, keeping in close touch with the societal body to stay tuned to the population's wavelength (the so-called "man in the street"), and rapidly taking action in the form of policy to give meaning and reality to the regime's presence – as well as endow it with legitimate attributes of state action. The effort to consolidate power externally is also present within the group as attribution of roles, restructuring, and dismissal of some actors are often enacted. In sum, the installation of the regime spells out a new reality often necessitating a major action to bestow upon it identity and to remove potential opposition. The process can be described as "a backstage institutionalization of political power behind the onstage agencies of government" (Abrams, 1988).

Power consolidation is not, however, solely confined to the period when a regime gains power. Periodically, the effort has to be repeated. Whenever the global situation which is the environment of the regime is undergoing a change, with the possibility of threats or at least major uncertainties about its future, a regime will seek to reaffirm its power. Generally, the greater the threat is, the more significant and urgent the effort will be. The guiding idea is to establish and then, whenever it appears to be necessary, reaffirm the regime's insulation from social forces, even if sometimes

64

the action might take the form of an alliance with the dominant classes in a sustained effort to avoid dispersal of power to civil society. Finally, resort to force is more often than not seen as an adequate strategy to implement these objectives, which can be articulated domestically as well as externally.

Economic Viability. A purely political and strategic concern such as power consolidation is reinforced and made to last if the regime is able to establish or perpetuate – if establishment was already accomplished by a previous regime – and maintain a certain level of economic viability. This aspect of regime security corresponds to the crucial economic test of the regime, that is, its ability or lack thereof to meet the socioeconomic demands of the population. By and large, survival of the regime is closely associated with the adequate providing of economic services to the population. Though tyrannical regimes have often survived when their people were being starved, it is a general rule that prolonged absence of economic viability ultimately spells certain doom for a regime. For the underlying rationale of the economic mission is the creation of a dynamic favorable to the regime in addition to the more general purposes of the state's economic activity, such as accumulation of wealth and reproduction of labor. Specifically, this means the association of economic success or at least satisfactory economic progress with the identity of the regime (i.e., the idea that were this regime to disappear, economic decay would surely follow). Nationalization of major local companies is an initial strategy often resorted to in that regard. Other effective measures include the creation of economic support systems directly linked to the ideology of the regime (food stamps, rationing under a political umbrella, and so on).

Threat Diffusion. This action constitutes the core of regime security. It consists in providing the regime with an adequate margin of security primarily staving off any danger to (i) its existence, (ii) its action, and (iii) the values attached to its identity (i.e., its founding myths). Deflecting threats is then the main agenda of the regime security dynamic. As the regime becomes impervious to attacks, it gains strength. And, in a mutually reinforcing circular movement, as it gains strength, it becomes more able to diffuse additional threats. Since the process takes place within a societal environment, regimes often attempt to link their own security with that of the whole of society. Creating or identifying a particular threat to regime as a danger to the whole community and its state is often resorted to as the best strategy to marshal endorsement and enlist support.[30] In that respect, threat diffusion resembles what Lasswell (1946) has dubbed "the socialization of danger."[31] In the Arab context, Dawisha points out that "Arab regimes have followed a two-pronged maxim: put fear in peoples' hearts but try to win their support, no matter how grudgingly given."[32]

Thus, the primary contribution of threat diffusion to the regime security ensemble is to neutralize constraints and pressures which otherwise would have afflicted the regime's action but also, down the line, its professed values and ultimately its physical presence. Obviating challenges of necessity also means the identification and recognition of actual challenges within or without the regime's environment. Attending to a situation which is not significantly problematic can easily disperse the action of the regime and reduce its security resources. It becomes a crucial test, then, to know which threats are more important. The performance of this crucial and sensitive task is equally consequential. Recognizing this leads to the realization that threats are multiform: political, social, economic, cultural, external, internal, global, regional, long-term, short-term, and isolated or pervasive.

Maintenance of Legitimacy. Maintaining legitimacy is an essential goal for a regime. It ensures its continued existence by linking both its actions and values to the idea that the community entertains of the state. Hence, legitimacy for a regime is always legitimacy by association. This is the very idea that the whole of regime security is determined by the parameters of state-building. Along these lines, Mastanduno *et al.* (1989) remark that:

66

While the survival of the state in the international arena requires the defense of the sovereignty and territorial integrity of the nation-state, domestically it demands that the state meet and overcome challenges from, and maintain the support of, societal groups and coalitions. *This is the case both for the state as an organization and for the incumbents who occupy dominant positions in the state apparatus at any given moment.* (Emphasis added.)

The enactment of regime security is a set of actions undertaken on the basis of a self-attributed righteousness. The performance of the functions unravels in the context of circumstances subjectively assessed by the regime's leaders. In effect, as Hugh Heclo (1974) notes, "Policy-making is a form of collective puzzlement on society's behalf; it entails both deciding and knowing." Accordingly, a regime also reappropriates the basic feature of the local legitimacy tenets that are ubiquitous in all facets of the polity.

Figure 2.1

The Analytical Framework

FOREIGN POLICY-MAKING PROCESS

⇑ (general decisional parameters) ⇑   ⇑ (particular decisional parameters) ⇑

STATE-BUILDING   ⇒ *(information flow)* ⇒   **REGIME SECURITY**
                          ⇐ *(adherence flow)* ⇐

• INSTITUTION-DEVELOPMENT	• POWER CONSOLIDATION
• NATIONAL CONSENSUS	• ECONOMIC VIABILITY
• DOMESTIC COHESION	• THREAT DIFFUSION
• CONTINUATION OF SOVEREIGNTY	• MAINTENANCE OF LEGITIMACY

Summary

This chapter has suggested that the state is an idea which is permanently being built by successive regimes in a country. The concept of state was discussed with regard to the nature of the explicandum as an idea and with regard to its reproduction over time. From a Hintzean-Hegelian perspective, it was proposed that this idea of state lends itself to a building process which is a prolonged effort to substantialize the state. That effort, state-building, is expressed in the foreign policy behavior of a country, and it can take the form of conflict and warfare.

Specifically, state-building is pursued through: (i) the establishment of institutions, (ii) the quest for and development of national consensus and domestic cohesion, and (iii) the maintenance of sovereignty. The general framework continuously established by these actions provides the stage for the efforts entertained by a regime to ensure its security. This regime security ensemble is fourfold: (i) power consolidation, (ii) economic viability, (iii) external and internal threat diffusion, and (iv) legitimacy renewal.

The two directing concepts are identified. State-building is permanent, general, and abstract. Regime security is temporary, specific, and empirical. In this case-study, Iraqi political history since 1921 provides the state-building parameter, and the Ba'thi regime in power in that country since July of 1968 is the one whose security is in question. The combination of these two concepts illuminates the decisionmaking processes at play amongst the Iraqi leadership during the 1990-1991 Second Gulf War. The aim of the next section is to demonstrate this.

NOTES

[1] Philip Abrams, "Notes on the Difficulty of Studying the State," *Journal of Historical Sociology* 1, 1 (March 1988), p.59. Also see Richard Marsden, "'The State': A Comment on Abrams, Denis, and Sayer," *Journal of Historical Sociology* 5, 3 (September 1992), pp. 358-377.

[2] Gabriel A. Almond argued that the devaluation of the concept of state was largely due to the waves of democratization and political mobilization that accompanied sociopolitical changes in the West at the turn of the century (Almond, 1988: 855).

[3] Most recently, the French debate has been essentially concerned with the issue of planetarization of the concept of state. See, for example, Ali Kazancigil, ed., *L'État au Pluriel - Perspectives de Sociologie Historique*, Paris: Economica, 1985; Bertrand Badie, *L'État Importé - L'Occidentalisation de l'Ordre Politique*, Paris: Fayard, 1992; Régis Debray, *L'État Séducteur - Les Révolutions Médiologiques du Pouvoir*, Paris: Gallimard, 1993; and Pierre Robert Baduel, ed., "État Moderne, Nationalismes et Islamismes," *Revue du Monde Musulman et de la Méditerranée* 68-69, 2/3 (1993), in particular Denis Retaillé's article, "L'État, le Territoire et les Relations Internationales: Nouvelles Approches Géographiques," pp. 41-64.

[4] Carl Joachim Friedrich, *Der Verfassungsstaat der Neuzeit*, Berlin: 1953, p.1.

[5] David Held, "Central Perspectives on the Modern State," in David Held *et al.*, eds., *States and Societies*, New York, New York: New York University Press, 1983, p. 42.

[6] For a poignant discussion of the inadequacy of the Weberian model for the Arab world see Louay Mounir Safy, "The Challenge of Modernity: The Quest for Authenticity in the Arab World," Ph.D. dissertation, Wayne State University (1992). Also see Bryan S. Turner, *Weber and Islam: A Critical Study*, London: Kegan Paul, 1974. Turner is concerned in particular with Weber's notion of patrimonialism in the Islamic context.

[7] Otto Hintze, "The Formation of States and Constitutional Development: A Study in History and Politics," (1902), in Felix Gilbert, ed., *The Historical Essays of Otto Hintze*, New York, New York: Oxford University Press, 1975, p. 159.

[8] Albrov (1970) and Blau (1970) have, for instance, showed how conflict in the bureaucracy – and beyond – is not accounted for by Weber. See Martin Albrov, *Bureaucracy*, London: MacMillan, 1970, chapter 3; and Peter Blau, "Weber's Theory of Bureaucracy," in Dennis Wrong, ed., *Max Weber*, Englewood Cliffs, New Jersey: Prentice-Hall, 1970.

[9] Otto Hintze, "Military Organization and the Organization of the State," (1906), in Gilbert (1975), p. 183.

[10] The fact that the state is an entity which always survives the different type of limitations – be they legal, societal, normative, or otherwise – that come to be imposed on it prompts us to understand "stateness" (i.e., the saliency of the state) as an essentially continuous quality, one resulting from a permanent action of construction and de-construction. It is important to point out that the international aspect of the state (sovereignty and autonomy) is affected by disturbances only conjuncturally, rarely structurally. Only the extreme case of defeat in war can sometimes lead to partition, as in the case of Germany in 1945. Generally, domestically-generated situations, such as revolutions and coups, yield changes in the form, attribution, and constitution of the state – never its very existence, the exception being secession, as was the case with the provinces of the former Yugoslavia after 1991.

[11] Reification of the concept of state is also the subject of criticism by Theodore J. Lowi who sees the state as a "residual category," something that cannot "be studied directly" (1988: 891). He emphatically denies it the status of variable (which Nettl, amongst others, had bestowed upon it).

[12] Roger Benjamin and Raymond Duvall, "The Capitalist State in Context," unpublished manuscript, University of Minnesota. Cited in Stephen D. Krasner, "Approaches to the State: Alternative Conceptions and Historical Dynamics," *Comparative Politics* 16, 2 (1984), p. 224. Benjamin and Duvall offer a similar classification in "The Capitalist State in Context," in Roger Benjamin and Stephen L. Elkin, eds., *The Democratic State*, Lawrence, Kansas: University Press of Kansas, 1985, pp. 19-57.

[13] Other definitions are, of course, possible. S.N. Sangmpam, for instance, recently emphasized the issue of power offering a definition of the state as "a set of relationships and interactions among social classes and groups as it is sustained, organized, and regulated by political power....[where] power implies the monopoly of the...means of...coercion and a set of institutions over a given territory" (1992: 401).

[14] Although his discussion is primarily about the problem of boundary between state and society, which he presents as "the defining characteristic of the modern political order," and although he is critical of the idea of the state as a "free-standing entity," Mitchell does concord with the notion of state as abstraction. Specifically, he argues that "the state appears as an abstraction in relation to the concreteness of the social, and as a subjective ideality in relation to the objectness of the material world" (1991: 95).

[15] In a society like the Iraqi one, the traditional, pre-modernization decision sites were tribal leaderships. Later, from the early 1930s on, rural landlords came to play a crucial socioeconomic and political role as well. Gradually, these two "sites" were integrated in the state-building process. For an influential statement on this question, see Hanna Batatu's monumental work *The Old Social Classes and the Revolutionary Movements of Iraq - A Study of Iraq's Old Landed and Commercial Classes and of its Communists, Ba'thists, and Free Officers*, Princeton, New Jersey: Princeton University Press, 1978. See also Batatu's "The Old Social Classes Revisited," in Robert A. Fernea and WM. Roger Louis, eds., *The Iraqi Revolution of 1958*, London: I.B. Tauris, 1991. Interestingly, in that article, Batatu concedes that one of the shortcomings of his book is his neglect of the state. He writes: "Roger Owen points to an important flaw in my book. He affirms that the state as a cluster of interacting institutions is not present in my study....I agree fully" (pp. 219-220).

[16] Friedrich Meinecke argued that it was Hegel who, by embracing reason of state as the soul of the state, legitimized Machiavelli's theory in modern political thought, in *Machiavellism - The Doctrine of Raison d'État and Its Place in Modern History*, Boulder, Colorado: Westview Press, 1965, p.350. Also see Michael Donelan, ed., *The Reason of States - A Study in International Political Theory*, London: George Allen & Unwin, 1978. Machiavelli's ideas were also lauded by Hintze in his "Military Organization and the Organization of the State" (Gilbert, 1975).

[17] Shlomo Avineri, *Hegel's Theory of the Modern State*, Cambridge, Massachusetts: Cambridge University Press, 1972, p.44.

[18] On that point, Heinrich Von Treitschke notes that "In state treatises, it is the will of the state which is expressed, not the personal desires of the individuals who concluded them," in *Politics*, New York, New York: MacMillan, 1916, vol. I, p. 15.

[19] Appropriately enough, Abrams later states that "The only plausible alternative I can see to taking the state for granted is to understand it as historically constructed" (1988: 80).

[20] Translation: [The state] is neither territory, nor population, nor mandatory body of laws. To be certain, all these sensitive fundamentals are not foreign to it, but the state transcends them. Its existence does not belong to the tangible phenomenology; it is of the order of the intellect. The state is, in the full meaning of the word, an idea. Having no other reality than conceptual, it exists only because it is thought.

[21] For Hegel, this tautology is crystallized in the fact that, for instance, the state elicits authority while simultaneously providing the means of this authority through institutional channels. In *The Philosophy of Right* (1821), he writes "So far as the authority of any existing state has anything to do with reasons, these reasons are culled from the forms of the law authoritative within it" (1971: 80).

[22] See Karl W. Deutsch and William J. Foltz, eds., *Nation-Building*, New York, New York: Atherton Press, 1963. Nation-building is in fact a concept derivative of nationalism. More recently, Andrew D. Smith argues that nation-building is the sole legitimizing activity of statehood; "State-Making and Nation-Building," in John A. Hall, ed., *States in History*, New York, New York: Basil Blackwell Inc, 1986, pp. 228-263. Also see John Breuilly, *Nationalism and the State*, Manchester: Manchester University Press, 1982; H. Seton-Watson, *Nations and States*, London: Methuen, 1977; and the seminal work of Charles Tilly, ed., *The Formation of National States in Western Europe*, Princeton, New Jersey: Princeton University Press, 1975, in particular Stein Rokkan's chapter, "Dimensions of State Formation and Nation-Building: A Possible Paradigm for Research on Variations within Europe," pp. 562-600. For an extension of Tilly's work to modern European conflict processes, see Karen A. Rasler and William R. Thompson, *War and State Making - The Shaping of the Global Powers*, Boston, Massachusetts: Unwin Hyman, 1989.

[23] Janice E. Thomson, *Mercenaries, Pirates, and Sovereigns - State-Building and Extraterritorial Violence in Early Modern Europe*, Princeton, New Jersey: Princeton University Press, 1994. Also see her "Explaining the Regulation of Transnational Practices: A State-Building Approach," in James N. Rosenau and Ernst-Otto Czempiel, eds., *Governance Without Government: Order and Change in World Politics*, Cambridge, Massachusetts: Cambridge University Press, 1992, pp. 195-218.

[24] Translation: The state does not die as such. Indifferent to the succession of rulers, it ensures the permanence of their acts insofar as, regularly performed, they can be imputed to it.

[25] On that aspect Zartman (1993: 240) remarks that "State-Building....implies the construction of an institutional and symbolic order that is strong enough to maintain and preserve itself."

[26] Robert C. Good, "State-Building as a Determinant of Foreign Policy in the New States," in Laurence W. Martin, ed., *Neutralism and Nonalignment - The New States in World Affairs*, Westport, Connecticut: Greenwood Press Publishers, 1962, pp. 5-8.

[27] See John H. Herz, "Rise and Demise of the Territorial State," in Heinz Lubasz, ed., *The Development of the Modern State*, New York, New York: The MacMillan Company, 1964, pp. 130-151. Herz demonstrates how under modern conditions states can act (militarily and otherwise) from center to center, thus de-emphasizing the sovereignty attached to the territorial dimension of statehood.

[28] The most explicit statement of the vision of war as a the foundation of the state is to be found in Heinrich Von Treitschke's *Politics* (1899).

[29] Blaise Pascal, *Pensées*, Paris: Gallimard, 1954, p.1152. Translation: The nature of power is to protect.

[30] For instance, Stephen C. Pelletiere demonstrates that the Ba'thi regime's decision in July 1986 to start staffing the army with university graduates and increase the involvement of urban centers' populations – previously shielded from the war which was almost exclusively limited to the front on the borders – significantly paved the way for Iraq's last victorious campaigns over Iran, which ultimately decided the fate of the First Gulf War. See *The Iran-Iraq War - Chaos in a Vacuum*, New York, New York: Praeger Publishers, 1992.

[31] Harold D. Lasswell, "The Garrison State," *The American Journal of Sociology* (January 1941), p. 461.

[32] Adeed Dawisha, "Reasons for Resilience," in Adeed Dawisha and I. William Zartman, eds., *Beyond Coercion: The Durability of the Arab State*, New York, New York: Croom-Helm, 1988, p. 277.

3

History of the Iraqi State

This chapter focuses on the history of the Iraqi state in the period ranging from its creation in 1921 to the eve of the 1990-1991 Second Gulf War. I also briefly look at the Arab state and identify the general patterns of its development as well as some of its prime characteristics. I argue that these characteristics are all found to a significant degree in the modern state of Iraq. Through a chronological overview of the successive regimes and episodes of that state, I highlight the specific issues of political instability, ethnic tension, and power struggles and their effects on Iraqi state-society relationships, as well as the Kuwaiti matter. These different parameters allow us to perceive the structure of the contemporary Iraqi body politic and the dynamics of the country's foreign policy as a reaction to the successive regimes' shared perception of the need to build a strong Iraqi state.

The Arab State

The existence of a significant intra-Arab polity in the relationships amongst the various Arab countries has often led to the consideration of the notion of an isomorphic Arab state (*dawla* or *daula*) whose characteristics are shared by the several Middle Eastern and North African countries. Although clearly reductionist in light of the idiosyncrasies of each country and the varying regional dynamics in the two Arab regions – the

Maghreb (Algeria, Libya, Mauritania, Morocco, Tunisia) and the Mashreq subdivided into three sub-regions; the Nile Valley (Egypt and the Sudan), the *Jazira* or Arabian peninsula (Saudi Arabia, the Yemen, Oman, Qatar, the United Arab Emirates, Bahrain, Kuwait), and the Fertile Crescent or Levant (Palestine, Jordan, Lebanon, Syria, Iraq) – this view does nonetheless rest on the existence of sociocultural, historical, economic, linguistic, communal, ethnic, religious, and political similarities as well as a high level of societal continuity.

The prime characteristic of the Arab state as shared by all these countries is that, due to colonizations alternatively conducted by France, Great Britain, Italy, and Spain, all contemporary Arab states belong to the twentieth-century modern era. None's formal constitution dates further back. Official independence by different states was achieved in the period ranging between 1918 (the Yemen) and 1971 (Bahrain, Qatar, United Arab Emirates), with a high incidence in the 1950s (Lebanon, Syria, Jordan, Iraq, Morocco, Sudan, Tunisia) and 1960s (Algeria, Mauritania, Kuwait, Libya). The conditions of the emergence of the Arab state are, then, fundamentally contemporaneous.

This modern nature and foreign intervention also define the second characteristic of the Arab state, namely, the primacy of its territorial aspect over the nationalistic component. In effect, "The Arab state is primarily a territorial state, merely defined as an extractive and coercive agency exerting its domination and authority over a given geographical area"[1] (Kienle, 1990). Initially, the reality of the Arab state was indeed merely territorial. An oblique testimony to that is that 16 out of 21 Arab countries still have pending territorial disputes. Over time, though, the state has been forced to engage in a host of societal operations to generate social support and foster a commonality of interests between itself and its society in order to endow itself, at least formally, with legitimacy.

But this process of recognition of the state by its society did not take place without impediments. A third characteristic of the Arab state explains the resistance (if not reluctance) of Arab societies to comply with the central authority: the existence of

74

allegiances by the citizens to other sociocultural fora than the state. The family, the tribe, and the local community have often enjoyed more sacred obedience from Arabs than has their state. Harmony and correspondence between state and society in the Arab world is still an ongoing process and an unresolved matter.

Whether colonial or local, the process of state construction in the Arab world has more often than not yielded the imposition of a fragile structure on a heterogeneous population. In the Maghreb, Mauritania was carved by France out of Spanish- and French-controlled Saharan areas of four Moorish tribal Emirates, and Moroccan and Algerian southern provinces possess historical, geographical, and human realities distinct from the coastal parts of these two countries – in addition to a pronounced Arab/Berber duality in both nations. In the Mashreq, King 'Abdallah's establishment in Transjordan – itself the result of 'Abdelaziz Ibn Saud's military conquest of the Hejaz between 1924 and 1932 and its attachment to the Najd (thus creating the contemporary Saudi ensemble) – was an obvious exogenous development in that part of Palestine. It was only made possible by the allegiance of the local tribal leaders to the Sharifian Prince. Similarly, 'Abdallah's brother, Faysal, was within months successively King of an ephemeral Arab kingdom based in Damascus and founder of the Hashemite dynasty in Iraq.[2] Clearly, the Arab state was seldom the result of a continuous and purely local process. This general characteristic explains both the state's initial disconnections with its society and its frailty as well as its lack of widely held founding myths.

Almost systematically, the establishment of the Arab state has also followed a pattern where an initially vague, all-encompassing *ancien régime* appealing primarily to traditional values was replaced by a nationalistic movement often but not always successful in gaining power. Beyond the strategic maneuvering of this sequential development, we can see that, because of its initial exogenous character, the Arab state has had continually to try to "make its case" to its community – first, with the conservative regimes, then through over-extended nationalistic arguments.

In light of the failure of the nationalists to meet the demands of statehood (that is, establish *de facto* independence for their countries) and resolve the crises plaguing

75

their economies, a third Islamist option for the Arab state has been in the making since the late 1970s and is picking up momentum in the 1990s. Whether the modern nationalist state will remain in place or whether it will be abruptly (but not necessarily violently) replaced by Islamist regimes remains to be seen. Burhan Ghalioun, for instance, argues that the days of the nationalistic state are all but over. New diverse forms of political mobilization (ethnic, confessional, or ideological) and the consolidation of the Islamist advance are redefining the existing state-society polity in the Arab world.[3] The transition from the nationalistic stage to the Islamist one is, he correctly points, really about the quest for progress and modernization of state and society.[4]

The lack of political participation which has been largely prevalent in the Arab world until the democratization wave began in the early 1990s, the monopoly of economic activity by a rentier and distributive state,[5] military might, and the absence of real class struggles (and class consciousness for that matter) – except in semi-industrial nations like Egypt, Syria, Iraq, and Algeria – make it possible for the state to remain autonomous. Yet although it is often crushing its society, the Arab state is not necessarily shielded from it. Indeed, the state's autonomy is a double-edged sword because it denies it lasting legitimacy. Domestically, legitimacy is achieved by way of wooing clientelistic networks who exchange support and activism in return for immediate socioeconomic favors and benefits. Because of the *ad hoc* nature of this type of relationship, government officials are able to check any class-based opposition that might develop as result of such arrangements.

The loyalty of the citizens is also commanded by the state through the use of foreign policy. In numerous instances, foreign policy behavior helps the state attend to a domestic situation. By engaging in foreign activity, policy-makers can do three things: (i) distract from internal conditions; (ii) appear to (or actually) act in the interests of the community by ensuring the safety and advancement of its external position; and (iii) create a rallying point for the community around a foreign issue. The pursuit of these goals confirms the thesis that

76

One factor which has always been, and continues to be a potent motivating force of foreign policy in Arab politics is the effort by Arab regimes to legitimize their rule by undertaking foreign ventures....This is not to suggest that the search for legitimacy necessarily motivates Arab leaders to embark on foreign ventures. However, given the environment in which Arab politics operate, it is easy to see why there is such a strong correlation between foreign policy and domestic legitimacy (Dawisha, 1990).

Cases in point are the 1980 Iraqi invasion of Iran and its 1990 annexation of Kuwait. Both events were sparked by domestic considerations linked with historical state-building concerns, namely the Shatt-al-'Arab question and the issue of Kuwait as an Iraqi province.

A fourth characteristic of the Arab state has been the prevalence of a one-man-dominated state system. As Ibn Khaldun remarked, it is in the nature of states that authority becomes concentrated in one person.[6] Although bureaucratic limitations do exist and socioeconomic parameters as well as political alliances constrain policy orientations, Arab leaders have indeed been able to enjoy a very large freedom of action. However, the legitimacy question remains a nagging constant. Lacking a universal particularisms-transcending legitimacy and suffering from the state's own lack of acceptance, Arab leaderships find themselves immersed in a cycle of legitimacy renewal – which they sometimes take down the risky road of foreign adventurism.

To be certain, the issue of the legitimacy of the Arab state has generated considerable debate.[7] Ibn Khaldun has emphasized the importance of the relationship between the power of the state and the actual recognition by society of that strength.[8] This *iltiham* (coalescence) is presented as the key to the state's *ghalaba* (domination) over its society. Thus, legitimacy primarily stems from a process of domination/recognition. And *iltiham* is fundamentally dependent upon the presence of strong ties – an idiosyncratic Arab notion introduced by Ibn Khaldun as *'asabiyya*[9] – between the members of the community which allows for the formation of the state as a transcendent notion. Simply put, Ibn Khaldun simultaneously posits the primacy of the all-encompassing state and the state's organic need for a legitimacy bestowed upon it by its community in order to function properly as leadership (*qiyada*). Elia Zureik showed that this legitimacy basis of the state gradually evolved from a traditional, purely tribal *'asabiya* to a modern form of patrimonialism so that the postcolonial Arab state is, at once, typified by the coexistence of pre- and postcolonial structures with state dominance as a common feature.[10]

More recently, Eric Davis' analysis is also instructive on the legitimacy subject. Focusing on oil-producing Arab countries, Davis (1991) argues that states in these countries have managed to escape the constraints of indigenous social and political forces, thus enabling them to try to establish a superstructural form of ideological legitimacy. The nationalist stage of the Arab state is the combined result, he argues, of three factors: (i) integration of these countries' economies into the world market; (ii) colonial rule; and (iii) the onset of oil production. He demonstrates that even though the oil commodity was available in the 1940s and 1950s to some dynastic regimes, such as the Hashemites in Iraq and the Sanussi in Libya, they were unable to use it in a manner so as to foster legitimacy. In contradistinction, their respective nationalistic successors initially succeeded in rallying their populaces around an ideology of progress and modernization through the use of petroleum wealth. For Davis also, the Arab state acquires legitimacy through mechanisms of statecraft whereby a state enhances its power and authority. Again, strength and acquiescence interact decisively to produce the historical and cultural parameters of legitimacy.

Although mentioned only in passing, a subtext of this discourse is that the process of legitimation can also take the form of an effort on the part of the state to reshape historical memory. A more explicit study of that thesis is Davis and Gavrielides (1991). Looking at the efforts of the Iraqi and Kuwaiti regimes to promote a historical memory, these two authors place the question of how knowledge of the past is transformed into increased power for the state at the center of the Arab state's continual search for legitimacy.[11] The argument is that traditional sources of legitimacy are revisited and appropriated by the respective regimes in an attempt to channel them in the body politic and institutionalize them in accordance with the regime's mobilizing

78

objectives. To that end, a specific understanding of the historical heritage (*al-turath*) is often formulated with an equally specific magnitude. Analogously, the past becomes politically salient and, most importantly, directly connected to the precise and immediate needs of each regime. This approach also implies that a process of ideologically mediated reexamination of the past – as well as the whole process of regime assertion itself – is in fact a two-way dialogue between the state (which is endowed with a continual history) and the regime (which seeks to refer to this history to situate itself and inscribe its action within the state's global parameters while at the same time adding to them). A good example of this is the 1988 Iraqi restoration of the ruins of the ancient city of Babylon. In a most unusual reconstruction plan, the foundations of the old palace were restored, and a new layer was built *over* the foundations. The inscription now reads that these are the ancient ruins of Babylon "restored during the time of Saddam Hussayn of Iraq." In sum, the regime forges its identity in the state's mold.

The Iraqi State

The four characteristics of the Arab state that were identified – (i) the modern aspect of the state due to colonial legacy, (ii) the importance of territorial questions, (iii) the tension between society and state, and (iv) the existence of a centralized leadership system – are eminently present in Iraq. They constitute the historical matrix of the Iraqi state that influenced directly the Ba'thi regime's policy-making process during the Second Gulf War.

Creation of the State and the Hashemite Monarchy. The process of Iraqi state construction began in 1921. At a meeting of French and British colonial powers held in Cairo, three former Ottoman provinces – Mosul (al-Mowsal, in Arabic), Baghdad, and Basra – were joined to form the Kingdom of Iraq whose monarch was chosen in the person of Faysal, one of the three sons of Hussayn the Sharif of Mecca and leader of the Great Arab Revolt against the Turks (1916-1919). The fusion of the three provinces into one administrative entity immediately emerged as an impediment to the construction of a new political reality. The intrinsic heterogeneity of the Iraqi state, due to the amalgam of peoples, was readily apparent to Faysal, who noted:

> In Iraq, there is still....no Iraqi people but unimaginable masses of human beings, devoid of any patriotic idea, imbued with religious traditions....connected by no common tie....prone to anarchy, and perpetually ready to rise against any government whatever. Out of these masses, we want to fashion a people which we would train, educate, and refine.[12]

Similarly, the Iraqi scholar Majid Khadduri (1973) wrote:

> The social structure of 'Iraq was divided into three principal parts. The first was the tribal and semi-tribal communities of the south, essentially a mixture of émigrés who entered the country in increasing numbers after the Arab conquests of the seventh century and intermarried with the natives. The second was composed of the urban centers in the middle of the Tigris-Euphrates valley. These centers had formed the backbone of the once highly civilized society of Islam's golden age....The third part of 'Iraqi society – the Kurdish community – had only become part of the country after World War I; it had never before been regarded as part of 'Iraq, since it formed a portion of the region known as Jazirat Ibn 'Umar. This non-Arab section, to say nothing of other religious and ethnic groups, added to the complexity of Iraq's social structure.

The post-World War I settlement in the Middle East region determined many a characteristic of the Iraqi state. The colonial powers made sure that the nascent Iraqi state would never become too powerful by creating the conditions of its vulnerability and exposure. Because, for instance, both the Tigris and the Euphrates rivers rise in the north, the country has always been dependent on Turkey and Syria on this crucial environmental matter. Equally important is the lack of access to the sea which prevents Iraq from enjoying the economic, political, and military benefits of being open to international waters – whereas Syria, Egypt, Jordan, and Saudi Arabia all have access either to the Mediterranean or the Red Sea.

Although the Iraqi state is only 76 years old, the history of the land dates back 6,000 years. Mesopotamia (the land between two rivers, from the Greek μεσοποταμια) was the name used by Europeans to refer to the area of the Euphrates and the Tigris rivers lying between the Gulf and Kurdistan. Mesopotamia is traditionally considered to be the area of biblical accounts: the Garden of Eden, Cain's murder of Abel, Noah's flood, and the Tower of Babel. Mesopotamia had also been the home of Sumerian (3000-2650 BC), Akkadian (2650-2450 BC), Urian (2400-2100 BC) and Babylonian empires (2000-1600 BC) with legendary kings like Hammurabi (1792-1750 BC), renown for his contribution in written law and government administration, and Nebuchadnezzar (605-562 BC) who conquered Jerusalem in 586 BC. Babylon was also home to one of the Seven Wonders of the World: the Hanging Gardens of Babylon. From 247 BC to AD 636, the region was under Persian rule by the Achaemenid, Parthian, Arsacian, and Sassanian empires, with an intervening Greek period under Alexander the Great (331-126 BC) and two Roman occupations (98-117 AD and 193-211 AD). On February 19, 636, the battle of al-Qadissiya – a locality south of Baghdad – consecrated Arabian rule in Mesopotamia, which had been initiated in 633 by the military campaigns of al-Muthana ibn Haritha and Khaled ibn al-Walid ("The Sword of Islam"). Following the fall of the Ummayad dynasty in Damascus (661-750), Iraq became from the 8th to the 13th century the capital of the Islamic Caliphate of the 'Abbassids (750-1258) where science, medicine, and commerce flourished under 37 successive Caliphs (starting with Abu al-'Abbas and ending with al-Mustasim Billah). The heyday of Baghdad took place under the reigns of Abu Ja'far al-Mansour (754-775), who built Baghdad in 763, and Haroun al-Rashid (786-809). During those centuries, Baghdad produced a world culture from the standpoint of its sources and its outlook.

The decline of the Caliphate began on February 13, 1258, when Mongol hordes led by So Hulagu, the grandson of Gengis Khan, invaded and burned down

Baghdad deposing the last of the 'Abassids, Mustasim. A second Mongol invasion led by Timur the Lame took place in 1384-1387. The Mongols held the country for three generations. They were followed by the Ottomans when, in 1534, Suleiman the Magnificent took Baghdad. Ottoman rule in Iraq lasted until October 1918.

This formidable succession of empires in Mesopotamia is regarded by the Iraqis as a source of pride and is often referred to in order to establish the country's heritage and the fact that contemporary Iraq is the custodian of deep historical roots. Nevertheless, the last four centuries spelled domination at the successive hands of Mongols, Turks, and British forces, and resentment, and were thus laying the ground for a genuine renaissance, that was facilitated by the Great Arab Revolt started by Hussayn the Hashemite on June 11, 1916.[13]

During World War I, Britain occupied the territory, prompting a disorganized Turkish retreat. General Stanley Maude's 100,000 troops penetrated Baghdad on March 11, 1917. Following US President Woodrow Wilson's "Fourteen Points" declaration in January 1918, the British, in agreement with the French, announced that they would allow for some form of self-determination in the territories they controlled in the Middle East. On March 8, 1920, following Damascus' fall to the Bedouin armies led by the Hashemites, a group of Iraqi nationalist leaders from the al-'Ahd society (founded in 1913) assembled in Damascus passed a resolution proclaiming Iraq's independence with 'Abdallah ibn Hussayn the Hashemite as its King. But, on May 3-5, 1920, convened at San Remo in Italy, British and French authorities decided that Iraq would become a British mandate.

In the meantime, the Arab populations inside Iraq were regaining the territories abandoned by Turkey and occupied by Britain after the Mudros armistice in October 1918. On June 3, the British garrison of Tel Afar, near the city of Mosul, was captured by Bedouin warriors of the Shammar tribe. The officers and their staff were massacred. On June 30, it was the turn of the Zawalem tribe to attack the city of Koufa. It, then, quickly became apparent that, in spite of the instauration of the mandate, the European powers were losing control over the territory. More significantly, Iraqi nationalist feelings gathered further momentum with the revolt that lasted from June 30 to the autumn of 1920. Reasserting their presence, the British disbursed twenty million pounds to put it down.[14] Still, the very idea of mandate was fiercely opposed by the Iraqis. The five main political parties – the *al-'Ahd al-'Iraqi* (the Iraqi Covenant), the *Harakat al-Istiqlal* (the Independence Movement), *al-Hizb al-Watani* (the National Party), *Hizb al-Sha'b* (the People's Party), and *Hizb al-Taqqadum* (the Vanguard Party) – all aimed at ending it. Sir Percy Cox remarked: "It was extraordinary with what aversion the mandatory idea had always been regarded in 'Iraq."[15] Similarly, Gertrude Bell, the Oriental Secretary to the High Commissioner in Iraq, euphemistically indicated that "the word mandate isn't popular."[16] In sum, the four-month revolt of 1920 simultaneously denoted (i) the Iraqi population's opposition to new tax measures introduced by Britain, (ii) its anti-British feelings, and, correlatively, (iii) its increasing sense of nationalism – which Faysal would balance with his Hashemite unionist attempts.

Then, at a Cairo meeting in March 1921, spearheaded by British Secretary of State for the Colonies Winston Churchill, the integration of the three former Ottoman provinces of Baghdad, Basra, and Mosul into a new political entity was decided.[17] Faysal ibn Hussayn, 39th lineal descendant of the Prophet Mohammad, became King of Iraq on August 23, 1921. Initially, the King resisted plans for a British-Iraqi treaty that would give control of most state prerogatives to the British.[18] Under pressure, he finally signed it on October 10, 1922. But for two years, he continued to undermine its adoption by the National Assembly. In the end, ratification of the treaty came on June 10, 1924. Hence, the country's establishment was very much tied to Britain's Middle Eastern designs.

As King of Iraq, Faysal had become head of the first Arab regime in Mesopotamia since the collapse of the 'Abbassid empire in 1248. The new Iraqi entity he was to lead was nonetheless beset by geographical and ethnic divisions that proved problematic to national integration and around which a modern state would be erected under a vast array of structural difficulties. The various cleavages (urban-tribal, modernizing-traditional, Sunni-Shiite, Arab-Kurd, north-center-south) were readily apparent to the political entourage of Faysal. This class was dominated by the presence of Sunni Arabs from Baghdad who had attended the Turkish military academies and who had later joined the Great Arab Revolt in Arabia and the *Shaam* (Greater Syria).[19] Two-thirds of the Iraqi Premiers between 1920 and 1936 had actively participated in the revolt against the Turks.[20] The Arab nationalism of these men served as a springboard for the construction of a nationalistic Iraqi identity with the idea of Arabhood as rallying point against internal heterogeneity. Faysal himself devoted sincere efforts in the construction of an Iraqi community of that nature – although he never ceased to cherish the idea of an integrated Arab kingdom under Hashemite rule. Clearly, the sectarian and ethnic cleavages were tied to issues of territorial concerns.

The construction of this Iraqi identity was given priority with an emphasis on an educational program that was meant to transcend the dynamics of conflict and cooperation between groups. This effort to foster a mentality above and beyond sectarianism was led by Sati al-Husri (1882-1968), who has been regarded as an innovating and aggressive educator.[21] The development of education was significant as the number of students rose from the all-time peak of 7,377 under Ottoman rule to 15,275 in 1922. By 1932, there were 37,472 enrolled students in Iraq. With a strong German nationalistic influence,[22] al-Husri and his followers (Fadhil Jamali and Sami Chawkat) promoted Arabhood through a common Arabic language that they systematically opposed to the various indigenous dialects. Since al-Husri's time, there has been a concerted effort at providing continuity to Iraqi nationalism taught in schools. All the regimes that followed have adopted this educational dynamic as something fundamental to Iraqi state-building.

State-building was equally pursued through the army, whose role was defined as early as March of 1927 when an unpopular universal military conscription was drafted and submitted to the parliament. (The Iraqi army had been formed on January 6, 1921 – a Military College was founded on July 19, 1921, followed in 1927 by a Staff College.) The bill, which was particularly resented amongst minorities and tribal chieftains and which was also regarded with suspicion by British authorities, announced Faysal's intention to rely on the army as the guarantor of Iraq's perennation. The development of the army was, in fact, so swift that by 1925 there were six infantry battalions, three cavalry regiments, and three batteries of artillery.

The emphasis on the development of education and the formation of armed forces were early testimonies to the concern about the establishment of the state beyond the formal idea of its mere physical existence. On June 30, 1930, Iraq was granted formal independence by Britain, although the treaty that was signed for the occasion provided for the stationing of British troops and close ties to Britain on a variety of matters including foreign policy. On October 3, 1932, a sovereign Iraq joined the League of Nations.

Ethnic strife quickly emerged as a testimony to the artificial nature of the new Iraqi ensemble as well as a major challenge to the authorities of Baghdad. In 1932, a Kurdish uprising could be put down only with the help of the British. That same year, on June 18, the leaders of the Assyrian community demanded autonomy – a move that was largely unpopular and led to a severe campaign against them starting on August 4.[23] It took a year for Baghdad to crush that rebellion, wiping out 60 of the 64 existing Assyrian villages. This episode turned out to be the first success for the Iraqi army, and it created a new national hero, Colonel Bakr al-Sidqi.[24] As result of the rise in popularity of the army, the conscription law was passed by the parliament in 1934. It took effect on January 1, 1936.

King Faysal died in the early hours of Friday, September 8, 1933, in Switzerland under mysterious circumstances.[25] He was succeeded by his son, twenty-one-year-old Ghazi, who pushed further his father's desire for total political independence for Iraq. As the champion of the Iraqi army, where he had been trained during his early days, Ghazi was able to rely on the nationalistic momentum and the prevalent anti-British feelings. But his youth and the lack of experience and political acumen allowed for leadership rivalries to come to the fore – in particular the ambitions of political pundits Nouri al-Sa'id and Yassin al-Hashemi.[26]

The Shiite tribal revolt of March to May of 1935, led by Sheikh Khawwan of the Banu Izraij, who had been incited by al-Hashemi, allowed the latter to become Prime Minister ousting al-Sa'id (who had held that office since 1930). Again, it was up to Colonel Bakr al-Sidqi to put the rebellion down. He took the rebel city of Rumaitha on May 16. Then, in early September, there was another uprising, this time by the Yazidis – a closed community from the Jabal Sinjar region (west of Mosul). Resenting the conscription, the Yazidis had petitioned for an exemption. Their rebellion was promptly brought to an end in October by al-Sidqi. Yet another short-lived revolt took place in June 1936 by the Agra' tribes led by Shaikh Sha'lan. Through these successive domestic adversities, the army's role as arbiter and rule-enforcer was getting national recognition. This, in turn, meant acceptance of the military's growing political role.[27] From then on, it was to be a symbol of the regime's legitimacy as well as a mechanism for fostering cohesion and loyalty (Simon, 1986).

With the tacit backing of King Ghazi, whose hold on office was becoming increasingly precarious, Colonel al-Sidqi organized a coup on October 29, 1936, against both al-Hashemi and al-Sa'id. As the new Commander-in-Chief of the armed forces, al-Sidqi turned against the young monarch who started losing power. This episode marked the first attempt at institutionalization of state authority through militarization in Iraq. It also revealed the permanent ethnic tension present in the Iraqi system. Indeed, al-Sidqi (a Kurd), his Turkoman attachés, and the new Prime Minister, Hikmat Suleiman, were opposed to the Arab nationalism professed by the Sunni royal court.[28] Under their guidance, the country turned towards Turkey as the new government made every move to distance itself from Arab politics of unionism – sentimental or otherwise.[29] Al-Sidqi also established a dictatorial rule that was widely resented around the country. In fact, he showed little interest in social progress. Opposition to his policies and style of government climaxed in Mosul on August 11, 1937, when he was shot dead, bringing his nine months rule to a brutal end. The pan-Arabist wing of the army took back power and Sidqi's followers were purged. A new government headed by Nouri al-Sa'id was formed and King Ghazi's control of political affairs reasserted.

In 1938, King Ghazi started calling for unification with Kuwait. Simon (1986) writes that "Ghazi continuously advocated the annexation of Kuwait by Iraq. He read letters [on his private radio station in the palace] violently attacking the British-sponsored Sheik of Kuwait and his family, calling his regime feudal, and suggested that the Kuwaitis look to Iraq for leadership." The small province of Kuwait had previously been part of the Ottoman *vilayet* (district) of Basra. In January of 1899, the local ruler of Kuwait, Shaikh Mubarak al-Sabah, signed a treaty with Britain recognizing his locality as an independent state under British protection but keeping his Ottoman title of *qa'immaqam* (governor). Britain, then, began discussing the status of Kuwait with the Sublime Porte when World War I broke out. A preliminary July 29, 1913, agreement about Kuwait was meant to pave the way for a more specific arrangement which never came.[30]

Initially, Ghazi found support amongst members of the Kuwaiti *majliss* (national assembly). But the assembly was dissolved on December 21, 1938, by the Emir, Ahmad al-Jabr. That, in turn, led to a March 1939 coup attempt against the Kuwaiti ruler. King Ghazi then moved troops to the border and ordered them to launch incursion operations. But Saudi and British deployments deterred the Iraqis from taking further action. Soon thereafter, on April 3, 1939, Ghazi died in a suspicious car accident.[31] To be certain, his sudden death dealt a serious blow to Iraq's fragile center of power as it did to the erection of a nationalistic state by a Hashemite regime using Arabo-Islamic symbolic attributes to enlist support of the eclectic Iraqi population.

Ghazi's Kuwaiti episode was prompted by a number of considerations. First, his nationalism and his growing popularity amongst both the army and the population made him confident that he could oppose Britain on the matter of the Emirate. Second, the King harbored a desire for revenge against Britain, which he believed had had a long history of betrayal towards his family including the killing of his father. Finally, the agitation with Kuwait made the political class rally around him for a while, at a time when the Iraqi state was becoming increasingly divided by leadership quarrels. (No less than six coups d'État took place in the period 1936-1941 (see table 3.1).) Thus, it would appear that domestic considerations of the security of his regime coupled with a historical consideration of the Iraqi state's rights – through his perception of the territories – account for King Ghazi's desire to annex Kuwait. A similar combination of factors would recur with further Iraqi attempts at the annexation of Kuwait in 1961 and 1990.

After the King's death, executive power was inherited by Prince 'Abdul-Ilah – Ghazi's brother-in-law, first cousin, and son of King 'Ali – the Regent for young Prince Faysal II, who was only four years of age at the time of his father's death. (When he came of age, Faisal II assumed full powers, on May 2, 1953.) Again, leadership rivalries were ignited, this time with the arrival in Baghdad of the Mufti of Jerusalem, Amin al-Husseini. The pro-German feelings of al-Husseini – that had caused him to be expelled from Palestine by the British – found resonance amongst the cabinet of the new Prime Minister, Rashid 'Ali al-Gaylani, to the displeasure of the Regent, 'Abdul-Ilah, supported by Nouri al-Sa'id. The conservative Regent (who harbored strong pro-British feelings) and al-Sa'id chose to side with the Allies, and they managed to replace al-Gaylani with Yassin al-Hashemi on February 3, 1941. The following April 1, al-Gaylani and his entourage of four disgruntled colonels – a group known as "The Golden Square" – reacted by organizing a coup against the Regent, forcing him to seek refuge in Hashemite Transjordan and request British assistance. On April 28, British troops attacked Basra and, on the morning of May 2, Iraqi positions were bombarded by the British Royal Air Force based at the al-Habbaniya airfield. Following Hitler's May 3 directive that "everything possible be done to provide al-Gaylani's government with military assistance" (Hirszowicz, 1966), Germany dispatched planes and military equipment to Baghdad on May 11. However, the Germans fled from their positions at Mosul and Kirkuk on May 29. The next day, al-Gaylani and his colonels, along with the Mufti, were forced out of power. They sought refuge in Iran via Mosul.

If anything, the reinstatement of Hashemite rule by force reflected badly on the monarchy. Seale (1965) argued that the episode of al-Gaylani's revolt corresponded to the divorce between the Hashemites and the nationalists. Indeed, from then on, popular resentment against the conservative rule of the Regent and Nouri al-Sa'id began gathering momentum. To be certain, Hashemite pan-Arabism in Iraq and the legitimacy of the monarchy were dealt a severe blow from which they never recovered. This explains the failed attempts at federation with Jordan in which Iraq engaged between 1942 and 1946 that yielded only the signature, on April 15, 1947, of a symbolic Treaty of Brotherhood and Alliance. More attempts at unity were made by al-Sa'id after Transjordan's King Abdallah was assassinated in Jerusalem on July 20, 1951. Abdallah's son, Talal, rejected the proposals, as did young Hussayn who became king on May 2, 1953.

In Iraq, the Hashemites had become estranged from their middle and lower classes which were gradually becoming receptive to the revolutionary themes developed by the Iraqi Communist Party (ICP) and the *al-Hizb al-Watani al-Dimuqrati* (National Democratic Party, NDP) led by a former companion of colonel Bakr al-Sidqi, Kamil al-Chadirji, and one Youssef Salman Youssef. Starting in the summer of 1946 and intensifying in 1947, the ICP began fomenting unrest in the north that led to a major uprising in 1948. As more concessions were made to the British – especially in the oil business – popular agitation and disenchantment with the royal authorities grew more intense. In the early 1950s, large segments of the population demanded the rescinding of the English-Iraqi Treaty.[32] To counter popular protest, martial law was imposed on November 23, 1952. A crackdown on opponents and a ruthless persecution campaign followed. By now, the issue was no longer the nature and viability of the federated Iraqi state but that of power-sharing and ideological politics. In the midst of all this, the army steadfastly remained an independent source of power.

The Regent and al-Sa'id tried anew to generate popular support by forming the Arab Hashemite Federation of Iraq and Jordan on February 12, 1958. In spite of a high level of integration of political, military, and educational matters, the two kingdoms maintained their sovereignties. Still, the federation was a genuine attempt on Iraq's part to increase its regional stance and counter the United Arab Republic created by Syria and Egypt two weeks earlier.[33] Thus, on February 4, 1958, the Iraqis decided to also invite Kuwait into the union. After London objected to the plan, Baghdad initiated direct talks with the Kuwaitis, first, secretly in Lebanon in April, then in Baghdad with the visit of the Kuwaiti Emir in May. When the Emir showed little interest, talk of military annexation of the Emirate resurfaced again. It was voiced by Prime Minister al-Sa'id himself, who had an official memorandum drafted on the subject.

The Federation with Jordan proved unsuccessful, and increasingly the regime of al-Sa 'id and the Regent was becoming unstable. Latent unrest culminated in the July 14, 1958, revolution that swept the Hashemites out of power. The coup was executed by the 20th Brigade Group of the Iraqi army along with Communist elements.[34] Young King Faysal II, the Regent, and most members of the Hashemite royal family were massacred in the Rihab Palace. Nuri al-Sa'id, who had managed to escape, was found and executed the next day. The mutilated bodies were paraded through the streets of Baghdad. In Amman, King Hussayn requested London's military assistance. Britain declined to intervene in Iraq but agreed to send two parachute battalions to Jordan. Simultaneously, 5,000 American marines were deployed in Lebanon.

The proximity in time between the threats against Kuwait made by al-Sa'id and the coup has given rise to suspicions about a British involvement in the overthrow of the Hashemites.[35] In any event, the revolution had been in the makings for years. The fall of the Hashemites underscored the fact that it was truly the end of an era. The legitimacy of the Iraqi state was no longer dynastic. From that event on, there arose a need to perpetuate a new form of state-society relationship based on the notion of a permanent revolutionary momentum. In that sense, the change of regime altered the legitimacy basis of the Iraqi state, which substituted a revolutionary-popular militaro-nationalistic founding myth for the monarchical-elitist religiously enhanced Hashemite order. In an analytical pamphlet written under a pseudonym, an informed British official remarked that for some time already there had been widespread resentment gathering against the excesses of the Regent. He noted: "A police state supporting an edifice of corruption; this is what their own state seemed to Iraqis."[36] Beyond the vision of a corrupt regime, it would seem that it was al-Sa'id and the Regent's failure to act on the perceived need of construction of the state in any significant manner, between their return to power in 1941 and the 1958 revolution, that precipitated events. Roger Owen correctly commented on this logic of failure:

> Try as they might, Nuri and his colleagues were unable to create a sense that they were at the center of a single, unique, coherent entity with an unchallengeable claim to universal allegiance....The result was a continual challenge to their position and, finally, their replacement by a coalition of military and civilian political interests temporarily united behind a project to monopolize an increasingly large share of Iraq's resources in order to create the powerful, united state apparatus thought necessary for promoting national development under the new banners of independence, anti-imperialism, anti-feudalism and social justice. In this sense, 1958 was the beginning not only of a process of political and social revolution but also the construction of a new type of Iraqi state.[37]

The Praetorian Regimes. Brigadier 'Abdelkarim Qassem and his aides – Colonel 'Abdelsalam 'Aref of the al-Jumaila tribe in the Ramadi province, and Naji Taleb – established a Supreme Committee of the Free Officers (SCFO) composed of fifteen Sunni officers of Baghdadi middle class background. The monarchy was abolished and Iraq's secession from the Arab Hashemite Federation of Iraq and Jordan announced. Qassem became President, Prime Minister, and Minister of Defense, and 'Aref Deputy-Prime Minister and Minister of Interior. The emergence of these men on the political scene confirmed the coming-of-age of a second Iraqi military generation following after the Sharifian entourage of the Hashemites. With them, political attention shifted to domestic concerns. Overall, Qassem's period emphasized Iraqi patriotism (*wataniya 'iraqiya*) at the expense of Arab nationalism (*qawmiya 'arabiya*).

91

A quick split developed between Qassem, who was hostile to unity with the United Arab Republic (UAR) of Egypt and Syria, and 'Aref, who was in favor of it. With the support of the ICP and the NDP, who were respectively awarded one and two ministerial portfolios in the new government, Qassem prevailed and kept Iraq to itself. Besides 'Aref, only the Ba'thists were in favor of unionism, but they enjoyed little influence on the policy process. To fight off their ostracization, the Ba'thists then decided to support 'Aref and had Michel 'Aflaq, founder of the Ba'th party, fly from Damascus to try to influence the new regime. 'Aref also found support amongst the Independence Party (IP) and the Muslim Brotherhood. Qassem, for his part, enjoyed the backing of the ICP, the NDP, and the Kurdish Democratic Party (KDP). On September 30, 'Aref was removed from his office and appointed Ambassador to Bonn. A few months later, he returned to Baghdad and was arrested on charges of plotting a coup. The strategic background of this episode between 'Aref and Qassem was the rivalry between Egypt and Iraq – a competition which was underscored by the simultaneous resignation on February 7, 1959, of six Iraqi cabinet members disavowing Qassem's policies of confrontation with Nasser.

Having gained control of the leadership and attempting to consolidate his power on a wider basis, Qassem then sought to open up to other political forces in order to ensure the security of his regime. On October 3, 1958, he initiated an opening towards the Kurds by allowing the return of their leader, Mulla Mustapha Barzani, who had been exiled to Iran under the monarchy. After his return, Barzani went along with Qassem's plans until 1961, whereupon, having reorganized his guerrilla troops, he started demanding autonomy for his region. Qassem's opposition to his requests led to renewed fighting. Open warfare broke out in 1961 with the Kurds getting Iranian support after 1965.

With regard to the Kuwaiti matter, Qassem initially decided to forego Iraq's claims on the Emirate. But when, on June 19, 1961, Kuwait became independent from Britain – as a result of the termination of the 1899 treaty – he reversed his position. On June 25, Qassem declared that Kuwait was part of Iraq's Basra province and called for its reintegration. He urged the Emir of Kuwait to collaborate as district *qa'immaqam*. The Iraqi President dispatched troops to the border – even though the unverified movements were later denied by the Iraqis.

Besides the historical argument, Khadduri (1969) has suggested that Qassem may also have been tempted by Kuwait's oil production, which, by 1960, had reached 80,573,627 tons a year. As King Ghazi had activated Iraqi territorial designs over Kuwait in a dual attempt to argue a historical situation and renew the political legitimacy of his faltering regime by rallying popular support around a national issue, Qassem simultaneously aimed at economic gains to endow his regime with a (Kuwaiti) dose of economic viability and domestic cohesion by acting as the custodian/pursuer of the Iraqi state's perceived rights.

At the request of the Kuwaitis, on June 30, 1961, 5,000 British troops arrived in Kuwait to deter Iraqi military action.[38] Afterwards, Arab forces from Jordan, Egypt, Sudan, Syria, and Saudi Arabia along with British contingents came to the rescue of Kuwait, forcing Iraq to abandon its designs over the Emirate. On July 20, 1961, Kuwait was admitted to the League of Arab States. The Iraqi representative's angry withdrawal in protest before the vote made it possible for the League to evade the unanimity rule for admitting new states. The admission of Kuwait into the Arab League was perceived as a humiliation by the Iraqi government, which announced through its Foreign Minister, Hashem Jawad, that it was recalling its ambassadors from the countries that took Kuwait's side in the issue. These included Jordan, Lebanon, Tunisia, India, Japan, and the United States. As with the attempt made by King Ghazi in 1938 and the one by Nouri al-Sa'id in 1958, the 1961 incident left the matter unresolved and ready to be reopened anytime – Qassem continued to voice the validity of his claims after the episode was over.

In many respects, 1961 was a dress-rehearsal for 1990. After two years during which it was riding the wave of the July 14 revolution, the new regime's popularity and control over local developments were faltering – just as Saddam Hussayn's government's legitimacy would dramatically decrease between 1988 and 1990. Kuwait was a way out for a regime that was becoming increasingly isolated. Action in Kuwait was bound to generate a rally around the President and renew his lease on the state. As was to be the case in 1990, and as it was in 1938, Qassem's operation in Kuwait was intrinsically tied to his regime's immediate politics – a regime, we should recall, primarily internally oriented – and a sincere belief in the Iraqi character of the Emirate through a combination of domestic orientation and historical perspective.

Besides the failure in Kuwait, Qassem's downfall was announced by the lack of improvement of the country's economic conditions – whereas national income had been steadily increasing in the period between 1953 and 1961.[39] A case in point is the agrarian reform law passed in September 1958 that dispossessed land owners of their properties but provided for no structural substitutes. Slowly, Qassem started losing his political allies, keeping only the Communists. So much resentment existed towards the President that one could remark that "Qassem had become unpopular with every class, community, or grouping of the population capable of influencing the balance of forces within the country" (Dann, 1969). A steady increase in student riots (in particular the National Federation of Iraqi Students' demonstrations in December of 1962) and union protests (such as the Baghdad taxicab drivers' strike of March 1961) set the stage for the regime's downfall. The writing was on the wall.

On Friday, February 8, 1963, Qassem was overthrown by a coup – known as the 14 of Ramadan coup – organized by a coalition of nationalists from the military and the Ba'th party whose militia, *al-Harass al-Qawmi* (the National Guard), played an important role in the preparation and execution of the operation. Following the change of power, a Communist witchhunt ensued. There is also substantiated evidence that the American Central Intelligence Agency (CIA) provided support to this coup.[40] An eighteen-member Revolutionary Command Council (RCC), initially known as the National Council of Revolutionary Command (NCRC), was established as the government's highest political authority. It was dominated by a large majority of Ba'thi officers. 'Abdelssalam 'Aref was appointed President and Ahmad Hassan al-Bakr, Prime-Minister. The Ba'thists, whose party counted only 300 members at the time, had succeeded in gaining power and placing one of their own, al-Bakr, in a high position. But already the tension between the civilian and the military was palpable in the cabinet. Ba'thi attempts at gaining operational control of the state apparatus met with fierce resistance by the military wing of the government. The contest between the two sides culminated in an open conflict, in the fall of 1963, with the Ba'th party seeing a large number of its sympathizers purged from the government. The Ba'thists gradually became isolated from the political configuration. Some influential Ba'thists, such as al-Bakr, who was promoted to vice-president, and his replacement as Prime Minister, Taher Yahya, remained in the cabinet, but their presence was simply window-dressing designed to keep further Ba'thi opposition at bay. A year later, the officers were in turn removed by 'Aref who appointed his brother, Brigadier 'Abdelrahman, Chief of Staff.

Having consolidated his regime's power base, 'Aref turned to foreign affairs and decided to settle the Kuwaiti matter in a less antagonistic fashion than his predecessors. On October 4, 1963, he signed with Kuwait a document recognizing Kuwait's sovereignty. Subsequently, Iraq extended formal recognition to Kuwait and introduced a series of economic measures designed to facilitate free trade between the two countries. To compensate for his faltering internal coalition, 'Aref sought external support in the form of an union with Nasser's Egypt. A Joint Presidential Council (JPC) was set up on May 26, 1964, to work on matters of unification between the two countries, and on September 5, contingents of the Egyptian army arrived in Iraq. On October 16, the JPC was transformed into a Unified Political Command (UPC). But Nasser's continued support of the Kurds and his desire to incorporate some of their leaders in the unity scheme gradually led to a deterioration of the Iraqi-Egyptian relationship. Hence, differences were made apparent when, on September 15, 1965, the new Iraqi Prime Minister, 'Aref 'Abdelrazzaq, attempted a failed pro-Nasser coup. He was replaced by a pragmatic civilian, 'Abdelrahman al-Bazzaz.

This praetorian era was marked by the struggles of a cabal of officers and a civic recession that was left unattended after a new leadership vacuum occurred. On the night of April 13-14, 1966, President 'Aref died in an accidental helicopter crash on his way to Basra. The cabinet and the National Defense Council (NDC) agreed at once to appoint his brother, Major General 'Abdelrahman 'Aref, as his replacement. Renewed power struggles and the increasing influence of Nasserist officers led to the resignation of Premier al-Bazzaz, on August 6, 1966. The latter was replaced by Naji Taleb, who in turn resigned in May of 1967, prompting 'Aref to take the premiership himself.

The political infighting amongst rival factions in this period spoke of an increasingly tenuous relationship between state and society. For their part, social and economic policies were characterized by chaotic and uncoordinated planning (Sluglett and Sluglett, 1987). The regime of the 'Aref brothers was essentially a transitional period, one with a strong emphasis on transnational dynamics as the power competition between Nasserists and Ba'thists took precedence over purely domestic issues.

The Ba'th Party Regime. The political vacuum and socioeconomic crisis created by 'Abdelssalam 'Aref's death had long been setting the stage for a Ba'thi countercoup. It took place on July 17 of 1968. The RCC was reduced to seven members. Hassan al-Bakr became President, 'Abdelrazzaq al-Nayef was appointed Prime Minister, and Ibrahim al-Daoud, Defense Minister. This time around the Ba'thists quickly disposed of their army co-conspirators – al-Nayef (sent as Ambassador to Morocco) and al-Daoud were dismissed on July 30 during a follow-up mini-coup – and early on established their power against the Communists and the Kurds. A period of severe repression against opponents ensued, and a failed coup attempt in January of 1970 led to more purges. By the summer of 1970, RCC membership had become limited to Ba'thists, and the army had been brought under the control of the party. Al-Bakr allied himself with the secretary-general of the party, Saddam Hussayn, to extend state power beyond the government and party apparatuses. An agreement was signed with the Kurds on March 11, 1970, and two prominent governmental positions offered to the ICP. A coalition formation, the National Progressive Front (NPF), was mounted to neutralize non-Ba'thi political activity. In spite of this swift and massive operation of

96

power consolidation, underground opposition to the new regime persisted, especially amongst Shiites in the south.[41]

Initially, a low profile was maintained in foreign affairs, especially vis-à-vis regional neighbors. Hence, relations were normalized with Saudi Arabia; and the regime abstained from intervening in the Jordanian-Palestinian war of 1970 although it had contingents stationed in Jordan at the time. By and large, Iraq's relations within the Middle East area were improving, except with Syria and Kuwait. Towards the former the Ba'thists pursued a vigorous policy of bellicosity – especially after 1973 – and with the latter the border question was revived in March of 1973 with an Iraqi military incursion into Kuwaiti territory. Domestically, instability proved endemic as another coup attempt led by chief of police Nadhim Kazzar was aborted on June 30, 1973.[42]

From 1968 on, there occurred an increasingly inward-looking orientation of the Iraqi polity, sustained by a militarization of the society – especially with the creation of a militia known as the Popular Army. The other major political development was the rise of the Tikritis, a Sunni tribal family from the northern city of Tikrit, and their monopoly on most government portfolios.

The Ba'thi regime undertook to reorganize the economy of the country. Major socioeconomic projects were launched and mobilization of national wealth was put forth as the panacea of a newfound nationalism. Agriculture and the oil sector became the twin pillars of the economic endeavor. The Iraqi Petroleum Company (IPC) was nationalized on June 1, 1972, and the rise of oil revenues subsequent to the 1973 war allowed for state resources to expand into other fields (construction, agriculture, manufacturing).[43] Oil revenues went from $487 million in 1968 to $6.7 billion in 1974 and $12.2 billion in 1979. For that matter, the financial gains made by Iraq in the early 1970s also spelled regime security for the Ba'thists. In effect, the association of economic prosperity with the new regime provided the Ba'thists with political viability.

All in all, there was between 1968 and 1980 a stabilization of the country through regulation of economic and political activity. After the nationalization of the IPC, the state became the largest employer in the country, with a high capacity of distribution – a case which prompted one analyst to conclude that the state itself came to function as bourgeoisie. By 1975, the problem of overhauling the socioeconomic system was being seriously tackled as, according to Francis Fukuyama, Iraq benefited both from the nationalization and the increase in oil production that ensued.[44] Besides major advances in the industrial sector – which saw an unparalleled growth between 1970 and 1980 – the Ba'thists oversaw the development of major programs of social welfare, health care (extended to most of the population by a 1971 law), education, and a vast array of free services like distribution of radio and television sets.

Table 3.1

Coups d'État in Iraq

DATE	PERPETRATOR(S)	DEPOSED AUTHORITY
October 29, 1936	Bakr al-Sidqi	Premier Yassin al-Hashimi
August 17, 1937	Amin al-'Omari and Sa'id al-Tikriti	Premier Hikmat Sulayman
December 25, 1938	Taha al-Hashemi and the "Seven Officers"	Premier Jamil al-Midfa'i
February 21, 1940	Nouri al-Sa'id and the "Golden Square" officers: Salah Eddin al-Sabbagh, Mahmoud Salman, Mohamed Fahmi Sa'id, and Kemal Chahib	The cabinet had resigned on February 18
February 1, 1941	The "Golden Square" imposes Taha al-Hashemi as Premier	Rashid 'Ali al-Gaylani had resigned on January 31
April 1, 1941	Rashid 'Ali al-Gaylani and the "Golden Square" colonels	Regent 'Abdul-Ilah and Premier Taha al-Hashemi
July 14, 1958	'Abdelkarim Qassem	Hashemite monarchy
February 8, 1963	'Abdelssalam 'Aref and Ba'thists	President Qassem
November 18, 1963	'Abdelssalam 'Aref	Ba'thi group in the government
July 17, 1968	Ba'th party	President 'Abdelrahman 'Aref
July 30, 1968	Ba'thi officers	First Ba'thi cabinet

98

Undeniably, the 1968 change brought to an end the period of regime instability and internecine quarrels that had characterized Iraqi political life since the fall of the monarchy and which underscored the weakness of the building process of state.[45] The concern with the elaboration of a modern state was present early on within Ba'thi ranks as a main policy concern. In the report of the eighth regional congress of the party, held in Baghdad on January 8-12, 1974, one can read the following:

> The next stage should include an intense and audacious activity to construct a modern revolutionary state....In the edification of this state, we will have to be concerned with the men and the techniques.[46]

On the political front, things were more difficult for the new regime. The Kurdish problem resurfaced again in 1972. The almost 20 million Kurds are present in Syria, Iraq, Turkey, Iran, and the southwestern part of the former Soviet Union.[47] Because they were denied a homeland of their own, which was promised to them by the British, the Kurds have been pursuing their dream of full independence for the past 75 years. In Iraq, their struggle was prone to be problematic for the central authorities in light of (i) the underlying federated nature of the country, (ii) the Kurds' opposition to Arab nationalism,[48] and (iii) because since the mid-1940s the city of Mosul, at the heart of the Kurdish area, had become a major strategic oil center.

Led by Mustapha Barzani, the Kurdish Democratic Party's (KDP) antagonism towards the Ba'thists came to the fore. The early pragmatism of the Ba'thists did not pay off. As part of their initial power-consolidation effort, they had proposed an agreement in 1970 recognizing the Kurdish right to autonomous rule in the three northern governorates of Irbil, Suleymania, and Dohuk. Admittedly, the new regime saw the Kurdish question as both a threat to the existence of the Iraqi state and an opportunity for foreign parties to meddle in Iraqi matters.[49] On March 11, 1974, the government announced that it would give limited autonomy to the Kurds; but by then relations between the central authorities and the different Kurdish groups had deteriorated. A Kurdish guerrilla war with Syrian, Iranian, Israeli and American

99

support followed.[50] The Kurdish military offensive was conducted by a new, more powerful Iraqi Kurdistan Front (IKF) led by Massoud Barzani, son of Mustapha Barzani. The Iraqi state's counter-offensive began in August of 1974. It continued intermittently until 1996.

In a parallel manner, a serious crackdown on Communists was conducted in 1978-1979. The latter had been cohabitating with the Ba'thists since 1971, but, by the end of the decade, relations had soured. In the spring of 1979, their last two ministers in the Government, 'Amer 'Abdallah and Mukaran al-Talabani, were stripped of their portfolios, and the newspaper of the Communist party, *Tareeq al-Cha'ab* (The People's Way) was ordered to cease publication.

Amidst efforts at insulating the regime from domestic contestation, the Ba'thi regime pursued its policies of normalization with its neighbors. In April of 1975, Iraq and Saudi Arabia settled their border dispute and created the Iraq-Saudi Arabia Neutral Zone.[51] A rapprochement was also negotiated with Syria in the fall of 1978 and winter of 1979. It led nowhere, although a vague and non-committal National Action Charter was signed on October 26, 1978, followed by the establishment of a Joint Higher Political Council. The relation was back to antagonism when an alleged Syrian-sponsored coup plot was discovered in Baghdad on July 28, 1979. The following August 8, twenty-two conspirators – five of whom were former RCC members – were sentenced and executed.

The agreement with Saudi Arabia left the Iraqi border with Kuwait the only unresolved territorial dispute in the Gulf area (besides the Abu Moussa and Greater and Lesser Tumb islands problem between Iran and the United Arab Emirates). (The border with Jordan was finalized in 1984.) From 1964 to 1967, a joint Iraqi-Kuwaiti border-delimitation committee had met several times inconclusively. In April 1969, Kuwait agreed to the stationing of Iraqi troops in its territory on the outskirts of the Iraqi port city of Umm Qasr. By December 1972, that force had become a significant military build-up. On March 20, 1973, these troops were involved in clashes with Kuwaiti elements at a locality known as al-Sameta. Two Kuwaitis were killed, and Iraq demanded sovereignty over the islands of Bubyan and al-Warbah. Two days later, the Kuwaitis asked for the withdrawal of the Iraqi force. The Iraqis resisted, but, on April 5, they were forced to leave Kuwait under international pressure. At least five other Iraqi incursions reportedly occurred between 1974 and 1980. Another joint committee was set up in July 1977 to settle the matter, but the deadlock persisted until the First Gulf War.

For Iraq, 1980 was a peak year. According to the International Monetary Fund, the country enjoyed a reserve of $5.3 billion. Investments represented a 33% share of the national budget. Oil revenues had reached $21.3 billion. The cities were blossoming with a wide array of services. Twelve thousand kilometers of asphalt (4,500 in 1968) had made those urban centers accessible to the rural population. Even in the traditionally neglected agricultural field, things had dramatically improved. With 750,000 tons, Iraq had become the world's premier date producer, capturing 70% of the market. The law on mandatory schooling, passed in 1976, had been in effect for a year, and with 452,365 students in primary classes, its effects were obvious.

Well on their way to modernizing their country's economy and society and in control of an army that was spectacularly multiplying – regular military forces went from 80,000 men in 1966 to 640,000 in 1984, and paramilitary ones from 10,000 to 650,000 in the same period (Picard, 1988) – and that had also been gradually ostracized from the policy-making process, the Ba'thists turned their state-building efforts towards the external realm.[52]

On July 16, 1979, Hassan al-Bakr resigned from the presidency for health reasons. He was replaced by Saddam Hussayn who at once became the new strong man of the regime swiftly installing his kinsmen at top governmental positions. On February 8, 1980, the new Iraqi President announced to the Arab countries an ambitious eight-point "National Charter" declaration that aimed at the installation of a new, more independent and assertive Arab order. Primarily, the declaration was a statement of political principles by the new Hussayn government. It was also an *a priori* justification of the war against Iran. Vaguely endorsed by Libya, Morocco, and

101

the Gulf States, the charter was nonetheless quickly forgotten by most of the Arab world.

By 1980, the Ba'thi regime had succeeded in contributing substantially and probably more than its predecessors (besides Faysal's founding efforts) to the building of a strong Iraqi state. Skowronek (1982) has pointed to four dimensions to assess a given state's nature: (i) the concentration of authority at the national center; (ii) the penetration of institutional controls from the governmental center throughout the territory; (iii) the centralization of authority within the national government; and (iv) the specialization of institutional tasks and roles within the government. The Iraqi state under the Ba'thists ranks high on all four of these dimensions. It is, then, reasonable to categorize it as a "strong" state. Similarly, according to Lentner (1984), the strength of a state is a factor of (i) resources, (ii) finances, (iii) bureaucracy, (iv) the protection of security, (v) the maintenance of order, and (vi) the provision of welfare. Here, also, the Ba'thi Iraqi state has a strong position on all six elements. Finally, Krasner (1978) locates state strength in the degree of social change engineered, and, according to Eric Nordlinger (1987), the Marxist tradition equates it with the ability to negate social demands. These also were two occasional characteristics of Ba'thi Iraq.

In sum, by 1980, the Iraqi state under the Ba'thi regime had become undeniably strong, enjoying immense oil revenues that it used to develop a massive authoritarian bureaucracy, which simultaneously allowed it to *control* the population but also provide it with good living standards, including some of the better educational and health programs in the Arab world. Also noteworthy is the role of the internal security apparatus, the infamous *al-mukhabarat* and the *istikhbarat* in diffusing threats to the regime of Saddam Hussayn. But, although the Tikriti group was undeniably in control of the governmental system, it is important not to exaggerate the political consequences of that notion. Eberhard Kienle (1990) explains:

> There is much talk about 'Alawi rule in Syria and Sunni rule in Iraq, but tempting though it is to adopt this view, it is nonetheless incorrect. Nor would it be more correct to infer from the frequent presence of military

officers at the helm of these states that the army as such is in control....[R]uling groups and their challenger....in Syria and Iraq, increasingly tended to be organized as Jama'at – as gangs or cliques. These draw their strength and cohesion from one or several kinds of informal ties which in the eyes of their members command and generate personal loyalty: kinship, camaraderie and intimate friendship, but also religious, regional or local factors.

The significance of this analysis is that it helps us understand that the emphasis on Tikriti rule in Iraq is essentially a gimmick. True, most of the leadership comes from that extended family. But to reduce the whole Ba'thi ensemble to a limited group is to misrepresent the role of the nationalists and their shifting alliance with the army since 1968, as well as the influence of tribal leaders. In addition, after an initial period of Tikriti omnipresence (1977-1984), nepotist excesses were fought hard in the mid-1980s, when the leadership realized that it was endangering social cohesion; especially in a wartime context. As we have seen, the multi-ethnic character of Iraqi society has systematically been a major concern to all Iraqi regimes. So to endanger it by opportunistic appointments and promotions was something that the Tikritis could afford only so much.

The First Gulf War. As far as the Iraqi authorities were concerned, the March 6, 1975, Algiers Protocol – which had been followed by a formal treaty signed in Baghdad on June 13, 1975 – about demarcation of the border between Iraq and Iran, was essentially meant to stop Iranian support to the Kurdish uprising.[53] The Iraqis had agreed to the middle-of-the-river demarcation desired by the Iranians in exchange for control of movements on the river and an end to Iranian-sponsored subversive actions at the border.[54] Indeed, within months, the Kurdish insurgency did collapse without Iran's support, but in 1979, with help from the new Islamic regime in Tehran, it started anew. By 1980, the Ba'thists, who had always been ill-disposed towards the accord and who were apparently waiting for a favorable conjuncture to denounce it as having been conjuncturally forced on them, had decided to revoke it and seek a more

103

controlled situation vis-à-vis the new regime in Tehran – at a time when Iran seemed the weakest.

To be sure, the frontier has been a source of dispute since the 17th century.[55] The Shatt-al-'Arab – a waterway at the confluence of the Euphrates and the Tigris rivers – border issue has its roots in the history of the conflicts between the Persian and Ottoman empires. Before the 1975 Algiers meeting between the Shah and Saddam Hussayn, four major agreements had been previously devised on the matter: the Treaty of Erzerum (1847), the Constantinople Protocol (1913), the Delimitation Commission (1914), and the July 4, 1937, Treaty. Roughly, the problem persisted because fundamentally the Iraqis understood the left bank of the Shatt-al-'Arab to be the boundary (thus giving Iraq sovereignty over the river) whereas the Iranians held the view that the deepest point in the middle of the river constituted the border.

Three reasons can be put forth to account for Iraq's decision to go to war with its neighbor.[56] First, Iraq was afraid of the repercussions of the successful Iranian revolution and in particular its possible appeal to Iraqi Shi'a, the country's largest religious group. Second, the perceived military weakness of Iran made the idea of a *blitzkrieg* victory, reminiscent of the Israelis' conduct of the 1967 Six-Day War, appealing to the Iraqi regime. Finally, war was seen as a way to remedy the historical problem of the Shatt al-'Arab, the resolution of which was, in the eyes of the Iraqi government, botched in Algiers. On top of that, Iranian rhetorical attacks against Iraq and the declarations of its intention to export the revolution were worrisome prospects for the Ba'thists, who felt that they were restraining themselves in the face of Iranian behavior.

On April 1, 1980, there was a failed assassination attempt against RCC member Tariq 'Aziz by a Shi'i member of the *al-Da'wa* clandestine Islamic party – one Samir Gaylan 'Ali, – at the Mustanssariya University in Baghdad. This was followed by another attempt on April 5 during the funerals of the group of students who were killed in the first attempt.[57] On April 17, the Ayatollah Khomeini urged the Iraqis to overthrow their government. Ten days later, the Iranian radio announced that Saddam

Hussayn had been killed. In a letter by the Iraqi Ministry for Foreign Affairs sent to the Iranian Embassy in Baghdad on June 14, the Iraqis protested repeated Iranian shelling of the border post of Mandali. Another letter dated July 10 made reference to 25 bombing instances of Mandali, Khanakin, and Zurbatiye. In the eyes of the Iraqis, all of this action constituted a *casus belli*.

Seeking to fend off more provocations and worried about the prospects of a *pax Iranica*, the Ba'thists began considering the abrogation of the 1975 treaty and going to war. Following a September 4 Iranian shelling of a small locality on the Iraqi border, the Iraqi government announced the abrogation of the 1975 agreement on the 17th. The defensive-offensive behavior of the Iraqi leadership and its understanding of its obligations to the Iraqi state are reminiscent of what Von Treitschke (1899) noted:

> When a state recognizes that existing treaties no longer express the actual political conditions, and when it cannot persuade the other powers to give way by peaceful negotiation, the moment has come when the nations proceed to the ordeal by battle.

On September 22, Iraq invaded Iran attacking simultaneously at eight different locations and bombing ten airfields – reportedly using all-Sunni troops. Officially, then, the war started on the 22nd. However, the Iraqis maintain that the hostilities had existed since the 4th.[58] Although the Iraqis expected a quick victory, it rapidly became clear that they had misjudged Iranian resolve. The war became a rallying point for the faltering Islamic revolution. The Iraqi strategy clearly underestimated the force of patriotic and Islamic fervor engendered by the Iranian revolution (Sluglett and Sluglett, 1987). Truly, it was a golden opportunity which the Iranian leadership immediately seized. But if the Ba'thists did not foresee the length nor the form of the war, they did realize beforehand its dual significance: (i) a way to preempt a domestic revolution that would in all likelihood have threatened seriously their regime's rule, and (ii) an opportunity to right the wrong they felt they had done to the Iraqi state in 1975 by acceding to Iranian demands on the border issue. To invoke both rationales, war looked to be an autonomy-enhancing act.

The First Gulf War turned out to be an eight-year-long and costly conflict to the Iraqi regime. In almost all areas, it brought to a halt the social and economic progress achieved between 1968 and 1980. The first part of the conflict ended in December 1980. Hostilities resumed after the winter with an Iranian counteroffensive in May 1981 that lasted through 1982. By July of that year, the Iranians had regained the military advantage and begun penetrating Iraqi territory. The Iraqis' initial reluctance to go all the way had cost them to lose the edge.[59] The war then became a stalled conflict along the entire 730-mile border during four years.

In that time-frame, a major domestic strategy of the Iraqi leadership was the routinization of war. Significant efforts were deployed to keep the conflict out of the cities and give the citizens the impression that the conflict was a remote affair. And, indeed, as one Iraqi observer who lived through the war put it: "It was strange how that war went on and on and yet didn't seem to affect our lives in Baghdad at all" (Sumaida, 1991). Another strategy of maintenance of legitimacy was to refer to the war as "Saddam's Qadisiyya" by analogy to the decisive battle in which the Arabs, led by Sa'd Ibn Abi Waqas, defeated the Persians of the Sassanid empire in AD 636. This landmark date has always been present in the Arab/Iraqi psyche as a testimony of Arabs' "superiority" over Persians (Cadiot, 1989). Thus it was only normal that 1,344 years later, the Ba'thi regime explored the symbolism emphasizing the idea of a modern-day Qadisiyya.

The threat of a second domestic front was diffused by an attempt to improve relations with the Kurds, who were given increased representation in the Iraqi Parliament, prompting IKF leader Jalal Talabani to declare: "At least we can talk to Saddam....Khomeini has killed 20,000 Iranian Kurds."[60] In addition, after 1980, in a disposition reminiscent of the Lebanese system, it was decided that the country's vice-president systematically be a Kurd (Taha Mohiedin Ma'rouf). But, as with the 1970 experience, the honeymoon was cut short. In 1984, Kurdish leader Talabani turned to

Tehran to ask for support for his guerrillas against Baghdad. Renewed Kurdish attacks in 1986 led to a severe reaction by the regime. A repression campaign known as *al-Anfal* (The Spoils) took place in 1988. In February of that year, the village of Halabja was bombarded with chemical weapons.[61]

Finally, there was an increasing centralization of power. From 1982 on, the RCC became limited to 9 members. Efforts were also put into fighting the external signs of political decay – signs that would further alienate the people and lead them to question the Iranian adventure. Technocracy was emphasized, anti-corruption measures were passed, and nepotism fought (the use of the al-Tikriti name, indicative of kinship with the President, was forbidden). In a parallel to the Ba'thist regime's attendance to its security, the First Gulf War undoubtedly was a state-building war for Iraq. The state was transformed into an entity serving a people with a common identity pursuing nationhood through a unifying war effort.

On February 14, 1986, the Iranians took the Iraqi Gulf peninsula al-Fao (or al-Faw). Unable to recapture it, the Iraqis adopted a static defense approach until they decided to bring the middle phase of the war to an end and launch a new military campaign dubbed *Tawakalna 'ala Allah* (upon God we rely), led by the Republican Guard and the army's VII Corps. The RCC decided to have the forces of Lieutenant-General Maher al-Rashid operate with a new, much more determined offensive strategy in order to replace their earlier attempt at wearing down the Iranians.[62] By 1988, the strategy was paying off as the Iraqis regained the upper hand. Analysts at that time were noting that Baghdad was capable of both sustaining its existing level of economic activity and continuing the war as long as it proves necessary.[63] Often ignored by a great many analysts, the decisiveness of this last Iraqi campaign is attested to by a 1990 US Army War College report cleared for public release. The report's detailed information, based on confidential information, is worth quoting at length:

> Commencing in April 1988, Iraq unleashed a *Blitzkrieg* that virtually
> wiped out Iran's army. Five major battles were fought between April and
> August 1988, and in each the Iranians were badly beaten. In the first

107

battle, 17-18 April, the Iraqis retook the Al-Faw peninsula which they had lost to Iran in 1986. The second battle saw Iran surrender land around the pressure point of Basra. The Iranians had seized the territory in 1987 after a desperate campaign that went on for over 3 weeks and cost them 70,000 casualties. The Iraqis took it back in 7 hours. One month later the Iraqis struck at Majnoon, the site of one of the Middle East's largest undeveloped oil fields. The Iranians occupied this site in 1984, and had threatened to pump it dry to exact reparations from Iraq for having started the war. Again, the Iraqis retook it in a matter of hours. The fourth battle occurred in the vicinity of Dehloran and effectively removed any remaining threat toward Baghdad. In the fifth and final battle, the Iraqis drove some 40 miles into Iran to Qasr-e-Sherin/Kermanshah. Iraq's military commanders apparently were prepared to penetrate farther, but were recalled by the civilian leadership. After the recall the war was essentially ended. Several minor engagements followed, but on July 18, 1988, Khomeini drank the 'poison cup' of defeat and agreed to a truce. The defeat of the Iranians was harsh.[64]

Similarly, Kenneth Timmerman (1991) writes:

The Iranian collapse at Fao that April led to a string of defeats in June and July....The Iraqis recaptured Majnoon and Fish Lake, then pushed the Iranians out of parts of Iraqi Kurdistan....In early July Iraqi troops stormed across the border, capturing 1,000 square kilometers of Iranian territory. The Iranians were so terrified of the advancing shock troops and their chemical weapons that they simply abandoned their equipment without a fight and fled. The Iraqis seized 570 artillery pieces and 1,478 armored vehicles, including more than 150 tanks. The booty was so extensive it took them weeks just to haul it back across the border.

Finally, Bob Woodward (1991) reports:

[I]n 1987 [Defense Intelligence Agency officer] Walter Lang saw his view confirmed as Iraq waged increasingly sophisticated warfare, killing as many as 20,000 to 30,000 Iranians in a single battle. In the last major ground battle of the war, the Iraqis killed 65,000 Iranians. At that point, Lang felt, Iraq could have moved its army anywhere into Iran. The Iraqis had chosen to consolidate their gains and had made peace in 1988, wisely so, in Lang's view.

As Michael Collins Dunn (1992) sums it:

> [There] is a stubborn refusal by many....to pay attention to how the Iran-Iraq war ended....Iraq destroyed the Iranian army as a fighting force in the last weeks of the war, and Iraqi forces were deep inside Iranian territory when Saudi Arabia and other Arab states persuaded Iraq to stop. Yet one continues to read that the Iran-Iraq war ended in "stalemate." It did not. Had it continued another month, some analysts believe, Iraqi forces would have taken some major Iranian cities. Kermanshah might have fallen in days. The Iraqi army fought well, destroyed its opponent, and won the war....[T]he Iraqis deserve credit for what they accomplished. For some reason, they have not generally received it, except from professional military analysts.

If indeed the first half of the war was undecided, the al-Fao offensive gradually broke the back of the Iranian war effort. In July of 1988, Iran accepted UN Security Council cease-fire resolution 598 but Iraq continued its advances for ten more days. Cessation of hostilities was decided on August 20, 1988.[65] Ultimately, the Iraqis lost close to 300,000 men and Iran 580,000.[66]

The Iraqi defeat of Iran has often been questioned. Notwithstanding the undeniable tremendous human, financial, and material cost, it must be established that the military victory was factual. In many ways, the situation was not unlike the Soviet victory over Germany during the Second World War – costly but decisive. Iraq survived the conflict intact but socioeconomically ravaged.

Table 3.3

The Regimes of the Modern Iraqi State

The Hashemite Monarchy	1921-1958

• King Faysal
(August 23, 1921-September 8, 1933)

• King Ghazi
(September 8, 1933-April 4, 1939)

• King Faysal II
(April 4, 1939-July 14, 1958)
[Regency of Prince 'Abdul-Illah
(April 4, 1939-May 2, 1953)]

The Militaro-Nationalist Period	1958-1968

• 'Abdelkarim Qassem
(July 14, 1958-February 8, 1963)

• 'Abdelsalam 'Aref
(February 8, 1963-April 13, 1966)

• 'Abdelrahman 'Aref
(April 14, 1966-July 17, 1968)

The Ba'th Era	1968-present

• Ahmad Hassan al-Bakr
(July 17, 1968-July 16, 1979)

• Saddam Hussayn
(July 16, 1979-present)

Summary

In this chapter, the Arab state was examined. Its basic characteristics were outlined as being (i) its modern nature due essentially to foreign intervention; (ii) the primacy of its territorial dimension; (iii) the existence of significant societal resistance to state authority; (iv) the domination of the one-man leadership system; and (v) the importance of the legitimacy issue. The combined presence of these elements gives added meaning, in the Arab context, to the correlation between statehood and historical significance. And, it is that correlation which provides the context for any policy-making instance. Hence, concern for historicity, as a postulation of continuity, and legitimacy – to be embedded in the state – emerge as often being the prime determinants of Arab regimes' policy-making processes, be they for domestic or foreign affairs.

The genesis of the Iraqi state and the problems that beset it were chronologically looked at. Chronic political restiveness due generally to the pursuit of state-building concerns perceived as historically rooted (Kuwait, Shatt-al-'Arab) and specifically to the successive regimes' attendance to their security appeared as the major characteristic of this state.

An often repeated story about the first Ummayad Caliph is telling about the nature of power in Iraq. Allegedly, on his deathbed, the Caliph Ma'awiyya advised his son and successor, Yazid, to give the people of Iraq a new governor whenever they asked for one. That was, he said, the only way to keep them quiet. The succession of regimes in twentieth century Iraq makes this advice relevant even under modern conditions. The seven Iraqi strong men were successively Faysal I, the Regent 'Abdul-Illah, Nouri al-Sa'id, 'Abdelkarim Qassem, 'Abdelsalam 'Aref, Ahmad Hassan al-Bakr, and Saddam Hussayn.

The salience of territorial concerns is also a major issue for the Iraqi state, one that was cyclically used by the different regimes to further their immediate organizational interests. With regard to legitimacy, Iraqis view their major foreign policy issues in terms of the state's unique geographic and historical setting (Helms,

1984). The fact that (i) Iraq is landlocked and (ii) that it is surrounded by countries that are hostile to it (except Jordan) account for most of its "defensive-aggressiveness." In addition, its frontier position highlighted by its history and its heavy emphasis on nationalism reinforces a perceived sense of responsibility vis-à-vis the Arab world.

NOTES

[1] For a discussion of the territorial aspect of the Arab state, see Bahgat Korany, "Alien and Besieged, Yet Here to Stay: The Contradictions of the Arab Territorial State," in Ghassan Salamé, ed., *The Foundations of the Arab State*, London: Croom-Helm, 1987, pp. 47-74. Korany correctly asserts that "The Arab territorial state is becoming increasingly implanted and naturalized. It is not an indigenous phenomenon and yet it no longer seems a foreign import."

[2] See Khaldun S. Husri, "King Faysal I and Arab Unity 1922-1923," *Journal of Contemporary History* 10, 2 (1975), pp. 323-340; Suleiman Mousa, "A Matter of Principle: King Hussein of the Hijaz and the Arabs of Palestine," *International Journal of Middle East Studies* 9, 2 (1978), pp. 183-194; and Reeva S. Simon, "The Hashemite 'Conspiracy': Hashemite Unity Attempts 1921-1958," *International Journal of Middle East Studies* 5 (1974), pp. 314-327.

[3] Burhan Ghalioun, "La Fin de l'État National," *Revue d'Études Palestiniennes* 54 (1995), pp. 91-99. For another opinion on this debate see Riccardo Bocco, "'Asabiyât Tribales et États au Moyen-Orient: Confrontations et Connivences," *Maghreb-Machrek* 147 (January-March 1995), pp. 3-12.

[4] Burhan Ghalioun, "Du Nationalisme à l'Islamisme: L'Impasse du Modernisme," *Défense Nationale* (July 1995), p. 20.

[5] On that aspect of the Arab state, see the work of Hazem Beblawi and Giacomo Luciani, eds., *The Rentier State*, New York, New York: Croom-Helm, 1987; Hazem Beblawi, "The Rentier State in the Arab World," in Luciani, ed., *The Arab State* (1990), pp. 85-98; Mohammad Duwaidar, *Al-Ittija' al-Rai' bi'l Iqtisad al-Misri* (The Rentier Orientation of the Egyptian Economy), Alexandria, Egypt: Munsha'at al-Ma'arif, 1983; Michel Chatelus and Yves Schemeil, "Towards a New Political Economy of State Industrialization in the Arab Middle East," *International Journal of Middle East Studies* 16, 2 (1984), pp. 251-265; and Rayed Khalid Krimly, "The Political Economy of Rentier States: A Case-Study of Saudi Arabia in the Oil Era, 1950-1990," Ph.D. dissertation, George Washington University, 1993. In spite of its many insights, the rentier state school has a tendency to neglect the state's exposure to purely political developments.

[6] Cited in Charles Issawi, *An Arab Philosopher of History*, London: John Murray, 1950, p. 114. For a discussion of Ibn Khaldun's work in the context of the study of international relations, see Ghassan Salamé, "'Strong' and 'Weak' States: A Qualified Return to the Muqaddimah," in Luciani, ed., *The Arab State* (1990), pp. 29-64; and Robert W. Cox, "Towards a Post-Hegemonic Conceptualization of World Order: Reflections on the Relevancy of Ibn Khaldun," in James N. Rosenau and Ernst-Otto Czempiel, eds., *Governance Without Government: Order and Change in World Politics*, Cambridge, Massachusetts: Cambridge University Press, 1992, pp. 132-159. As Michael Hudson (1977: 43) noted "[His] writings convey an uncanny sense of modernity to the twentieth century reader."

[7] See for instance Michael C. Hudson, *Arab Politics - The Search for Legitimacy*, New Haven, Connecticut: Yale University Press, 1977; Salamé, ed., *The Foundations of the Arab State* (1987);

Adeed Dawisha and I. William Zartman, eds., *Beyond Coercion: The Durability of the Arab State*, New York, New York: Croom-Helm, 1988; Nazih N. Ayubi, *Over-Stating the Arab State: Politics and Society in the Middle East*, London: I.B. Tauris, 1996; Khaldoun Hasan al-Naqeeb, "Social Origins of the Authoritarian State in the Arab East," in Eric Davis and Nicolas Gavrielides, eds., *Statecraft in the Middle East - Oil, Historical Memory, and Popular Culture*, Miami, Florida: Florida International University Press, 1991, pp. 36-70. For an overview of the Arab debate about the state, see Talal Asad, "Ideology, Class, and the Origin of the Islamic State," *Economy and Society* 9, 4 (1980), pp. 450-473; Fahmi Jadaane, "Notions of the State in Contemporary Arab-Islamic Writings," pp. 112-148, and "*Al-Watan* and *Al-Umma* in Contemporary Arab use," pp. 149-174, both in Salamé (1987).

[8] Much insight about the Arab state is to be found in the work of Ibn Khaldun. I purposely confine myself here to a single aspect of his monumental work.

[9] This concept, which has alternatively been translated as "*esprit de corps*," "solidarity," "sense of tribal solidarity," "group feeling," and "group consciousness," has often been discussed but it is still not precisely pinned down in Western social sciences. As Cox (1992: 153) correctly notes: "The concept of '*asabiya* in Ibn Khaldun is the subject of as much discussion and shades of meaning as the concept of *virtù* in Machiavelli. It has been roughly but probably inadequately translated as "group feeling".... '*asabiya* is the form of intersubjectivity that pertains to the founding of a state....and in this respect '*asabiya* has (for a Westerner) some relationship to Machiavelli's *virtù*." Although Ibn Khaldun's ideas are indeed present throughout Machiavelli's discourses (particularly with regard to the evaluation of religion in relation to the state), the difference is that "[Both of them] share an impartial empiricism....But Ibn Khaldun inquires into the origin and development of the state in order to find and formulate an underlying law." [Erwin I. J. Rosenthal, *Political Thought in Medieval Islam: An Introductory Outline*, Cambridge, Massachusetts: Cambridge University Press, 1958, p. 108.]

[10] Elia Zureik, "Theoretical Considerations for a Sociological Study of the Arab State," *Arab Studies Quarterly* 3, 3 (Summer 1981), pp. 229-257.

[11] On the political use of culture in contemporary Iraq, see Amatzia Baram, "Culture in the Service of *Wataniyya*: The Testament of Mesopotamian-Inspired Art in Ba'thi Iraq," *Asian and African Studies* 17 (November 1983), pp. 265-313. Also see Chantal Foucault, "L'Archéologie au Service du Pouvoir," in Pierre Robert Baduel, ed., *Crise du Golfe - La Logique des Chercheurs*, Aix-en-Provence, France: Edisud, 1991, pp. 10-15. It is of no small significance that the annual budget of the Iraqi Ministry of Culture went from $2 million in 1975 to $30 million in 1981.

[12] Confidential memorandum dated March 1933. Cited in Abdulrazzaq al-Hassani, *Tarikh al-Wizarat al-'Iraqiya* (The History of Iraqi Cabinets), vol. 3, Sidon, Lebanon: Matba'at al-'Irfan, 1953, p. 289.

[13] Stephen Longrigg (1958: 53) points out that "the Iraq of 1500-1900 never became Turkish in culture or sentiment, still less in blood or language." In an earlier work, Longrigg (1953: 2) similarly noted that "The progress which Turkish culture had made in some 'Iraqi circles detracted little from the Arab character which [Iraq] shared equally with the backward provinces of the Hijaz, the Yaman, and North Africa."

[14] The human cost was 8,450 Iraqi and 2,105 British casualties (al-Marayati, 1961: 18).

[15] Cited in Foster, *The Making of Modern Iraq*, p. 97.

[16] Lady Florence Bell, ed., *The Letters of Gertrude Bell*, New York, New York: 1927, p. 593.

[17] In fact, as early as 1259, the Mongols had divided the territory into three provinces: (i) "Iraq" in the center and center-east including some of the southern region, (ii) the "Jazirah" in the north from Mosul to Irbil, and (iii) the mountainous regions. As Longrigg (1953: 1) notes, the central province was always the most important: "Baghdad had always held primacy over the two other renowned cities of 'Iraq, Mosul and Basra; and even in 1900, after Mosul had emerged finally as a wilaya in 1879 and Basra in 1884, the Wali of Baghdad was by every standard the senior of the three governors."

[18] See Philip Willard Ireland, 'Iraq - A Study in Political Development, New York, New York: The MacMillan Company, 1938, esp. pp. 201-221. A testimony of Iraq's strong desire for independence is that it was the only mandate territory to establish treaties with other countries.

[19] See Ernest C. Dawn,. "The Amir of Mecca: Al-Hussayn ibn 'Ali and the Origin of the Arab Revolt," Proceedings of the American Philosophical Society C4, 1 (1960), pp. 11-34. For instance, the first Minister of Defense was Ja'far Basha al-'Askari, the former commander-in-chief of the Hashemite army of the Hejaz (Arabia).

[20] All twelve of them were Sunnis and, except three, Baghdadis. See Tarbush (1982).

[21] See William L. Cleveland, The Making of An Arab Nationalist - Ottomanism and Arabism in the Life and Thought of Sati' Al-Husri, Princeton, New Jersey: Princeton University Press, 1971, especially pp. 59-77, "Institutionalizing Nationalism: Iraq, 1921-1941"; and Mohammad Abdelrahman Bourj, Sati' al-Husri, Cairo: Dar al-Kitab al-'Arabi, 1969.

[22] See H.C. Englebrecht, Johann Gottlieb Fichte: A Study of his Political Writings with Special Reference to his Nationalism, New York, New York: Columbia University Press, 1933; and the works of Gottfried Von Herder and Ernst Moritz Arndt. The claim that Husri has borrowed much of his ideas from Europe was refuted by Walid Kazziha in "Another Reading into Al-Husari's Concept of Arab Nationalism," in Marwan R. Buheiry, ed., Intellectual Life in the Arab East, 1890-1939, Beirut, Lebanon: American University in Beirut, 1981, pp. 154-164. The German influence was also strong on the Iraqi officers who, according to Simon (1986: 27), "were impressed with the technical and military education disseminated by....the [German] General Staff system which instilled order and respect for efficiency by elevating the methods of war to the level of a science." More recently, German theories of nationalism have been identified as having had a significant impact on the Ba'th theory of Arab nationalism. Al-Dmour (1991) establishes the relationship with regard to the definition of nationalism, the roles of culture and language, the emphasis on national unity, the concept of national mission, and the commitment to the idea of collectivity. See Khaled Mohammad al-Dmour, "The Influence of the German Romantic Theory of Nationalism on the Ba'th Theory of Arab Nationalism," Ph.D. dissertation, the Southern Illinois University at Carbondale, 1991.

[23] Hemphill (1979: 106) sums up the prevalent feeling about the Assyrians: "To Iraqi[s], the Assyrians were a standing affront to all that the newly independent kingdom stood for, perpetuating Iraq's disunity, and inviting continued British interference. This Christian minority, foisted upon Iraq by the Mandatory, was unwilling to assimilate, and the Iraqis were not over-eager to dissuade them. Iraqi accounts reflect a sense of exasperation with a strange people of a strange faith who persisted in regarding themselves as British protégés, and who were openly contemptuous of independence."

[24] For an extensive, if polemical, Assyrian account of these events, see Yusuf Malek, The British Betrayal of the Assyrians, Warren Point, New Jersey: The Kimball Press, 1935, esp. pp. 213-262. Also see Khaldoun Husri, "The Assyrian Affair of 1933, Part I," International Journal of Middle East

Studies 5, 2 (1974), pp. 161-176, and "The Assyrian Affair of 1933, Part II," *IJMES* 5, 3 (1974), pp. 344-360; and R.S. Stafford, *The Tragedy of the Assyrians*, London: Allen & Unwin, 1935.

[25] Although the issue was never resolved, the King was reportedly poisoned by his Indian nurse, acting on British orders. See Tarbush (1982), pp. 240-241.

[26] Despite the fact that there is a wide consensus as to the important and positive role played by Faysal I in the building of a modern Arab state – Khadduri (1960: 7), for instance, noted that "Faysal's role in building up the Iraqi state can hardly be exaggerated" – it should be borne in mind that his Hejazi origin was not always accepted. Iraqi historian Wafik Raouf (1992: 17), for instance, argues that the imposition of Faysal was an initial state-building error in that it did not reflect the profound aspirations of the local population.

[27] Tarbush (1982) attributes the first forays of the Iraqi army into politics to three crucial events: (i) the Assyrian uprising, (ii) the death of King Faysal, and (iii) the events of 1936. See his chapter 5, pp. 95-120. This confirms J.C. Hurewitz's thesis that the army usually comes to occupy the power vacuum that inter-communal divisions create. See Hurewitz, "Soldiers and Social Change in Plural Societies: The Contemporary Middle East," in V.J. Parry and M.E. Yapp, eds., *War, Technology and Society in the Middle East*, London: 1975.

[28] The most complete treatment of this period is to be found in al-Hasani, *Tarikh al-Wizarat al-'Iraqiyya*, 1953-1967.

[29] See Ahmad A. R. Shikara, *Iraqi Politics, 1921-1941: The Interaction Between Domestic Politics and Foreign Policy*, London: LAAM, 1987; and Majid Khadduri, "The Coup d'État of 1936: A Study in Iraqi Politics," *The Middle East Journal* 3 (1948), pp. 270-292.

[30] For a comprehensive historical review of the complex border issue and the various and often contradictory agreements it was subjected to, see David H. Finnie, *Shifting Lines in the Sand - Kuwait's Elusive Frontier with Iraq*, Cambridge, Massachusetts: Harvard University Press, 1992. Also see Michael B. Bishku, "Iraq's Claim to Kuwait: A Historical Overview," *American-Arab Affairs* 37 (Summer 1991), pp. 77-88; and Majid Khadduri, "Iraq's Claim to the Sovereignty of Kuwayt," *New York University Journal of International Law and Politics* 23, 1 (Fall 1990), pp. 5-34.

[31] Rumors about a British-ordered assassination led to a mob lynching of the British Consul in Baghdad, G.E.A. Monck-Mason, on April 6. Raouf (1992: 30) argues that by eliminating Ghazi, Britain would have secured a strategic area at the eve of World War II.

[32] On the nature and functioning of the British mandate, see Philip W. Ireland, *Iraq: A Study in Political Development*, London: Jonathan Cape, 1937; Elizabeth Monroe, *Britain's Moment in the Middle East, 1914-1956*, London: Chatto and Windus, 1963; and Daniel Silverfarb, *The Twilight of British Ascendancy in the Middle East: A Case Study of Iraq, 1941-1950*, New York, New York: St. Martin's Press, 1994.

[33] Fawzi Mellah, for instance, argues that this strategic aspect of the union was in fact its sole purpose. The Hashemites, he argues, could not afford to have Nasser at their borders. See *De L'Unité Arabe - Essai d'Interprétation Critique*, Paris: L'Harmattan, 1985, pp. 135-137. Also see Bruce Maddy-Weitzman, "Jordan and Iraq: Efforts at Intra-Hashimite Unity," *Middle Eastern Studies* 26, 1 (January 1990), pp. 65-75.

[34] See Ismail al-Arif, *Iraq Reborn: A Firsthand Account of the July 1958 Revolution and After*, New York, New York: Vantage Press, 1982.

[35] See Mufti (1993), pp. 167-169. Mufti highlights the fact that, as soon as he took power, Qassem adopted a cooperative attitude on the important national matter of Kuwait's independence. The issue is rendered more ambiguous by the rumor that a 1957 secret agreement between Iraq and Britain specified that Kuwait would be integrated into Iraq at the time the 1899 Treaty expired (Rondot, 1963: 318). Also see the testimony of a member of the monarchical regime on this point: Khalil Kanna, *L'Irak, Hier et Demain*, Beyrouth: Éditions Dar al-Rayhani, 1966, p. 299.

[36] Caractacus (pseudonym of Frederick John Snell), *Revolution in Iraq - An Essay in Comparative Public Opinion*, London: Victor Gollancz Ltd, 1959, p. 29.

[37] Roger Owen, "Class and Class Politics in Iraq before 1958: The 'Colonial and Post-Colonial State,'" in Robert A. Fernea and WM. Roger Louis, eds., *The Iraqi Revolution of 1958 - The Old Social Classes Revisited*, London: I.B. Tauris, 1991, pp. 169-170.

[38] See Mustapha M. Alani, *Operation Vantage: British Military Intervention in Kuwait, 1961*, Surbiton, England: LAAM, 1990.

[39] Khaldoun Haseeb, *The National Income of Iraq: 1953-1961*, London: Oxford University Press, 1964, p. 14. This is a comprehensive and particularly detailed study of the economic conditions in Iraq during the 1950s.

[40] See Edith Penrose and E.F. Penrose, *Iraq: International Relations and National Development*, London: Ernest Benn Limited, 1978, p. 288. Also see CARDRI (1986: 32).

[41] See Hanna Batatu, "Iraq's Underground Shi'i Movements: Characteristics, Causes and Prospects," *The Middle East Journal* 35, 4 (Autumn 1981), pp. 578-594.

[42] Unsuccessful coups took place in Iraq on the following dates: December 9, 1959 (Rashid 'Ali al-Gaylani and tribal leaders); September 12, 1965 ('Aref 'Abdelrazzaq leading army and air force elements); June 29, 1966 ('Aref 'Abdelrazzaq with Nasserite elements from the army); January 20, 1970 (military leaders led by 'Abdelghani al-Rawi and Saleh Mahdi al-Samarrai); June 30, 1973 (civilian faction of the Ba'th party led by Nadhim al-Kazzar, director of the Internal Security Services); July 18, 1979 (pro-Syrian group including Muhiabdel Hussayn, Mohammad 'Ayach, 'Adnan Hussayn, and Mohammad Mahjoub); February 1990; May 4, 1991 (Lieutenant-General Barek Abdallah); March 1995 (Wafiq Samarrai, head of military intelligence, and Kurdish groups); and July 1996 (unidentified Republican Guard officers with CIA support). This list is not exhaustive.

[43] See Michael E. Brown, "The Nationalization of the Iraq Petroleum Company," *International Journal of Middle East Studies* 10 (1979), pp. 107-124. The IPC was renamed the Iraqi Company for Oil Operations (ICOO).

[44] Francis Fukuyama, *The Soviet Union and Iraq Since 1968*, Santa Monica, California: The Rand Corporation, 1980.

[45] Yves Schemeil, "Le Système Politique Irakien Enfin Stabilisé," *Maghreb Machrek* 74, (1976). Similarly, Axelgard (1988: 19) wrote: "For the first time since the death of Faisal I in 1933, an Iraqi

116

regime had appeared that seemed to have the potential to make a historic contribution to the consolidation of the Iraqi state."

[46] Arab Socialist Ba'th Party, *Revolutionary Iraq - 1968-1973*, Report adopted by the Eighth Regional Congress of the Arab Socialist Party of Iraq, Baghdad: January 1974, p. 303.

[47] See Joyce Blau, *Le Problème Kurde: Essai Sociologique et Historique*, Brussels: Center pour l'Étude des Problèmes du Monde Musulman Contemporain, 1963; Hassan Arfa, *The Kurds: An Historical and Political Study*, London: Oxford University Press, 1966; P. Kreyensbroek and S. Sperl, eds., *The Kurds - a Contemporary Overview*, New York, New York: Routledge, 1992; and Ali Beha Kahan, *Les Kurdes d'Irak*, Beyrouth: 1994.

[48] See Amatzia Baram, "Qawmiyya and Wataniyya in Ba'thi Iraq: The Search for a New Balance," *Middle Eastern Studies* 19, 2 (April 1983), pp. 188-200. In an interview with *Le Nouvel Afrique-Asie* 46-47, July-August 1993, Tariq 'Aziz expressed the opinion that since 1961, the Kurds have always resisted integration and created difficulties for the Iraqi state, especially in times of crises (1975, 1980, and 1991).

[49] Sa'd Jawad, "Recent Developments in the Kurdish Issue," in Niblock, ed., *Iraq: The Contemporary State*, p. 49.

[50] See Michael Gunter, "Mulla Mustafa Barzani and the Kurdish Rebellion in Iraq: The Intelligence Factor," *International Journal of Intelligence and Counterintelligence* 7, 4 (Winter 1994), pp. 465-474; and Jason Morris, "Begin Airs Secret Israeli Aid to Kurds as Reminder for Iraqis," *The Christian Science Monitor*, 6 October 1980, p. 11. Barzani died on March 2, 1979, in Washington, D.C.

[51] An additional agreement was signed with Saudi Arabia in 1981, followed by two more protocols in 1982.

[52] Baram (1990: 243) notes: "*Army officers were gradually excluded from political power in lower institutions, and the army officers' corps increasingly became a professional body with very little involvement in politics.*" In 1975, Saddam Hussayn was saying: "*We should be fully conscious of the decisive weight of two interdependent factors with their own mutual political effects: a solid economic base and an effective military capability.*" ["The National Potential and International Politics," p. 72.]

[53] In fact, Iranian support went beyond supplying arms to the Kurds. Pelletiere (1992: 9) reports that by 1975 the Iraqis were directly clashing with some Iranian paramilitary troops.

[54] Kienle (1990: 87-88) remarks: "Ironically, by recognizing Iran's dominant position in the Gulf, this agreement enabled the Iraqi regime to strengthen its own internal and regional position economically as well as politically and finally to challenge Iran again. In the long term Iraq, by giving a little, gained more."

[55] C.J. Edmonds, "The Iraqi-Persian Frontier: 1639-1938," *Asian Affairs* 62, 2 (June 1975), pp. 147-154. The animosity between the two countries also has a far-reaching history. The state of Iraq was not, for instance, granted recognition by Iran until May of 1929, eight years after its creation. See Khalid Izzi, *The Shatt-al-'Arab Dispute: A Legal Study*, London: Third World Center for Research and Publication, 1981.

117

[56] Among other explanations, Crawford (1992: 344-345) offers three pertinent justifications for the conflict: (i) Iran's political and military provocations (thus war, on the part of Iraq, was a rational response to threat), (ii) war as a rational choice of means to achieve a change in borders, and (iii) centuries-old ethnic conflict between Arabs and Persians. Helms (1984: 4), for her part, argues that "the deeper cause of the war was a perceived threat *to the Iraqi Ba'thists and to the Iraqi state* arising from revolutionary Iran." (Emphasis added).

[57] *Al-Da'wa* would later be credited with two other assassination attempts against Saddam Hussayn and his entourage: in July of 1982 at Dujayl and in September 1987 at Baquba.

[58] Interview with Iraqi officials, Baghdad, August 1994.

[59] This reluctance had a purely political rationale, with an emphasis on long-term historical and statehood-related concerns. In an interview granted to *Le Monde* on August 22, 1981, Tariq 'Aziz explained: "Our military strategy reflects our political objectives. We want neither to destroy Iran nor occupy it permanently because that country is a neighbor with which we will remain linked by geographical and historical bonds and common interests. Therefore, we are determined to avoid taking any irrevocable steps."

[60] Cited in Nader Entessar, *Kurdish Ethnonationalism*, Boulder, Colorado: Lynne Reinner Publishers, 1992, p. 79.

[61] Although it took place during a clash between Iraq's and Iran's armies, the massacre of Halabja has been generally imputed to the Iraqi side. Yet on December 19, 1990, *The International Herald Tribune* published an article entitled "US Study Finds No Proof of Iraqis Gassing Kurds," in which it cited a declassified US Army War College report which questioned Iraq's sole responsibility in the massacre.

[62] According to Stephen C. Pelletiere (1992), the key development was an extraordinary congress of the Ba'th party held in July of 1986 at which a secret military solution was planned. It rested on a newly-established synergy between the generals and the civilian leadership geared towards a maximal use of technology and means of modern warfare on a larger scale than previous operations. By detaching their thinking from international considerations and the interests of their closest allies – both the United States and the Soviet Union preferred a political rather than military solution – the Iraqis achieved "a conclusion that was one of the more astonishing military upsets in recent history" (p. 112). Pelletiere's work is a convincing and well-researched major reinterpretation of the First Gulf War and, in particular, of how the 1988 threshold planted the seeds for the 1991 conflict.

[63] Jonathan Crusoe, "Economic Outlook: Guns and Butter, Phase Two?," in Frederick W. Axelgard, *Iraq in Transition - A Political, Economic, and Strategic Perspective*, Washington, D.C.: Center for Strategic and International Studies of Georgetown University, 1986, p. 53.

[64] Stephen C. Pelletiere, Douglas V. Johnson II, and Leif R. Rosenberger, *Iraqi Power and US Security in the Middle East*, Carlisle Barracks, Pennsylvania: The Strategic Studies Institute of the US Army War College, 1990, p. 1. Also see Richard Juppa and Jim Dingeman, "How Iran Lost/Iraq Won the Gulf War," *Strategy and Tactics*, March-April 1990.

[65] See G. H. Jansen, "Why Rafsanjani Has Opted for Peace," *Middle East International*, 22 July 1988, p. 3; G.H. Jansen, "The Gulf War: Iraq Continues the Punishment," *Middle East International*, 5 August 1988, p. 5; and Shahram Chubin, "The Last Phase of the Iran-Iraq War: From Stalemate to Ceasefire," *Third World Quarterly* 11, 2 (April 1989), pp. 1-14.

[66] Samir al-Khalil (pseudonym of Kanan Makiya), *Republic of Fear: The Inside Story of Saddam's Iraq*, New York, New York: Pantheon Books, 1989, p. 259.

4

Iraqi Policy-Making During
the Second Gulf War

This chapter articulates the state-building/regime security framework in conjunction with the foreign policy making process of the Iraqi government during the 1990-1991 Second Gulf War. Four major decisions were taken by the Iraqi authorities – the decision to invade Kuwait (8/2/90), the decision to internationalize the conflict (8/12/90), and the decisions to reject the two withdrawal ultimata (1/15/91 and 2/23/91). In a review of these decisions, I argue that the decisionmaking sequence was in general conditioned by the requirements of both state-building and regime security. However, as the crisis evolved towards a certain military confrontation with an American-led international coalition, the Iraqi authorities increasingly gave more importance to their regime's survival.

The Decision to Invade Kuwait

The immediate events leading to the invasion of Kuwait are of great significance. They follow an extraordinarily insistent logic. In the two-year period between the end of the war with Iran and the second Gulf conflict, the Iraqi regime was trying to establish anew all four elements of its regime security: power consolidation, economic viability, threat diffusion, and legitimacy renewal. If indeed Iraq had won a military victory over its Iranian neighbor, the costs of this victory were domestically high to the Ba'thi regime. But, in trying to consolidate its power, meet the demands of economic viability, diffuse the short- and long-term threats to its existence, and, most of all, maintain its legitimacy, the regime set in motion a sequence of events that culminated in the invasion of Kuwait.

The post-First Gulf War period turned out to be a more volatile and uncertain time than the conflict with Iran itself. The very fact that Iraq did not lose the war meant a kind of victory that would incite further expansion of the military potential. Hence, what transpired in those two years of living dangerously can be summed up as follows: emboldened by a war that it had won against all odds (including its own), the Iraqi regime endeavored to reestablish itself both domestically and regionally. A new, more assertive Iraq was emerging. Liberalization measures were taken at home and an effort to lead the Arab world – more immediately the Mashreq part of it – was pursued. But, as the new policy orientation failed to rapidly show tangible results, in the face of the enormity of domestic reconstruction tasks and regional resistance to the Iraqi leadership designs by the Gulf countries and competition by Egypt, the Ba'thi regime decided to take a major action that would provide it with national consensus as well as further its interests internally and externally.

At the time, the government of President Saddam Hussayn was faced with several challenges. The most salient of these tests was the faltering of social cohesion in the wake of the First Gulf War and the decline of living standards. After an exhausting and costly conflict, Iraq found itself beset by economic uncertainties. The sacrifices endured by the population for almost a decade meant that the social fabric was overstretched (al-Jabar, 1991). Similarly, the state's regulative and distributive capabilities were seriously endangered. Approximately $130 billion had been spent on the war effort and, due to the deterioration of industrial production and living standards, $63 billion had to be invested in reconstruction projects. Moreover, 13 million date trees had been destroyed during the war, seriously undermining agricultural production. With an estimated debt of $80 billion, (and an annual $10 billion service) Iraq's problem was clearly financial.

In such a context, the Kuwaiti decision to raise its oil production to make up for the unused Iraqi quota set by OPEC could only make matters worse for the Iraqis. Gradually, Kuwait emerged as the new *bête noire*. Its "insulting" wealth and its reluctance to cooperate with financially-strapped Iraq in need of a respite were to provide the key to a restoration of nationalistic feelings. The uneasiness was summed up in general terms by President Hussayn during one of his speeches:

> We reaffirm that what we have always stressed; namely, that our intentions are not affected by our military capability, but rather, our capability corresponds to our intentions, which constantly emphasize that what we need is not permanent fighting, but permanent peace. *When we resort to fighting, we do this only when fighting is indispensable to an honorable peace and a dignified life.*[1] (Emphasis added.)

That kind of rhetoric was surprising from a country that was only a few months away from the end of an eight-year-long conflict. Then, in 1989, the government announced a vast liberalization program. In fact, major privatization measures had been enacted since 1987. These included tax breaks, reduced price control, and privatization of state-owned services. With the new batch of dispositions, political pluralism and democratization measures were also discussed.

That the aim of the policies was an effort at domestic cohesion and national consensus is demonstrated by the fact that a rehabilitation of the monarchy took place. The tombs of the Hashemite kings were restored at the occasion of a state visit by King Hussayn of Jordan – who, by now, had become Iraq's main regional ally. To register its new regional status abroad, Iraq supervised the creation of a new Arab sub-ensemble with Jordan, Egypt, and North Yemen, the Arab Cooperation Council (ACC). Following after the Union of the Arab Maghreb (UMA), in which Algeria, Libya, Mauritania, Morocco, and Tunisia had united in February of 1989, the ACC was in fact designed as a time-delayed response to the all-powerful Gulf Cooperation Council

(GCC) of Saudi Arabia, Kuwait, Qatar, Oman, the United Arab Emirates, and Bahrain. Iraq also signed a non-aggression pact with Saudi Arabia in March of 1989. These early moves signified a multiform reasserting of Iraqi ambitions.

Besides the economic crisis *per se*, domestically, the major challenge to the Iraqi regime was demobilization of the army. The huge arsenal and the manpower that the war with Iran had yielded meant that a real "social atomic bomb" was coming back to the cities.[2] In effect, the armed forces had gone from 110,000 in 1974 to 444,000 in 1979 to 900,000 in 1987. But of the 1,000,000 soldiers Iraq had in 1988, only 250,000 had been demobilized by August 1990.[3]

It is fair to say that for the first time since 1961, the army was regaining a major say in political matters. With battle-hardened soldiers moving about the cities, the Ba'thi regime had to take measures to diffuse that threat. Hence, to take care of the soldiers, their salary was increased and military programs were expanded. Yet the political machinery could not enlist the support of the army so easily for the latter was beginning to threaten the regime's very organizational interests. Truly, the army had become the melting pot where all contradictions were cross-cutting each other. No longer on the front and deprived of economic opportunities, soldiers were turning into a fluid social group. One Iraqi observer describes the phenomenon:

> After the war ended, there were many unemployed soldiers about, more than a few of them whom turned to crime to support themselves and their families. Others sold their weapons. A whole new market grew (Sumaida, 1991).

The only problem for the Ba'thists is that this erratic social group was a powerful one. Indeed, as Sumaida goes on:

> [It] was only a matter of time before Saddam shifted again. He had a million-man army with nothing to do....He would have to find something to keep them busy before they turned their thoughts to the presidential palace, the way armies do when they have time on their hands.

By that reckoning, the invasion of Kuwait would then have represented a bail-out for the regime. At the same time, and because the awakened issue – Kuwait's appurtenance to Iraq – dealt with nationhood through territorial assertiveness, Iraqi state-building was reproduced by legitimizing references to history. Indeed, the importance of the crisis for the Iraqi state is not to be underemphasized. The three-way interaction between regime, army, and state lies at the bottom of the August 2, 1990, decision to invade Kuwait. It is also the continuation of a historical pattern in Iraq.

To sum up then, societal cohesion was being endangered by an economic crisis, the financial difficulties of the state, and a returning army. As the regime saw it, it had become imperative to contain society's increasing discontent. The invasion of Kuwait was also a bid to channel that discontent on the basis of a new-found Iraqi patriotism (*wataniya 'Iraqiya*) that had become a strong enough rallying point since the defeat of Iran – but which needed to be reactivated.[4] Surely, the Iraqi leadership was understanding that "the more unstable, ineffective, and divided the civil society becomes, the greater is the likelihood of military intervention" (Tarbush, 1982). Tellingly, the invasion of Kuwait was initiated by the Iraqis in order to regain national cohesion and quash internal dissensions.

Von Clausewitz said that war is the continuation of policy by other means. The August 2, 1990, invasion of Kuwait by Iraq is no exception. It emanated from domestic and foreign policies that were in the making since 1988 and that were dramatically accelerated during the first half of 1990. A review of that complicated period shows that some dramatic development was impending. Specifically, the Iraqi regime's need to attend to domestic developments and a desire to establish itself regionally (militarily and politically) heralded the invasion of Kuwait.

The opening salvo of the sequence leading to the invasion of Kuwait occurred on February 7, 1990, when Lieutenant-General 'Amer Hamoudi al-Sa'di announced that Iraq was ready to launch two different domestically-produced satellites; al-'Abid and Tammuz I. Iraq was making it known to the world that it intended to bid for a new international role. The following February 12, US Deputy-Secretary of State John

Kelly and US Ambassador to Iraq April Glaspie met for ninety minutes with President Saddam Hussayn in Baghdad. Kelly called Hussayn "a force of moderation" in the Middle East. But, three days later, an editorial on the Arabic service of The Voice of America broadcast in the Middle East castigated Saddam Hussayn's "ruthless secret police regime" and called him a vicious dictator. Ambiguity and tension with the United States and their regional allies continued when, at a meeting of the Arab Cooperation Council, held on February 24 in Amman, the Iraqi President voiced his country's displeasure with the conservative behavior of the Gulf States; and he lashed out against the policies of the United States in the Arab region. Hussayn spoke of the need for the Arab world to reassess its strategic objectives after the end of the Cold War:

> The continued US presence in the Gulf is due to the fact that the Gulf, in view of the developments witnessed in international politics and in the prospect of the oil market and of the increasing need for oil by the United States, Europe, Japan, and perhaps even the Soviet Union, has become the most important spot in the whole world....The country, therefore, that succeeds in wielding the biggest share of influence over the region, through the Arab Gulf and its oil, will secure to itself an unchallenged supremacy as a superpower.[5]

Fifteen years earlier, Hussayn was making the same predictions:

> Once we concede that world politics have entered a new formative phase, we must then step up our efforts and increase our potential for planning and execution to consolidate our position and strengthen our role on this globe at the time and place of our choice.[6]

The sum total of these manifestations constituted a logical sequence of statements speaking of Iraq's new geostrategic aims – based, to be certain, on long-standing ambitions. Starting in the spring, the events would become even more specific in terms of Iraq's newfound assertiveness.

At the time, a host of underground intelligence maneuvering was taking place. This quiet policy aspect is attested to by three episodes that became public. On March

15, an Iranian-born British journalist, Farzad Bazoft, who was on a reporting mission for the London-based *The Observer* was hanged on spying charges.[7] Bazoft had been investigating an explosion that had taken place at the al-Qaqaa military-industrial complex. On March 22, the Canadian-born scientist Gerald Bull who had been contracted by Iraq to build a supergun was assassinated in his home in Brussels.[8] And, on March 28, on their way to Iraq, 95 nuclear triggers (electronic detonator capacitators) designed in Salem, Massachusetts, were seized by the British police at Heathrow airport in London.

On April 2, at a ceremony honoring the armed forces, President Hussayn threatened to burn half of Israel with chemical weapons if he were to be attacked by that country. Saddam Hussayn's declaration struck a chord amongst the Arab peoples who almost at once started seeing Hussayn as the champion of the oppressed Arab masses.[9] The very next day, Israel launched a satellite in orbit as a response to the Iraqi threat. The probe, Ofek II, was believed to be a military reconnaissance unit.[10] The Iraqis continued their warnings saying that they would retaliate with their full might against anyone who attacked them or an Arab country. On April 18, speaking to Arab delegates, President Hussayn specifically declared, "He who launches an aggression against Iraq or the Arab nation will now find someone to repel him." Ten days later, *The New York Times* featured an editorial entitled "Baghdad Rages On" in which the newspaper remarked that "President Hussein's actions become more threatening."[11]

In an interview given to the Cairo daily *Al-Ahali*, Iraq's Deputy-Prime Minister, Taha Yassin Ramadan, denounced the campaign against Iraq and explained it by Iraq's victory against Iran. He argued that an Israeli attack against his country had been planned for some time.[12] Later, Iraqi Foreign Minister Tariq 'Aziz would say that his country was expecting such an attack in March and April 1990. Referring to the 1981 Israeli attack on the Osiraq I Iraqi nuclear reactor,[13] an Iraqi official told me: "We wanted to show them that this was not 1981, that now we can respond."[14]

Yet the Iraqi announcements continued to meet with ambiguous and contradictory American and Arab responses. On April 12, a group of US senators led by Robert Dole met with Saddam Hussayn in Mosul. The senators expressed concern about Iraq's weapons program but again the tone was conciliatory. They also apologized for the February 15 Voice of America broadcast. A month later, National Security Council aide Richard Haas visited Baghdad expressing "Washington's desire to continue to seek friendship with Iraq." At an Arab League Summit held in Baghdad on May 28, President Hussayn expressed displeasure with the United Arab Emirates and Kuwait's financial behavior towards Iraq. In public and private meetings with their Arab counterparts, the Iraqis made it clear that if a settlement was not reached soon, they would be ready for a total confrontation. The full configuration of Iraq's ambitions was emerging. Yet the response of both Americans and Gulf Arabs alike were tentative at best. Attentive to the US perception of his regime's regional policies, on July 4, Saddam Hussayn sent a message to President George Bush urging a US-Iraqi relationship based on mutual trust.

On July 11, at an OAPEC meeting, Iraq submitted a proposal for higher oil prices that was rejected by the ministers. At the same time, Kuwaiti overproduction – drawn primarily from the Rumaila oil field which is contiguous to Iraq – continued. On July 15, Iraqi Foreign Minister Tariq 'Aziz sent a letter to the secretary-general of the Arab League, Chadli Klibi, lodging an official protest against Kuwait's actions vis-à-vis his country. In the letter, 'Aziz writes:

> The aggression of the government of Kuwait against Iraq has been twofold; by encroaching upon our territories and oil fields, and by stealing our national wealth, such action is tantamount to military aggression. The Kuwaiti government's deliberate attempts to bring down the Iraqi economy is an aggression no smaller in its consequences than a military aggression.[15]

Two days later, in a speech celebrating the 1968 revolution, President Hussayn lashed out against Arab states "conspiring" against Iraq. In particular, he articulated Iraq's grievances towards Kuwait: "Reducing the price of oil....to the current low price....has resulted in Iraq's losing $14 billion dollars annually at a time when several billion dollars could complete much of what has been suspended or postponed in the life of

128

the Iraqis."[16] He added: "O God almighty, be witness that we have warned them. If words fail to protect Iraqis, something effective must be done to return things to their natural course and to return usurped rights to their owners."

Fully aware of Baghdad's offensive potential and temerity, on July 20, Israeli Defense Minister Moshe Arens visited US Secretary of Defense Richard "Dick" Cheney to express concern about Iraqi behavior. However, according to James Baker (1995), Israel's intelligence service, the Mossad, concluded (and passed on to its American counterparts) that Iraq's moves were only designed to dissuade an Israeli attack. Still, in Tel Aviv, many Israeli analysts were remarking at the time that the climate of July 1990 reminded them of the period preceding the 1967 Six-Day War.[17]

On July 21, on the basis of satellite pictures, the Defense Intelligence Agency (DIA) estimated that a force of 30,000 men was massing at Kuwait's borders. A week later, the number would rise to 100,000. Nonetheless, on July 24, the US Department of State's spokesperson, Margaret Tutwiler, unambiguously declared: "We do not have any defense treaties with Kuwait and there are no special defense or security commitments to Kuwait." On July 25, this message was reinforced by the US Ambassador in Baghdad April Glaspie who told President Hussayn:

> I have lived here for years. I admire your extraordinary efforts to *rebuild* your country. I know you need funds. We understand that and our opinion is that you should have the opportunity to *rebuild* your country. But *we have no opinion on the Arab-Arab conflicts, like your border disagreement with Kuwait.*[18] (Emphasis added.)

To be sure, the Hussayn-Glaspie meeting turned out to be a controversial one. It has been regarded as either denoting an American diplomatic blunder or more sinister plans. In any event, it resulted in giving the direct impression to the Iraqis that American reaction to an attack on Kuwait would be minimal. That the Iraqis chose to believe that remains as bewildering as the American pronouncements themselves.

As Ali (1993) notes, the US Ambassador made five serious mistakes during her meeting with Hussayn: (i) she did not warn the Iraqi President that the United States were aware of the concentration of Iraqi troops near Kuwait, (ii) she told him that some Americans (from oil-producing states) agreed that the price of the oil barrel should go up to $25, (iii) she failed to dissuade him from invading Kuwait, (iv) she told him that her country had no opinion on the border dispute between Iraq and Kuwait, and, finally, (v) she informed him that the US had no defense treaty with any Gulf country. Indeed, the optimistic cable that the Ambassador sent to Secretary Baker after the meeting is entitled "Saddam's Message of Friendship for President Bush."

For reasons we have yet to fathom, and keeping aside conspiratorial theories,[19] whether Glaspie's behavior was akin to diplomatic blunder or enticement has been inconclusively debated. For shorthand purposes, to say the least, the United States displayed significant ambivalence towards Iraq in those last crucial hours before the invasion. (During the whole duration of the conflict, the US Department of State would prevent the Ambassador from making public declarations.)[20] Moreover, the Bush administration could have hardly missed the Iraqi disarray signals as they were explicitly expressed by the Iraqi Ambassador to the United States in an op-ed article published in *The New York Times* on May 4.[21] In an interview granted to a Turkish newspaper after the war, President Hussayn explained that he did indeed interpret Glaspie's stance as non-committal:

> I....said: 'We do not want you to be involved'....They said they would not interfere. In so saying, they washed their hands. What response should I have waited for? We entered Kuwait four days later....What was the problem? They had said that they would not intervene.[22]

Further apparent US "washing of hands" came to Hussayn on July 28. In a presidential message from George Bush, drafted by the National Security Council, the American President wrote to his Iraqi counterpart:

> I was pleased to learn of the agreement between Iraq and Kuwait to begin negotiations in Jeddah to find a peaceful solution to the current tensions between you. The United States and Iraq both have a strong interest in

130

preserving the peace and stability of the Middle East. For this reason, we believe these difficulties are best resolved by peaceful means and not by threats involving military force or conflict (Baker, 1995).

Finally, on July 31, in congressional testimony, in response to a question by Representative Lee Hamilton, Assistant Secretary of State John Kelly declared that the United States did not have a treaty commitment to defend Kuwait – thus *de facto* removing any remaining US disincentives for Iraq's invasion of Kuwait.

On the same day, Kuwaiti and Iraqi delegations met inconclusively for two hours in Jeddah, Saudi Arabia. Iraq's senior delegation was composed of RCC Vice-Chairman, Ezzat Ibrahim al-Douri, Deputy-Prime Minister Sa'doun Hamadi, and a prominent Ba'th party leader and Saddam Hussayn's relative, 'Ali Hassan al-Majid. The Kuwaitis refused to yield to Iraq's demands to lease the islands of al-Warba and Bubyan and pay Iraq $10 billion for war losses. According to one version of the meeting, the Kuwaitis offered to loan $9 billion – holding on the remaining $1 billion to humiliate Iraq – and demanded a formal border agreement as precondition.[23] When the infuriated Iraqi delegates refused, the meeting was adjourned. The failure of this last round of negotiations was not surprising. By now, an agreement had almost become impossible. Pelletiere (1992) explains the process of radicalization:

> [W]ar is set off by a change in the dynamics of the dispute in which the parties have become embroiled. It must be that at a point in the negotiations, the ante is upped to a dangerous level....When this occurs, the exchange ceases to be rational; the opponents have locked themselves into an escalatory spiral that drags them along, willy-nilly.

Yet, and although Kuwait had placed its armed forces on alert since July 20, the Emirate still thought an invasion unlikely. That perception spoke of a somewhat tenuous grasp of reality on the part of Kuwait's rulers. To be certain, Iraq's covetous attitude towards Kuwait had been reemerging since the mid-1980s. A 1990 Ministry of Information presentation of the country listed "maintenance of territorial integrity" as the first objective of Iraq's foreign policy.[24] After the war, the Iraqis started protesting the facts that: (i) Kuwait had been making incursions into Iraqi territory during the First Gulf War, (ii) Kuwait had been slant-drilling oil wells in the disputed area, and (iii) the Emirate refused to wipe off its wartime loans to Iraq.[25]

At approximately 2:10 a.m. (Kuwaiti time), August 2, 1990, Iraqi troops entered Kuwait. It was a two-pronged fast and decisive operation lasting seven hours. The decision to invade Kuwait had then followed an incremental logic. Despite the many uncertainties that still surround the issue – for it is indeed all a matter of conjecture at this point – one might wonder: Did Iraq consider a limited operation? According to the Egyptian historian Mohammad Heikal (1992):

> The original intention had been to seize only the islands and the oilfields, but Saddam Hussein had had second thoughts at the end of July....Saddam argued that a limited operation would leave the al-Sabah family in power in Kuwait, and they would undoubtedly mobilize world opinion and use their relationship with Washington to ensure a US military response. Kuwait would then become a US base threatening Iraq. It seemed better to move decisively.

It is interesting to establish a parallel with the 1961 operation of President 'Abdelkrim Qassem:

> When the crisis broke speculations were advanced that Qassem did not really wish to annex Kuwait, but that he had a hidden purpose. It was asserted that *he wanted to increase his bargaining power* in other spheres; that he wished to counteract UAR influence in Kuwait by *a demonstration of strength*; or that he thought he would be able *to extort money* from the ruler (Dann, 1969). (Emphasis added.)

Such a threefold reasoning can equally account for Saddam Hussayn's 1990 operation as the decisive factors in opting for a full invasion. It would also appear that, in many ways, the Second Gulf War is a repetition of the first one with Iran. If anything, it

132

follows the same logic: a question of internal stability combined with far-reaching historical boundary disputes. Political marginalisation of the army would have led to a swift loss of the regime's insulation especially as the equation between regime and prosperity had become absent. In order to keep the opposition at bay, then, the Iraqi leadership reawakened the "Kuwait question." Thus, the logic of the financial issue and that of strategic matters gradually combined:

> The fusing of these questions in Iraqi thinking and propaganda was a step-by-step process. And while there are indications that the Iraqi leadership had been toying with the idea of invading Kuwait since 1988, only gradually did Baghdad come to see such an invasion as the solution for all its problems.[26]

Other explanations of the August 2 invasion have been put forth that make reference to this combination of immediate (i.e., regime security) and remote (i.e., state-building) factors. According to Christian Daudel, seven variables account for the invasion: (i) the historical formation of Kuwait, (ii) the permanent claims on Kuwait by Iraq, (iii) the project of a better access to the Gulf for the Iraqi state, (iv) the end of the war with Iran, (v) the political future of Saddam Hussayn in the Arab world, (vi) the formidable power of the Iraqi army, and (vii) the management of oil wealth.[27] The first three elements relate to state-building issues whereas the next three are tied to the Ba'thi regime's security. The oil issue is, for its part, equally present in both decisional constellations. Similarly, Faleh 'Abd al-Jabbar argued that the invasion was the result of a mixture of domestic-Iraqi, regional, and international phenomena with internal Iraqi dynamics being the most important set of factors.[28] Finally, another proponent of this view noted that

> President Hussein may also have had reasons for the invasion that were additional to his oil-related grievances with Kuwait. The stalemate in his war with Iran may have incited him to try once again for a realignment of the regional balance of power. It is useful to recall that Mesopotamia (Iraq), Persia (Iran), and Egypt, and occasionally the Arabian Peninsula

133

as well, have been disputing, without resolution, hegemonial regional overlordship since the Sumerian Sargon tried to achieve it around 2500 BC.[29]

Further testimony to the notion that the decision to invade Kuwait sprang from a combination of long- and short-term considerations is provided by the Iraqi leaders themselves who were consistently arguing the idea that the settlement of the Kuwait matter was postponed as the various Iraqi regimes had to attend to other national security matters. The two dimensions were indirectly referred to by Iraq's Foreign Minister Tariq 'Aziz himself who noted that the goals behind the decision to invade were "to unite [with Kuwait], to become one after the long separation, and to resolve [Iraq's] economic problems with a lung open to the sea."[30] Along those lines, in the course of his meeting with the US Ambassador April Glaspie, President Hussayn remarked:

> Since [1961], the Kuwaiti government has been stable while the Iraqi government has undergone many changes. Even after 1968 and for ten years afterwards, we were too busy with our own problems. First in the north, then the 1973 war, and other problems. Then came the war with Iran which started ten years ago.[31]

Hussayn went on to make the correspondence between past and present clearer. As it appears, the Iraqi state's history is, in effect, of immediate relevance to his regime's security requirements:

> I say to you clearly that Iraq's rights....we will take one by one. That might not happen now or after a month or after one year, but we will take it all. We are not the kind of people who will relinquish their rights. There is no historic right, or legitimacy, or need for the UAE and Kuwait to deprive us of our rights. If they are needy, we too are needy.

134

The Decision to Internationalize the Conflict

As was the case with the First Gulf War, Iraq entered Kuwait without having a well-thought plan about how to bring the matter to a satisfactory settlement.[32] This may be attributed in part to the swiftness with which the invasion was undertaken. After the failure of an initial withdrawal plan and some oscillation, and following surprisingly swift and strong US and UN efforts to reverse the invasion,[33] the Iraqis decided to *expand* on the invasion and play for larger geostrategic stakes.

On the afternoon of August 3, King Hussayn visited Baghdad and secured an agreement from President Hussayn about settling the matter of the invasion within an Arab framework – specifically in the course of a meeting that was to be held in Jeddah the evening of Saturday the 4th of August or on Sunday the 5th. The initial withdrawal plan arranged by King Hussayn, and reportedly blessed by the Kuwaitis,[34] failed because the Iraqi condition agreed to by the King – namely, that no Arab public condemnation occur before the pull back – was not met when Egypt issued a separate statement denouncing the invasion.[35] On August 3, Iraq had indeed announced that it was going to withdraw its troops from Kuwait the next day. An official Iraqi news agency aired this statement by the spokesman of the RCC:

> If there are no threats against Iraq or Kuwait, Iraqi forces will start to withdraw tomorrow [August 4]. A plan to withdraw from Kuwait has already been approved.

According to Israeli author Amatzia Baram (1994), the evacuation of a tank brigade was shown on Iraqi television on August 5. But after the Egyptian announcement – which had angered and disheartened King Hussayn who perceived it as a deliberate sabotage meant to undermine his mediation – all bets were off and the scheduled Iraqi withdrawal was canceled.[36]

The failure of this initial mediation plan has been regarded by the Iraqi leadership as the proof of the existence of an Arab and American campaign directed

135

against their country. In a letter sent by Tariq 'Aziz to the foreign ministers of the Arab world and the world at large on September 4, 1990, the Iraqi official held the US and their Saudi and Egyptian allies responsible for the cancellation of the August 4 meeting. He remarked:

> This summit, which was to be held during the evening of Saturday, the 4th of August, or on Sunday the 5th, did not take place because of the intervention of the United States of America on the very day for which the Arab summit had been scheduled. President Bush asked his Defense Secretary to visit Saudi Arabia seeking the King's approval for US forces to be invited to Saudi Arabia. The US Defense Secretary arrived in Jeddah on the morning of 6 August and the US forces began entering Saudi Arabia on 7 August, the very next day. The speed with which this operation was started confirms two basic facts. The first, is that there was a ready-made US military plan to ensure US domination of the Gulf region....The second fact is that the United States deliberately aborted an Arab solution to the problem proposed for discussion at the planned Jeddah Summit of 5 August, 1990.[37]

Then, at the suggestion of Syria, an Arab League Emergency Summit was held in Cairo on August 10. In the course of this controversial and heated meeting, the Egyptians managed to have the League pass a majority resolution formally condemning Iraq – although during a private encounter prior to the official ceremony President Mubarak had informed the Iraqi delegation that the intention was only to foster a dialogue between the various parties.[38] In point of fact, the Cairo summit resolution was in violation of article 5 of the Arab League charter which stipulates unanimity as the preferred voting procedure on such matters.[39]

The Iraqis were so confident that no major Arab opposition to their plans would emerge from the summit that they refrained from conducting consultations with the different delegations to inquire about their stances; whereas the Kuwaitis made sure that they talked to everyone present.[40] Since, ultimately, Tunisia, Jordan, Libya, Algeria, Mauritania, the Yemen, Sudan, and the PLO, either boycotted the meeting, abstained, expressed reservations, or voted against the resolution condemning Iraq, it seems that a more resolved and better coordinated diplomatic effort by the Iraqi delegates could have yielded more satisfactory results for their country. In the end, in the face of Egyptian and American condemnations, Iraq's position became more radicalized. (In fact, the sparks of rivalry between Egypt and Iraq, as well as the signs of Mubarak's personal antipathy towards Saddam Hussayn, had appeared long before.)[41] The stage was set for more deadlocks in this crisis.

Beyond immediate and short-term governmental agendas, the failure of these early mediation efforts was essentially due to the existence of simultaneous and conflicting views of the Arab order. Egypt, for instance, has long had its own outlook centered around a close relationship with the Gulf States, while, starting in the early 1980s, Jordan had attempted to play an objective role based on King Hussayn's understanding of the dynamics of Iraqi politics – a country where his Hashemite cousins had reigned for 37 years. In the new Kuwait crisis, Jordan endeavored to help the Iraqis without antagonizing the major powers.

Still, the Iraqis were committed to find a formula for withdrawal that would give an appearance of having achieved limited aims. On August 12, President Saddam Hussayn made a speech in which he offered to withdraw his troops from Kuwait in exchange for a comprehensive settlement of all outstanding territorial issues in the Middle East. Specifically, he declared:

> I propose that all issues of occupation, or the issues that have been
> depicted as occupation in the entire region, be resolved in accordance
> with the same bases, principles, and premises to be set by the UN Security
> Council, as follows: First, the....withdrawal of Israel from the occupied
> Arab territories in Palestine, Syria, and Lebanon, Syria's withdrawal from
> Lebanon, a withdrawal between Iraq and Iran, the formulation for
> arrangements for the situation in Kuwait....Second,....the immediate
> withdrawal from Saudi Arabia of US forces....Third, all boycott and
> siege decisions against Iraq shall be frozen immediately.[42]

The offer was immediately rejected by the United States and the other members of the coalition. Most Arab governments – even those that did not oppose Iraq as categorically as Egypt, Syria, and the Gulf countries – also saw the offer as a hurriedly devised strategy to prolong Iraq's stay in Kuwait and, accordingly, treated it as such. Some Arab leaders even saw it as a publicity stunt forcing a nexus between tangentially related issues.[43] The Syrians, in particular, ruled out any comparison between their presence in Lebanon and Iraq's invasion. Syrian Foreign Minister Farouq al-Shara' accused the Iraqis of drawing Israel into Arab-Arab matters.[44] Yet the seeds of "linkage" had been sown (Freedman and Karsh, 1993). Iraq's army was trapped in Kuwait and the proposal was a way to get it out in a most grandiose way.[45]

Establishing a linkage between the various regional issues would have enabled Hussayn to (i) gain the emotional support of Arab masses and (ii) score a political victory – even as the troops were withdrawing. What had indeed happened was that, once the invasion had taken place and since, in the eyes of the Iraqis, the problem had been blown out of proportion, the Ba'thi regime sought to temporize in order to legitimize its action vis-à-vis the Arab world. By placing Iraq's action in Kuwait on the same level as Israel's annexation of the occupied territories, the Iraqi government was aiming at expanding its regional role – even at the cost of appearing as an expansionist power violating international law and, most significantly, even as it was equating itself with its traditional Israeli enemy. This apparent paradox in fact masks the dual Iraqi objective that laid at the basis of the August 12 proposal. Namely, (i) securing the regime's domestic position by using the physical and symbolic attributes of the state in a regional crisis whose configuration was internationally expanded, and (ii) using the crisis (through war and, now, diplomacy) as an autonomy-enhancing strategy for the Iraqi state. A cardinal feature of this reasoning was that, for the Ba'thists, sovereignty of their state spelled betterment of position in the international system. In effect:

> Lier la libération du Koweït à celle de la Palestine ne vaut pas
> négociation, mais s'impose simplement comme un mode de communication
> internationale. Celle-çi devient, à son tour, le seul objectif final recherché
> de façon réaliste (Badie, 1992).[46]

Moreover, by invoking the possibility of accommodation, the Iraqi government was in fact saying that the situation created by its invasion of Kuwait was no longer a zero-sum game. In essence, the approach was a combination of aggressiveness and readiness to cooperate. In that very sense, the August 12 decision was an added objective to the policy-making process that led to the invasion. The political feasibility of this improvised objective rested on the recognition that the new situation was part and parcel of a complex and multiform regional configuration wherein geostrategic processes were interwoven.

Nevertheless, the Iraqi leadership, even as it was offering a comprehensive solution, was aware of the American resolve to act decisively to reverse the invasion of Kuwait. In the course of his January 9, 1991, Geneva meeting with US Secretary of State James Baker, Foreign Minister Tariq 'Aziz explained:

> [S]ince the onset of events, we have expected military action from you against us. Despite all of this, we espoused the positions that we have chosen. We have constantly called for meetings and talks.[47]

Whether or not the Iraqis understood the global post-Cold War changes is a question that many analysts have posed and, for the most, answered negatively (see the review in chapter one). Yet we have seen here that, as early as February of 1990, Iraq was urging its Arab allies to rearrange their strategic priorities in the face of the US emergence as sole superpower. The question then begs itself: Were the Iraqis expecting the coalition to express interest in the August 12 proposal; or was it simply a way of briefly achieving international diplomatic parity and getting their message across? To be certain, the rejection of the proposal by the world community was perceived as a humiliation by the Iraqis. It also reinforced their beliefs about the existence of a "double-standard" used to judge similar acts by Israel and the Arabs in an asymmetrical manner:

> On August 12, 1990, President Saddam Hussayn announced an initiative

139

in which he called for all outstanding issues in the region to be settled on the basis of the same criteria and principles. He expressed his genuine hope that this initiative would open the door for just and peaceful solutions of all the problems in the region. Western states, however, rejected this initiative even before perusing it or making any inquiries about it, thus confirming the double-standard they apply to regional and international disputes in comparison with their position towards Israel.[48]

Later, at the Geneva meeting with James Baker, 'Aziz would try to revive the linkage issue. Although it was clear by that time that the August 12 proposal had been rejected by the various parties to the crisis, 'Aziz's words speak of a genuine hope that the Iraqi leaders seemed to have vested in the viability of their diplomatic offer:

What you are saying is the following: 'I reject linkage.' We have heard this. I would like to tell you in all sincerity , however, that effecting a linkage in this regard would be a realistic move. It is a vital issue in this region. If we are to realize security, stability, and peace, we have to deal with all of these issues. You are asking me to implement certain Security Council resolutions. But there are other Security Council resolutions which have remained unimplemented. No armies have been sent to enforce these resolutions. We are pained and infuriated by the double standards used with regard to the region's issues. We demand the implementation of uniform standards.[49]

No less instructive is 'Aziz's reaction to Soviet President Gorbachev's warning to him that linkage between the issues would never be accepted by the United States. In that meeting, held in Moscow on September 5, the Iraqi Minister angrily replied:

[S]o what is your role, you in the Soviet Union?.... You are *demanded* to side with us....[Y]ou are supposed to adopt a program of linking between all the region's issues and acknowledge that it is high time to tackle the Mid-East disputes.[50] (Emphasis added.)

Even though, by mid-August, Iraq was already facing a resolved coalition that had made it clear through the unprecedented swift adoption of several specific UN Security

Council resolutions demanding an immediate and unconditional withdrawal (see the chronology), the August 12 démarche could have been successful.[51]

According to Faleh 'Abd al-Jabar, it rested on three sound elements: (i) it addressed real problems; Israel's failure to withdraw from the occupied territories, the continuing Syrian presence in and control of Lebanon, the unequitable distribution of oil amongst Arab countries, and, now, the presence of Western troops in the Middle East, (ii) since the 1970s, there had been a leadership vacuum in the Arab world that became increasingly apparent in the 1980s after Israel's invasion of Lebanon and the United States' bombing of Libya, and (iii) economic frustration and political alienation made most Arab societies resentful of their governments.[52] Had the proposal been accepted, let alone implemented, it would have represented a sufficient victory for Hussayn, answering both regime and state concerns. Thus it can be said that the August 12 proposal – if maybe politically naive – was not necessarily insincere.

Paradoxically enough, the Second Gulf War generated a new dynamic of peace in the Middle East.[53] In the immediate aftermath of the conflict, an Arab-Israeli peace conference was held in Madrid on October 30, 1991. It gave birth to a celebrated yet incomplete two-part peace accord between the Palestine Liberation Organization – renamed the Palestinian National Authority – and Israel signed in Washington on September 13, 1993, and September 28, 1995. In 1994, a more comprehensive normalization took place between Israel and the Hashemite Kingdom of Jordan.

The Decision not to Abide by the January 15, 1991, Deadline

On November 29, 1990, the United Nations' Security Council passed resolution 678 authorizing the use of "all necessary means" to evict Iraqi troops from Kuwait if they did not withdraw before the following January 15. The malleability of the formula meant the recourse to the use of force if the set deadline was not complied with. The day after the adoption of the resolution, US President George Bush offered to meet with Iraqi Foreign Minister Tariq 'Aziz and proposed to send his Secretary of State, James Baker, to Baghdad. After much maneuvering, a meeting between the Foreign Minister and the Secretary of State was held in Geneva on January 9, 1991. The Iraqis had hoped to use that Geneva meeting to start a *de-escalation* process, at the end of which they would have withdrawn their troops from Kuwait but only after January 15. To have complied with the deadline would have meant more than "losing face" for Iraq. The Ba'thi regime's legitimacy would have surely been questioned domestically – thus setting the stage for uprisings and/or coups – and the state's sovereignty as well as its regional stance would have been significantly curtailed. To avoid such developments, and in the face of the US-led UN coalition's resolve not to negotiate and thus to initiate a military conflagration, the Iraqi leadership decided to let the ultimatum pass without ordering a withdrawal. This *de facto* rejection of the ultimatum was the most important Iraqi decision of the Second Gulf War, although it was one that had not been considered initially.

The Geneva meeting was a crucial meeting most of the time too briefly considered in the literature on the Gulf war. Oftentimes, reference is only made to Foreign Minister 'Aziz's refusal to transmit a letter from President Bush to President Saddam Hussayn on the grounds that the letter's language was insulting.[54] Beyond this diplomatic episode, the fact is, after months of standoff, the Iraqis became urgently interested in a negotiated settlement. Having released the remaining Western hostages on Christmas Day and thinking that the crisis should now be de-escalated, they sent a delegation of high officials to Geneva in the hope of painstakingly initiating a negotiation process.[55] One that would leave them with a symbolic political victory – as was the case with the First Gulf War. This disposition is demonstrated by a brief statement made by Tariq 'Aziz upon arrival at the Geneva airport on January 8:

> I would like to say that I have come in good faith. I am open-minded and I am ready to conduct positive, constructive talks with Secretary Baker if he shows the same intention....If there is a genuine sincere, serious intention to make peace in the whole region of the Middle East we are

ready to reciprocate. If we are going to hear the same kind of talk that has been reiterated over the last few months then we are going to give the proper answer.

As was the case with the August 12 proposal, this was a combination of readiness to cooperate and aggressiveness. To underscore the view, the next day, during the meeting with Baker in room D of the Hotel Inter-Continental's Salons des Nations, 'Aziz declared:

[W]e really want to talk. We have not talked since the beginning of the crisis. As is known, our two peoples are heading for a confrontation and it would be useful, before getting engaged in one, to explore the possibilities of establishing some understanding between our two countries. I prefer that we inform each other of our attitudes in a civilized manner that demonstrates mutual respect, and if God helps us reach understanding, that would be alright. If we fail, and this is not my wish, then each of us will know his way.[56]

The meeting lasted 6 hours and 46 minutes. Although the world expected a breakthrough, the encounter was unproductive. Within five minutes of Baker's announcement that "regrettably" he had not heard anything new from the Iraqi delegation, oil prices had jumped from $23.35 to $31.[57] Nonetheless, at various points during the talks, 'Aziz had suggested a follow-up meeting – a scenario that would have, in fact, been enough of a symbolic success for Iraq: "We are meeting now, and if God grants us success, we may pursue our work in the future."[58] As the meeting was winding down, the Iraqi Foreign Minister added: "If you are interested in further talks,....then talks would be possible" – but, again, he remained steadfastly defiant telling his American counterpart: "If you have made a decision to go to war, then you can carry out this decision at any time."[59] Although the contours of their calculation still remain vague, a respite or a postponement of the deadline seems to be what the Iraqis were after. Nevertheless, the US rejected the offer for further talks on the grounds that it was too late and that the January 15 deadline was real. Save for the UN resolutions, the American delegation had in fact very little interest in pursuing a settlement road with the Iraqis. In his book *The Politics of Diplomacy* published in October of 1995, Secretary Baker confirms this:

> I assumed the talks would be unsuccessful and that within a matter of days, we would be at war. Most of the very pessimistic opening statement I delivered at a press conference after the meeting was in fact drafted the day *before* our talks. (Original emphasis.)[60]

Despite last minute diplomatic efforts – such as the visit of UN secretary-general Javier Pérez de Cuellar to Baghdad and a more serious French effort – as well as a strong worldwide current of opposition to the war, the deadline passed announcing the coming conflict. Fragmentary evidence suggests that a French proposal brokered by President François Mitterand's special adviser Edgar Pisani was formally accepted by the Iraqis on the night of January 13-14. On the 14th, Pisani and French Foreign Minister Roland Dumas were to fly to Baghdad aboard the *Concorde*. Once in the Iraqi capital, a joint French-Iraqi announcement would have been made to the world. But, as Howorth (1994) reports, "that visit never took place because, before Concorde could leave for Baghdad on 14 January, Pérez de Cuellar had persuaded Mitterand that Saddam Hussein could not....be trusted." Besides the French initiative, there also was an unreported attempt by Yasser 'Arafat to secure a promise on the evening of the 14th; and in late January the Jordanian Prime Minister, Mudar Badran, secretly traveled to Baghdad but was not received by President Hussayn.[61]

Held in Baghdad on the 13th, the meeting between President Hussayn and secretary-general Pérez de Cuellar echoed the one between 'Aziz and Baker. Although, upon returning to New York, Pérez de Cuellar reported to the Security Council that the Iraqi President had refused to order his troops out of Kuwait, it would appear that had the UN diplomat pursued his mission more vigorously and with some commitment he would have secured an agreement from Hussayn. Indeed, the officially never-released transcript of the meeting reveals an affable Hussayn willing to hear arguments

144

and propositions much like his Foreign Minister interacted with James Baker. Phyllis Bennis, who had access to the text of the meeting, noted:

[O]f even more significance is the general tone of the conversation as a whole, and especially the remarks of Saddam Hussein. The Iraqi leader's statements, while not making explicit promises, do not reflect a rejection of diplomatic possibilities. There is a certain amount of flexibility, an apparent willingness to consider diplomatic alternatives based on an Iraqi withdrawal from Kuwait, possibly linked with a broader regional settlement. Whether these possibilities might have become realities will never be known; all that is certain is that the unequivocal "no" indicated in the secretary-general's report to the Security Council is not reflected in the meeting's unauthorized transcript.[62]

In the end, with regard to this particular decision, the Iraqis were, it seems, well aware of the nature of the confrontation. They chose to go all the way because domestically and historically they felt they had no other choice. Spelling capitulation, a withdrawal at this stage and under the conditions set by the coalition was tantamount to suicide for the Iraqi regime.

Also, in the particular context of this crisis, the proclivity to cross the bridge to military hostilities was not a giant leap for the actors involved because of the initial act of aggression (i.e., the invasion of Kuwait) and the swift US military deployment. Matthews (1993) points out to the in-built propensity for a military resolution of this crisis – that there was an entropic dynamic of war. In other words, escalation came as easily to the Iraqis as it came to the Americans because none was deterred by the idea of a military clash.

In that sense, the argument that Iraq misunderstood the resolve of its adversaries is misguided. In fact, at the press conference following his meeting with Secretary of State James Baker, Foreign Minister Tariq 'Aziz addressed that very point:

[Baker] spoke at length about his government's assumptions of miscalculations by Iraq. And when I came to that point, I made it clear to him that we have not made miscalculations. We are very well aware of the situation. We have been very well aware of the situation from the very beginning. And I told him that we have heard a lot of talk on his side and on the side of President Bush that 'the Iraqis have not gotten the message, they don't know what's going around them' etc.... I told him 'if we had met several months ago I would have told you that we do know everything. We know what the deployment of your forces in the region mean. We know what the resolutions you imposed on the Security Council mean. And we know all the facts about the situation, the political facts, the military facts, and the other facts.' So talking about miscalculations is incorrect.[63]

Inexorably, in meetings with Arab counterparts, the Iraqis were indeed emphasizing that they knew what they were doing.[64] Analogously, in the course of his meeting with Baker, 'Aziz declared: "We are an active government that works a great deal, reads, analyzes, and follows up."[65] Why, then, did Iraq choose to engage in a war it could not militarily win? The answer, I believe, is that the decision to reject the January 15 ultimatum was formulated in light of the course of events. The most cogent reason propelling non-action on the deadline is a feeling of fatalism that had developed amongst the Iraqi leadership. Following the Geneva failure, it became clear to the Iraqis that no matter what they did – besides an immediate withdrawal; something that they could not bring themselves to do – the conflict was going to erupt.

Their perceptions were, it seems, well-founded. In a book published in the spring of 1995, the former French Defense Minister Jean-Pierre Chevènement revealed that, as early as August 9, 1990, President George Bush had personally informed him of his intention to go to war to stop the risk of a too powerful Iraq.[66] In an interview with Saddam Hussayn, conducted by Chevènement for the same book, the President of Iraq explains:

I never had any illusion about the United States' resolve to go to war. They would have done it *no matter what*....As early as August 3 and 4, the deployment of American troops ruined the possibility of an Arab solution....We always had the impression that, *no matter what we did*, the United States were decided to hit and destroy Iraq. This is the reason why we have preferred to await the attack in Kuwait, because if we had withdrawn and had been hit, while still being prisoners of the embargo,....we would have demoralized our sincere patriots. Whereas, by accepting to be hit in Kuwait, we only had against us...traitors.[67] (Emphasis added.)

Similarly, in an interview with *The Washington Post* done after the conflict, Foreign Minister Tariq 'Aziz confided that, by December 1990,

Kuwait was no longer the main question. It was only a detail. The United States saw a historic chance to impose its power in the region after the Soviet Union's decline. We developed a fatalistic feeling about the war. We found ourselves in a position where we could not do anything about it.[68]

Finally, US Secretary of State James Baker's recollection of how his Geneva meeting with the Iraqi Foreign Minister ended confirms the idea of the Iraqi leadership's fatalism:

I will never forget the look in Aziz's eyes as we shook hands at the end of the meeting. He didn't appear angry or aggressive, but fatalistic.

The Iraqis had in fact followed a self-paralyzing strategy, and they found themselves locked into a set of cognitive imperatives that operated to preserve their belief system. This paralysis, which led them to reject the January 15 deadline, was the result of two considerations guiding every move they were making:

(i) a withdrawal before the deadline would have seriously undermined the regime's security;

(ii) a withdrawal under January 15 conditions would have been costly to the Iraqi state whose building would have been curtailed by the formulation of a new regional configuration specifically denying Iraq's geostrategic ambitions.

147

These were the fundamental threats which the Iraqi leadership chose to avoid at the cost of a gigantic war. With regard to the first element, the regime was already losing its economic viability before the invasion and now it was under an already five-month-long embargo. For the three other components of regime security – power consolidation, threat diffusion, and maintenance of legitimacy – it was make or break time. By rejecting the ultimatum (and thus engaging in war), the regime was primarily seeking to enlist the support of its population, especially as the country became the target of foreign attacks. To maintain its physical presence, and having established a supranational-to-local continuum, the government could not afford to back down and withdraw its troops before the deadline. Ofra Bengio (1991), for instance, has noted that such strategy resulted from the combined outcome of the regime's self-perception, severe domestic problems, and Iraq's longtime aspirations.

In a parallel manner, Iraq's sovereignty would have been dealt a heavy blow if the country had accepted the consequences of withdrawal without, at least, engaging in a defensive fight. It was obvious to the Iraqi leadership that *a posteriori* loss of sovereignty following defeat is fundamentally different than *a priori* acceptance of ultimatum conditions. Following the war, Tariq 'Aziz commented on this aspect:

> After January 15, there was a military battle. Before January 15, retreat
> ....meant a political and morale collapse...*This collapse would have a
> domino effect*....when you give in politically, it means you have lost your
> cause even before putting up a fight.[69] (Emphasis added.)

By the same token, national consensus and domestic cohesion within the Iraqi society would have been shattered by the regime's acknowledgment that it was acceding to external pressure. Finally, the process of institution-development, which in this case meant the establishment of the state's muscle and assertiveness – a political doctrine of wide-ranging domestic appeal – would have taken a step back. The state as custodian of internal order and external protector of domestic reality had to be reproduced in the face of challenges – even if it meant engaging in a suicidal fight. Hence, the only

148

insurance for the Iraqis that their regime would survive, and that they would further their historical claim by fighting for it was to go to war. This combination of fatalism, stoicism, and sense of obligation towards history is the construal of the problem. It was expressed by 'Aziz when he had met with Baker:

> What is more important is that we know our determination. We feel that we are victims of injustice. This is our feeling and when a people have such a feeling and when a war is imposed on them they will fight. Yes, you are a great power and you have the capabilities of other countries but do not doubt at all my people's determination to remain steadfast. *We are living in an era where feelings and history are interlinked... There is a feeling of tranquillity if war breaks out.*[70] (Emphasis added.)

Instead of de-escalating the conflict – their initial strategy from early December to mid-January – the Iraqi leaders sought further domestic and Arab legitimacy through an escalation within the war itself. They would let the coalition attack them and then they would "give the proper answer" by attacking Israel in order to undermine the position of the Arab portion of the allies. Contrary to what has been widely written, the strategy was sound. No Arab regime could have domestically withstood the test of fighting another Arab country alongside Israeli troops (see below). Nevertheless, by extending its protection to Israel, the US successfully diffused that scenario.

At 2:38 a.m. (Baghdad time), January 17, 1991, the Second Gulf War began between Iraq and a coalition of twenty-eight countries.[71] It lasted 44 days with 5 days of ground war.

The Decision to Reject the February 23, 1991, Deadline

After a month of fighting, the Iraqis chose to go back to their initial de-escalating strategy. Their Scud missile attacks having failed to get Israel involved in the conflict – thereby changing its Arab configuration – and their invasion of the Saudi locality of

Khafji (see below) having failed to provoke an early ground war which would have given them the opportunity to seize the military advantage before the coalition forces could be fully ready for an offensive, the Iraqis initiated a negotiation process through their former Soviet ally. Thus doing, they hoped to secure an agreement that would have ensured them the minimal objective of embargo lifting. Faced with an American refusal to condone the Soviet plan and the announcement by President George Bush of a 25-hour withdrawal ultimatum, the Iraqis repeated the January 15 deadline decisionmaking process letting the new deadline pass without ordering a withdrawal of their army divisions inside Kuwait. Only this time the stakes were higher for a regime that had to maintain significant troop build-ups at its frontiers with Kuwait, Iran, and Turkey. Hence, in this last decision, as war was no longer avoidable, regime-security took precedence over state-building.

On February 10, the Soviet President announced that he was sending his personal emissary, Primakov, to Baghdad in search for a way out of the ongoing military hostilities. Two days later, Primakov met with Hussayn who accepted the principle of an announcement on Iraq's part of willingness to withdraw in exchange for a coalition cease-fire. Accordingly, on the 15th, Iraq offered to remove its troops from Kuwait. Its offer was linked to three main demands echoing the August 12 proposal: (i) an Israeli withdrawal from the occupied territories, (ii) a Syrian pull out from Lebanon, and (iii) the departure of all coalition forces from the Gulf region. Hussayn also announced that he was sending 'Aziz to further explore the matter with Moscow. Calling the offer "a cruel hoax," the Bush administration rejected it and implied that the United States would not, in fact, be satisfied until the Iraqi regime was removed from office. After a February 18 preliminary visit by the Iraqi Foreign Minister, on the night of February 21-22, Tariq 'Aziz and Soviet President Mikhail Gorbachev met in Moscow for 2 hours and 20 minutes. They emerged with an agreement in which the Iraqi government announced its full and unconditional withdrawal from Kuwait to begin a day after cessation of hostilities and which would occur in a fixed time frame to be specified later. In exchange, the Iraqis asked for the removal of UN economic

150

sanctions after two-thirds of their forces had withdrawn and a full lifting of the Security Council resolutions after completion of the withdrawal. The next day, at 10:43 a.m. Washington time (6:43 p.m. in Baghdad), President George Bush set his own conditions:

(i) a large scale Iraqi withdrawal to begin by noon Saturday 23, Washington time;

(ii) Kuwait City to be cleared by Monday 25 and the government restored;

(iii) all Iraqi troops out within 7 days; and

(iv) POWs and remains of allied servicemen returned by noon Monday, Washington time.

The tone of the US administration was uncompromising. It in effect meant a total break with Iraq with whom the relationship had once been an alliance.[72] It left the Iraqis with an either/or option similar to the January deadline – a difficult choice that led to Iraq's refusal to make any concessionary announcements.[73] On one aspect at least, the American position bore the badge of consistency in that it corresponded to what James Baker had told Tariq 'Aziz during their meeting in Geneva:

[F]rom our point of view, there will be no halt. In case of a conflict, there will be no UN truce creating a breathing space or negotiations. You must have heard, over the past months, that if a conflict erupts it will be huge and will not be another Vietnam.[74]

The Iraqi leaders had become fully aware that the Bush administration was out to unseat them. Thus, they invested major efforts in the Soviet-sponsored scenario of evacuation. Due to necessity, the span of objectives had shrunk to regime continuation. But the Iraqi leadership's reliance on the Soviet government made sense since, by James Baker's own account, coordination and joint policy-making between the US and USSR had been unprecedented during this crisis.[75]

151

Two hours after the American announcement, at 1:00 p.m. Washington time (9:00 p.m. in Baghdad), Kremlin spokesman Vitaly Ignatenko announced that a revised tentative agreement was agreed to. The Soviets declared that after getting the maximum from the Iraqis, they were confident that Iraq would accept a three week pull out and a four day period, rather than two, to leave Kuwait City. "We've got the maximum we can achieve," said Ignatenko. Nevertheless, the Soviet bid was rejected by the United States because "it [did] not constitute an unequivocal commitment to an immediate and unconditional withdrawal." Although his cooperation, and especially that of his Foreign Minister Eduard Shevardnadze, had been vigorously sought and valued in the early stages of the crisis, Gorbachev was now being cast as a side-player by the American authorities. At 9:55 p.m. Baghdad time (1:55 p.m. Washington time), a spokesman from the Iraqi Ministry of Information denounced the ultimatum and criticized the Americans for escalating the conflict. The next day after the deadline passed, the US released a statement announcing that "Military action [would] continue on schedule and according to plan." In fact, the ground phase of the war had already started several hours ago.

The second ultimatum was therefore passively rejected.[76] By its very terms and style of delivery, it was simply unacceptable to the Iraqis for, again, its acceptance represented a major security dilemma. An Iraqi woman interviewed as the deadline was passing said the following: "Until yesterday, I was really hoping that everything will be solved. But today we realize that, if it is like that, *let it happen.* Any ordinary person thinks like this. *We don't have another choice.* We put whatever we can do and it became very difficult on this stage (sic)."[77] During his July 25 meeting with Ambassador April Glaspie, Saddam Hussayn had explained this martyr rationale in the face of intractability and a nothing-less-than-surrender scenario:

> You can come to Iraq with aircraft and missiles but do not push us to the point where we cease to care. And when we feel that you want to injure our pride and take away the Iraqis' chance of a high standard of living, then we will cease to care and death will be the choice for us. Then we

152

would not care if you fired 100 missiles for each missile we fired. Because without pride life would have no value.[78]

Clearly, the Iraqis preferred to be defeated rather than humiliated. It would not be amiss to claim that a withdrawal without an all-out fight – or the illusion of one, since the Iraqi troops had in fact begun their withdrawal in mid-February – would have meant a serious loss of legitimacy for the regime.

Two other practical variables determined the decision to let the ultimatum pass without respecting it. On the one hand, the situation of the troops in Kuwait had almost become independent from the central command in Baghdad. To conduct an orderly evacuation in the time demanded – one day – was almost impossible since the US bombings had succeeded in inflicting serious damage to communication lines between Baghdad and the front. On the other hand, it was necessary that at least minor clashes occur between the armies in order for the frustration of the Iraqi troops to be diffused. An encounter would have forestalled the chances of a revolt by the army. Overall, a simple withdrawal was no longer possible. As Stephen Pelletiere (1992) demonstrates:

> Under ordinary circumstances, Saddam might yet have been able to extricate himself from the dangerous impasse to which he had brought matters; he should have had the option of retreating....[T]his was not the case. Because of the enormous power of the US military, once the air war commenced, Saddam's army was trapped inside Kuwait.

In all likelihood, the Iraqi army would have revolted. Evidence to support this theory is available. An Iraqi intelligence report warned about the possibility of a rebellion by the army in case of a withdrawal from Kuwait (Alia and Clerc, 1991). To have troops return without combat to Iraq after seven months of martial rhetoric was something that the regime could not afford. Hence, security considerations held primacy in this particular decision. But even in the midst of such a volatile situation, concern for the historical rights of the Iraqi state were on the mind of the leadership in Baghdad. Indeed, the recalling of the troops was rationalized by a sense of realism – in the face of

153

a 28-country-strong coalition – and the promise to survive to fight another day. Attempting a classification of the Iraqi outcome priorities for the crisis, Matthews (1993), for example, argues that, out of the various scenarios, a "non-violent withdrawal from Kuwait" ranked as the worst outcome for the leadership in Baghdad.

Faced with an increasingly untenable position, Iraq chose nonetheless to announce that it was evacuating Kuwait. But it did so only after the deadline had passed and following two days of combat. In fact, the deadliest Scud attack came three days into the ground war when, on February 26, an Iraqi missile hit the al-Khobar barracks in eastern Saudi Arabia killing 28 American soldiers and wounding another 101.

The symbolism of defiance and of *bellum perpetuum* was the last argument the regime was making.[79] In this sense, more than any of the other decisions, February 23 represents the full implementation of the whole defiance strategy. In other words, the contextual rationality of the regime's security needs gained ascendancy over the absolute rationality of state affirmation; although, there existed a ceaseless interplay between the two realms during the whole duration of the conflict.

The Iraqi strategy was in reality designed to seal-off the conflict and bring it to a rapid end. Yet though in the immediate aftermath of their decision to reject the ultimatum, the Iraqi leaders felt the need to withdraw their troops in order to maximize their chances of survival, it, nonetheless, seems that they never really felt that their regime would totally collapse. This faith in their ability to maintain composure in the face of real threats to their regime's security was explicitly articulated by Tariq 'Aziz to James Baker when the two diplomats had met in Geneva:

> You said that if Iraq does not do so and so then the current leadership will
> not be able to decide the future of Iraq; that there will be others. I think
> that is a miscalculation by you. Leadership in our country is not something
> easy. It is true that our system is not like yours. However, those who reach
> the leadership in Iraq and who stay for a long period as we have should
> have very strong reasons for remaining for such a period of time. I tell you
> without boasting, and despite the insult contained in your comments about

this subject, I tell you that the current leadership will continue to rule Iraq now and in the future.[80]

Time and again, we encounter the state-building/regime security argument. Here, implies 'Aziz, the regime is secure because it adheres to and perpetuates the history of the land while adapting it to contemporary conditions:

> I believe you know that Iraq as a people is 6,000 years old during which states, kingdoms, and empires were set up and leaders existed and contributions were made to human civilization. *We are the grandsons of these people*. It is true that we live in this age and that we are affected by it *but we have our own values in administering the country's affairs.*[81] (Emphasis added.)

Ensuring the survival of the regime also meant controlling the whereabouts of the army as well as its actions. The fact that the Iraqi troops were nowhere to be found in Kuwait when coalition forces entered Kuwait, and that a mere week later they reappeared in Iraq to crush one major rebellion in the north and unrest in the south of the country has so far been incomprehensible. Various explanations have been put forth. Pelletiere (1992), for instance, offered that:

> What [Saddam] appears to have done is to allow the army to decompose. From roughly the last week in January there was a steep climb in desertions; whole units simply melted away. There seems to have been no attempt on Saddam's part to interfere with this process. At the same time, as soon as the cease-fire was declared, the army reconstituted itself inside Iraq. The proof of this was the speed and effectiveness with which the army put down the so-called rebellions.

In addition, the withdrawal was made easy by the fact that the Iraqi troops inside Kuwait were much less than the 547,000 originally announced by the coalition. The number was in fact 183,000, of which 63,000 were captured by the Americans.[82] It is also very possible that the Iraqi regime saw the issue as an opportunity to rid itself of some of the least useful troops, i.e., aging veterans of the war with Iran and those elements whose loyalty was questionable. The concept of "Saddam's throwaway divisions," articulated in the book *Triumph Without Victory* (1991), certainly accounts for many an ambiguity about the war's confused and confusing last week.

As for the rebellions themselves, they confirmed the validity of the regime's concerns about its security at this crucial juncture. Kurdish guerrillas started a major offensive against governmental troops and within a week captured a dozen cities in Iraqi Kurdistan. In the south, the situation was more ambiguous. There, it appears that agitation by local Shiites combined with disgruntled (and armed) soldiers coming back from the Kuwaiti front to create the conditions for a revolt. Nevertheless, it would seem that the scale of the operation could not have been massive unless Iranian elements participated. This assessment was confirmed by Foreign Minister Tariq 'Aziz in an interview conducted after the conflict. 'Aziz acknowledged that 6,000 to 10,000 Shiite soldiers joined the revolt that was fomented by Iraqi Shiites from Iran.[83]

Four Other Defining Decisions

Finally, a word must be said about four other minor yet consequential decisions taken by the Iraqi leadership during the crisis and war: (i) the decision to free the hostages, (ii) the decision not to use the airforce during the war, (iii) the decision to attack Israel and Saudi Arabia with Scud missiles, and (iv) the decision to launch a ground attack on the Saudi city of Khafji. By and large, these four decisions have befuddled analysts of the Gulf conflict. I believe that they followed from specific, context-sensitive strategic considerations.

The decision to free the hostages. The action of freeing the remaining hostages, including some 2,000 Western nationals, announced on December 6, 1990, and enacted on December 25 was the first tangible de-escalation measure taken by the Iraqis to initiate a settlement to the crisis. By showing good will, the Iraqi leadership hoped that coalition governments would reciprocate enabling them to pursue the diplomatic road with minimal guarantees. Also, down that road was the Geneva meeting upon which the Iraqis were investing a lot of hopes. In addition, there is increasing evidence that Iraq had been advised to do so by its closest Arab allies. A high-ranking official from a North African country known to maintain good relations with Iraq informed me that, sometime in the fall of 1990, his country was asked by French and Spanish officials to relay to Baghdad the message that if the hostages were released, chances for military action would be drastically reduced, if not at all eliminated.[84] In the course of an internal meeting held within the leadership of the Ba'th party after the war, Hussayn is said to have regretted the liberation of the hostages. The objectives of reducing the level of international opposition and disrupting the coalition's unity had not, he said, been reached.[85]

The decision not to use the airforce. Understanding the might of the coalition air armada, the Iraqi leadership chose not to send its 700+ airforce aircrafts to face coalition fighter planes. Before the war started, 75% of the Iraqi airforce fleet was parked in hardened shelters, "some of them reputed to be the strongest in the world" (Bin Sultan and Seale, 1995). Only a few were sent on combat missions. (The result of the air war was 28 Iraqi airplanes shot down in air-to-air combat to three US planes and 38 coalition jets shot down by Iraqi ground fire.) Then, 135 Iraqi jets were sent to Iran in late January and early February.

According to the Saudi Joint Forces Commander: "The episode of the mass exodus of Iraqi planes to Iran – one of the most curious of the war – remains something of an aberration to this day." In fact, it was a two-pronged political and strategic maneuver by the Iraqis. On the one hand, with a full capacity in the shelters, they were sending these planes for protection to the only neighboring country – besides Jordan – that was not siding with the coalition. The flight road to Jordan was too dangerous and both Iraqi and Jordanian authorities were reluctant to have the kingdom involved in the hostilities at this late stage of the conflict. On the other hand, interception of the planes over the Iranian border by coalition forces would have probably drawn Iran in the conflict. This constituted an added incentive. In sum, this decision was primarily one of *kriegsraison* (military necessity) but in the same way it carried a political calculation. It is also worth noting that – historical concerns being ever present in Iraqi decisionmaking process – Baghdad was keen on preventing a repeat of the bombing of most of the Egyptian airforce by Israel in 1967. The existence of a pronounced competition with Egypt over Arab leadership and regional military might have precipitated this decision. Sumaida and Jerome (1991) put it simply:

> Every Arab leader had a vivid memory of how the Israelis had destroyed the Egyptian airforce while it was still on the ground in 1967, and the humiliation still burned. For Saddam, it had become more important to protect his squadrons than actually use them. The symbolism was what mattered.

Ken Matthews (1993) concurs:

> It is likely that the 'lesson' of the Arab-Israeli war of 1967 in which 75 per cent of Egyptian aircraft were destroyed on the ground when the Israelis achieved complete surprise did not go unlearnt by the Iraqis.

The decision to attack Israel and Saudi Arabia with Scud missiles. After hostilities had begun at 2:38 a.m. (Baghdad time), January 17, Iraq's first offensive action during the conflict was the simultaneous launching on the following night of a barrage of Scud missiles aimed at both Saudi Arabia and Israel. The Scud campaign against these two countries continued until the very last hours of the war. (In addition, one missile was also targeted at Bahrain.) The attacks constituted an integral part of the Iraqi war effort. The Iraqi leaders' intention to consider Saudi Arabia and Israel as party to the war were, in effect, voiced early on during the crisis. In Geneva, 'Aziz had told Baker that "it is certain that [the parties that will participate in the war] are the United States, Iraq, Saudi Arabia, and Israel."[86]

With regard to Israel, the attacks were explicitly planned and formally announced all along. During the press conference that followed his January 9 meeting with US Secretary of State Baker, Tariq 'Aziz was asked if, in the case hostilities began, his country would attack Israel. His answer was an unambiguous "yes, absolutely yes." Indeed, on the evening of January 18, a first wave of 8 Scud missiles was launched on Tel Aviv and Haifa. The next day, another 5 Scuds were fired at Tel Aviv. Further attacks followed on January 20, 22, and on the 23rd a missile aimed at Ramat Gan killed three and wounded ninety-six. In total, 39 Scuds were launched at Israel during the 44 days that the conflict lasted.

The attacks had a twofold reasoning. First and foremost, they were designed to provoke the Israeli authorities into ordering a retaliation mission which would have *de facto* drawn Israel into the war. That in turn would have led to a reconfiguration of the conflict whereby the Arab members of the coalition (Saudi Arabia, Egypt, Syria, Morocco, and the Gulf countries) would have found themselves fighting an Arab country alongside their fiercest enemy, Israel. Iraq would have then succeeded in putting these regimes (primarily, Syria, Egypt, and Saudi Arabia) in an otherwise untenable position both domestically and regionally. Just like the hostage decision, this was an effort at fracturing the coalition.

Second, ever pregnant with history, the calculations of the Iraqi leadership were also a form of retribution for Israel's June 7, 1981, destruction of the French-built Iraqi nuclear reactor Osiraq 1. At the time, enfeebled by their involvement in the Arabistan/Khuzistan offensive against Iran, the Ba'thists were unable to retaliate. Here was an opportunity to exert revenge. Indeed, in the last week of the war, 6 Scuds were fired at the Israeli Dimona nuclear reactor in the Negev desert. However, little is known about this particular strike.

The attacks on Israel were a win-win scenario for Iraq. They could only either draw Israel or paralyze it. The best case scenario being that Israel would not be able to

159

restrain itself – an objective almost achieved and one whose pursuit certainly made strategic sense. Indeed, after the January 18 and 22 attacks, the Israeli Cabinet came close to ordering retaliation. On the 19th, Defense Minister Moshe Arens telephoned US Secretary of Defense Richard Cheney to unsuccessfully request the IFF (identification-friend-or-foe) electronic codes to prevent collisions between American and Israeli planes. And, in the book *The Samson Option* (1992), Seymour Hersh reports that for the second time in its history Israel went on nuclear alert following the first wave of Scud attacks.[87]

Israel's involvement would have certainly widened the conflict's configuration. If Israel did not respond, forced to assume a defensive posture, its deterrent position in relation to the Arab states might erode.[88] In the end, if only symbolically, the myth of an all-powerful Israel was for all purposes shattered by the 1991 Iraqi Scud missiles that constituted the first air attack on Israeli cities since the country's creation in 1948. In addition, Israeli Foreign Minister David Levy's public statement that any Iraqi attack on Israel would be considered an act of war rendered an absence of retaliation harder to justify.

Israel's inaction – in reality the result of very strong US pressures and shuttle diplomacy by Deputy-Secretary of State Lawrence Eagleburger who arrived in Tel Aviv on January 20 – was a bitter disappointment to the Iraqi leaders. Notwithstanding, the effect on the Israeli population was dramatic: "[T]he six weeks in early 1991 [turned] into...a harrowing psychological ordeal for the civilian population. There was a maddening dichotomy between proven military prowess on the one hand and a sense of utter impotence on the other" (Shlaim, 1994).

The attacks on Saudi Arabia were equally twofold. First, they were designed as immediate military retaliation in a purely strategic aspect. The Americans were conducting the war from the Saudi kingdom and, as far as the Iraqis were concerned, that was were the front would be. Indeed, the deadliest Scud attack of the war was the one that hit the US barracks at al-Khobar. Second, the missiles carried a message to the Saudis about their present and future vulnerability. The idea was to bluntly terrorize the

Saudis and make them regret the invitation extended to the Americans. To make a point about Saudi Arabia's strategic vulnerability, 43 Scuds in total were fired by Iraq – four more Scuds than the 39 launched at Israel.

Even though, the decision to attack the Saudis came rather easily to the Iraqis, it is nonetheless important to note that in the initial phases of the crisis, the Iraqi leaders went out of their way to reassure the Saudis about their country's lack of predatory intentions towards the kingdom. One month after the invasion of Kuwait, Tariq 'Aziz declared:

> In view of the spurious allegations concerning the so-called Iraqi threats to Saudi Arabia, we have affirmed in every way available to us that there is no Iraqi threat to Saudi Arabia or to any other country in the Gulf. We have made clear our willingness to provide all necessary guarantees required to that effect, whether on the bilateral level or within the framework of the League of Arab States. We have also stated that we would not object to Saudi Arabia calling in Arab forces for assistance or protection, if the Saudis were afraid, although we still see no basis whatsoever for this fabricated fear.[89]

Yet underscored by a strategic rivalry, financial competition, OPEC-related struggles, and conflicting styles of regional hegemony, the relationship between the two countries was never truly positive. And, if it is evident that the more recent cohabitation between revolutionary-secular, USSR-backed Ba'thi Iraq and conservative-religious, US-protected Saudi Arabia was always difficult, it is worth remembering that:

> Iraqi-Saudi rivalry did not originate with the 1968 Ba'th coup in Baghdad. Some of its basic ingredients are geopolitical and go back to the ancient symbiotic relations between fertile Mesopotamia and the arid Arabian Peninsula. Since the inception of Hashemite rule, modern Iraq in 1920, Saudi-Iraqi relations were dominated by the historic possibility between the House of Saud and the Hashemite family, which held power in both Iraq and Transjordan.[90]

The decision to launch a ground attack on Khafji. By the end of January, the Iraqis devised a strategy to seize the military initiative from coalition forces and draw them in a ground war earlier than the latter had planned to. Although its importance was not recognized at the time, the invasion of Khafji was a major attempt at redrawing the configuration of the conflict in favor of Iraq. After the war, General Bernard E. Trainor and Michael R. Gordon (1995) would correctly point that

> *The battle of Khafji [was] the most important clash of the six-week Persian Gulf War*....Khafji was one of a series of border engagements at the end of January that took Schwarzkopf and his top commanders completely by surprise. Although characterized at the time as a minor skirmish, *the two-day clash was the war's defining moment.* Schwarzkopf's failure to grasp the significance of Khafji was one of the general's greatest oversights. His war plan was never revised to take account of the lessons of the battle and that omission contributed mightily to the escape of the Republican Guard when the allies' land offensive was launched more than three weeks later. (Emphasis added.)

On January 29, two Iraqi battalions from the 15th Brigade of the 5th Mechanized Division in Kuwait launched a three-pronged attack on Saudi Arabia, capturing the north-east coastal city of Ras al-Khafji. At about 10:25 p.m., the Iraqis crossed the border. At 11:00 p.m., a tank column from the 1st Mechanized Division of the IV Iraqi Corps descended towards Umm Hajul. At the same time, a mechanized infantry battalion of 45 vehicles began driving the coastal highway and charged into Khafji overrunning coalition positions. A third Iraqi attack was launched by the 20th Mechanized Brigade and the 26th Armored Brigade between Khafji and al-Wafra backed by a 10 mile long supply column. Directed at a major US logistics base manned by the Marines in Ras Mishab, this repulsed attack was meant as the principal operation involving 25,000 troops. Little is known about this episode and it remains a hidden battle. The Iraqi attacks continued with an amphibious landing force – backed by 17 vessels – which was sent down the coast aiming to cut off Khafji. The Iraqis occupied and held the city for 36 hours. American, Saudi and Qatari forces launched two failed

162

counterattacks. Then, on February 1st, after significant reinforcements had been dispatched, coalition forces were able to recapture the city (Taylor, 1992; Schwarzkopf, 1993; Gordon and Trainor, 1995; Sultan and Seale, 1995; and interviews).

Hence, the strike on Khafji was clearly an attempt by the Iraqis to seize the momentum of the conflict and take their opponents by surprise with a full-scale assault. In that sense, it succeeded.[91] The Iraqis achieved a genuine element of surprise and induced some embarrassment on the part of the coalition forces (Matthews, 1993). The strategy behind the attack rested on the rationale that, since war had already started, it was imperative to render it costly, lengthy, geographically extended, and in the short-term counter-productive for the United States. In fact, a 1,000-vehicle strong Iraqi column was moving southwest of Khafji several days after the city had been recaptured by allied forces. Since the initial operation was decided at the highest levels – Saddam Hussayn had reportedly traveled to Basra on January 27 to review the plan with the head of the III Iraqi Corps, Lieutenant-General Salah Abu Mahmoud – it is fair to assume that the design was more ambitious than the emblematic aspect of the operation.

Summary

Four decisions have been discussed in this chapter as being most significant with regard to both the development of the Gulf conflict itself overarching Ba'thi regime security and the continuity of the Iraqi state: (i) the invasion of Kuwait on August 2, 1990; (ii) the démarche to settle the matter on August 12, 1990; (iii) the rejection of the first withdrawal ultimatum on January 15, 1991; and the refusal to abide by the second ultimatum on February 23, 1991. If all four decisions simultaneously answer to both state-building and regime security constellations, I have offered that, as military hostilities increased and diplomatic options failed, the decisionmaking process grew more concerned with the security of the Ba'thi regime. Finally four secondary decisions – the release of the hostages, the grounding of the airforce, the launching of missiles on Saudi Arabia and Israel, and the attack on Khafji – were briefly looked at in an attempt to shed some light on the strategic and political elements that determined them.

The factors shaping all of these decisions have been systematically established as a twin set of considerations by the Iraqi leadership: the general reproduction of the Iraqi state-building process and the more immediate furtherance of the regime's domestic and regional interests. This combination was meant to allow for the maintenance of the physical presence of both state and regime. The state-related territorial issue acted as a permanently operating factor while the security dilemmas of the regime provided the opportunity and the immediate rationalization. Unable to reap the fruits of the invasion of Kuwait as it initially envisioned them, the Ba'thi leadership sought to maximize its and the Iraqi state's short and long-term autonomy-enhancing objectives. An assessment of this policy-making process is the subject of the next chapter.

NOTES

[1] Saddam Hussayn, "President Saddam Husayn Delivers Army Day Speech," Baghdad Domestic Service, 5 January 1990, United States Foreign Broadcast Information Service - Near East and South Asia (FBIS-NES), "Daily Report," January 5, 1990, p. 16.

[2] Interview with Iraqi author Faleh 'Abd al-Jabar, Cairo, December 10, 1993. The formula is his.

[3] Al-Jabar (1991: 35) puts the number of demobilized soldiers at 150,000.

[4] The main paradox in this transitional period is that: "....inasmuch as the discontent was growing, the organized structures capable of mobilizing that discontent into political action were diminishing" (al-Jabar, 1991: 32).

[5] Saddam Hussayn, "Speech at the ACC Summit, 24 February 1990," in Ofra Bengio, Saddam Speaks on the Gulf Crisis - A Collection of Documents, Tel Aviv: The Moshe Dayan Institute for Middle Eastern and African Studies, 1992, pp. 37-49.

[6] Saddam Hussayn, "The National Potential and International Politics," p. 68.

[7] Bazoft confessed on Iraqi television on October 31, 1989. See the transcripts of his confession in FBIS-NES, November 1, 1989. Also see "Death of a Journalist: The Spy Bazoft," chapter 18 of Simon Henderson, *Instant Empire - Saddam Hussein's Ambition for Iraq*, San Francisco, California: Mercury House, 1991, pp. 204-216.

[8] There are three alternative scenarios for the death of Bull. The first is that he was murdered by the Israeli intelligence services, the Mossad, to prevent him from completing work on the missile-firing gun. The second is that the scientist was eliminated by the Iraqi secret service, al-Mukhabarat, to insure that he would not be divulging information about the supergun. Finally, the Iranian intelligence agency could have killed Gerald Bull since his supergun was equally dangerous to Iran as it was to Israel. None of these explanations has so far been substantiated by anyone.

[9] Alan Cowell, "Iraq Raises its Volume and Arab Hopes," *The New York Times*, April 4, 1990, p. A6.

[10] Joel Brinkley, "Israel Puts a Satellite in Orbit A day After Threat by Iraqis," *The New York Times*, April 4, 1990.

[11] Also see Nadim Jaber, "The Iraq-West Confrontation: Background and Reactions," *Middle East Report*, April 13, 1990, pp. 3-4.

[12] Taha Yassin Ramadan, "Ramadan on 'Planned Israeli Attack'," *Al-Ahali*, May 16, 1990.

[13] See Amos Perlmutter, Michael Handel, and Uri Bar-Joseph, *Two Minutes Over Baghdad*, London: Vallentine Mitchell, 1982.

[14] Interview, Baghdad, August, 28, 1994.

[15] Tariq 'Aziz, "Note to the Secretary-General of the Arab League, July 15, 1990" (Salinger, 1991: 223-234).

[16] Saddam Hussayn, "Saddam Speech Marks Revolution's 22nd Anniversary," Baghdad Domestic Service, July 17, 1990, FBIS-NES, July 17, 1990, p. 22.

[17] "Proche-Orient: Les Risques d'un Conflit," *Le Point* 930, July 16, 1990, p. 14.

[18] "The Hussayn-Glaspie Transcript," (Bennis and Moushabeck, 1991: 395). Ambassador Glaspie's eight-page reporting cable on the meeting is still classified by the US Department of State. Also present during the meeting were Foreign Minister Tariq 'Aziz and Ambassador-translator Sa'doun al-Zubaydi both of whom I met twice for the purposes of this work.

[19] See Sami Yousif, "The Iraqi-US War: A Conspiracy Theory," in Haim Bresheeth and Nira Yuval-Davis, eds., *The Gulf War and the New World Order*, London: Zed Books, 1991, pp. 49-69.

[20] Roxanne Roberts, "The Silence of a Diplomat: April Glaspie and Iraq," *The Washington Post*, March 15, 1991. Nevertheless, Secretary of State James Baker would meet privately with the Ambassador and ask her to brief him in preparation for his Geneva encounter with Foreign Minister 'Aziz.

[21] Mohamed al-Mashat, "Why do they Lie about Iraq?," *The New York Times*, May 4, 1990.

[22] Saddam Hussayn, interview with *Hurriyet* (Ankara), February 10, 1992, reprinted in FBIS-NES, February 13, 1992, pp. 22-23.

[23] Interviews, New York (July 1995) and Amman (September 1994).

[24] Ministry of Information and Culture, *Iraq 1990*, Baghdad: Dar al-Mamun, 1990, p. 97.

[25] Martin Yant, *Desert Mirage - The True Story of the Gulf War*, Buffalo, New York: Prometheus Books, 1991, p. 75. In October of 1990, the Iraqis released a letter reporting on a visit by Kuwaiti officials to CIA director William Webster in November 1989. The document, which the Iraqis found in Kuwait's Foreign Ministry after the invasion, stated that "We agreed with the American side that it was important to take advantage of the deteriorating economic structure in Iraq in order to pressure on that country's government to delineate our border." The memorandum was distributed to the UN Security Council.

[26] Amatzia Baram, "The Iraqi Invasion of Kuwait: Decision-Making in Baghdad," in Amatzia Baram and Barry Rubin, eds., *Iraq's Road to War*, New York, New York: St. Martin's Press, 1993, p. 9. Also see Amatzia Baram, "Calculation and Miscalculation in Baghdad," in Alex Danchev and Dan Keohane, eds., *International Perspectives on the Gulf Conflict 1990-1991*, New York, New York: St. Martin's Press, 1994, pp. 23-58.

[27] Christian Daudel, "Origines et Contextes de la Crise du Golfe," in *Crise du Golfe: Les Changements Stratégiques*, Paris: FEDN, 1990, p. 14.

[28] Faleh 'Abd al-Jabar, "Roots of an Adventure - The Invasion of Kuwait: Iraqi Political Dynamics," in Victoria Brittain, ed., *The Gulf Between Us - The Gulf War and Beyond*, London: Virago Press, 1991, pp. 27-41.

[29] Andre Gunder Frank, "A Third-World War: A Political Economy of the Persian Gulf War and the New World Order," in Hamid Mowlana *et al.* eds., *Triumph of the Image - The Media's War in the Persian Gulf: A Global Perspective*, Boulder, Colorado: Westview Press, 1992, p. 9.

[30] Sa'd al-Bazzaz, *Harb Tawlad Oukhra: Al-Tarikh al-Sirri li Harb al-Khalij* (A War Gives Birth to Another: The Secret History of the Gulf War), Amman: al-Ahliyya, 1992, p. 30.

[31] "The Hussein-Glaspie Transcript," (Bennis and Moushabeck, 1991: 392).

[32] It is striking that twice in a decade the Iraqi leaders seem to have ignored Carl Von Clausewitz's astute maxim that: "No one starts a war – or rather, no one in his senses ought to do so – without first being clear in his mind what he intends to achieve by that war and how he intends to conduct it." To be fair to the Iraqi leaders, they did have an idea about how to reach certain objectives. But, one has to reckon that that idea appears to have been only tentative and based on too many conditionalities.

[33] In less than three weeks, the US had fielded 7 combat-ready brigades, 3 carrier battle groups, and 14 tactical fighter squadrons. See Joseph S. Nye, Jr., "US Regional Security Strategies for the Middle East," *The Brown Journal of World Affairs* 2, 2 (Summer 1995), p. 72.

[34] Interview, Amman, September, 2, 1994.

[35] See "Opportunity Lost," chapter four of Heikal (1992), pp. 249-270.

[36] Heikal (1992: 265) reports that "King Hussein felt he had made a breakthrough and was eager to tell Mubarak." And, according to Salinger and Laurent (1991: 116), when the King knew of Mubarak's action "[He] was shattered. He felt humiliated. In the King's eyes, the Egyptian communiqué was all part of a vast conspiracy." The King himself later said: "I phoned President Mubarak and told him about my breakthrough, but by that time there was already an Egyptian statement. I was furious" (in Heikal, p. 266). The Iraqis, for their part, believed that it was the Saudis' lack of response to their openings that most seriously torpedoed this initial intra-Arab solution. See Fred Moore, *Iraq Speaks - Documents on the Gulf Crisis*, Palo Alto, California, p. 42. The Iraqi assessment finds confirmation in James Baker's remarks: "From the outset, the Saudis were the most aggressive member of the coalition....The Saudis not only wanted American troops in their soil; they privately hoped a diplomatic resolution couldn't be reached. They didn't just want Saddam ejected from Kuwait; they wanted him destroyed. For them the *only* solution was an American-led war that would annihilate Saddam's military machine once and for all. From the start, they were always advocates for the massive use of force" (Baker, 1995: 289). (Original emphasis.)

[37] Tariq 'Aziz, "The Kuwait Question," p. 11.

[38] Ibid. Many saw in that meeting an Egyptian revenge for the November 2, 1978, Baghdad meeting convened by the Arab League to condemn and expel Egypt from its ranks after President Sadat had signed the Camp David accords. History, it would appear, is an ever-present factor in Arab political policy-making.

[39] Of course the Iraqi invasion of Kuwait was itself a violation of the Arab state system principles of independence and sovereignty, as well as of the Charter of the United Nations.

[40] Interview with an official delegate to the summit, Rabat, September 17, 1994.

[41] Interview, Amman, September 2, 1994.

[42] Saddam Hussayn, "Saddam Husayn's Speech on 'Linkage' - 12 August 1990," (Bengio, 1992: 125-126).

[43] Interview, Amman, September 3, 1994.

[44] Also see Michael Eppel, "Syria: Iraq's Radical Nemesis," in Baram and Rubin, eds., *Iraq's Road to War* (1993), pp. 177-189.

[45] As Bengio (1992: 25-26) correctly points out, the Iraqi regime was finding itself faced with three tasks: (i) maintaining control over Kuwait, (ii) standing up to the growing international coalition, and (iii) dealing with the socioeconomic and political domestic consequences of the invasion.

[46] Translation: "To link the liberation of Kuwait to that of Palestine does not equal negotiation. [Linkage] imposes itself as a method of international communication that in turn becomes the only final objective realistically pursued."

[47] "Minutes of the 'Aziz-Baker Meeting," Iraqi News Agency (INA), published between January 9 and January 14, 1992. Reprinted in FBIS-NES, 92-009, p. 28.

[48] "'Aziz, "The Kuwait Question," p. 13.

[49] "Minutes of the 'Aziz-Baker Meeting," p. 31-32.

[50] *The Baghdad Observer*, March 16, 1992.

[51] On the functioning of the coalition, see, for instance, Andrew Bennett, Joseph Lepgold, and Danny Unger, "Burden-Sharing in the Persian Gulf War," *International Organization* 48, 1 (Winter 1994), pp. 39-75. For its part, Iraq was attempting to extricate itself from previous conflict situations in order to focus on the crisis at hand. Thus, at the same time that the linkage proposal was being made, the Iraqi government hastily patched up its strained relationship with Iran and proposed a final resolution of the First Gulf War bringing matters to pre-1980 conditions.

[52] Faleh 'Abd al-Jabar, "The Gulf War and Ideology: The Double-Edged Sword of Islam," in Haim Bresheeth and Nira Yuval-Davis, eds., *The Gulf War and the New World Order*, London: Zed Books, 1991, pp. 215-216. Similarly, Sharam Chubin considered that "Saddam's strategy nearly worked....On the regional level his calculations were not far from the mark." ["Regional Politics and the Conflict," in Danchev and Keohane, eds., *International Perspectives on the Gulf Conflict* (1994), p. 16.]

[53] Whereas in the period right before the invasion of Kuwait, the US-PLO and Israel-PLO negotiations were at an all-time low. Indeed, on June 20, 1990, the United States had decided to suspend all talks with the Palestinians following a failed commando attack on an Israeli beach.

[54] During the press conference that followed the meeting, 'Aziz explained the letter matter: "At the beginning of the meeting, Secretary Baker told me that he carries a letter from his President to my President and he handed over a copy to me. I told him 'I want to read this letter first.' And I read it....carefully and slowly and I knew what is was about. I told him 'I'm sorry, I cannot receive this letter.' And the reason is that the language in this letter is not compatible with the language that should be used in correspondence between heads of state. I have no objection that Mr. Bush would state his position very clearly. A serious exchange of letters between leaders and politicians can, or should, contain the position of each party. But when a head of state writes to another head of state a letter and if he really intends to make peace with that head of state or reach genuine understanding, he should use a polite language. And politeness does not contradict with substance. Therefore,....I declined to received it" (CNN, January 9, 1991). After the Iraqi refusal to take the letter, the Americans left it on the table where it stayed until the meeting ended. Afterwards, it was removed by Sandy Charles, a National Security Council staffer part of the US delegation. On January 8, Baker had met with French President François Mitterand who, upon reading the letter, remarked: "This is a tough letter....It leaves Saddam Hussein no option but total surrender" (Baker, 1995: 371). Finally, I have been told by a high-ranking Iraqi official present at the Geneva meeting that the copy of the letter that was published a few days later by *The New York Times* was substantially different in content. This new version was less harsher and less offensive to the Iraqi President.

[55] Besides Foreign Minister Tariq 'Aziz, the Iraqi delegates included: Barzan al-Tikriti, Ambassador to the UN in Geneva and half-brother of President Hussayn, Nizar Hamdoun, Deputy-Foreign Minister, Riyad al-Qaysi, Ambassador at the Foreign Ministry, and Sa'doun al-Zubaydi, Ambassador-translator at the Foreign Ministry.

[56] "Minutes of the 'Aziz-Baker Meeting," pp. 26-47.

[57] James Baker, "Address to the National Press Club," C-Span, October 11, 1995.

[58] "Minutes of the 'Aziz-Baker Meeting," p. 37.

[59] Ibid., pp. 43-44.

[60] Secretary Baker assessed the meeting as follows: "To his credit, Tariq 'Aziz was thoroughly professional, from start to finish. It was cool and as direct a discussion as I can remember – and totally unproductive....[W]e were never going to negotiate down from the Security Council resolutions. There was no question in my mind – we were going to war.... 'Good-bye, Mr. Secretary,' he said. 'Perhaps we'll meet again.' 'Good-bye, Mr. Minister,' I replied. I felt no animus toward him whatsoever. He had done a very credible job with an extraordinarily bad brief." (Baker, 1995: 363).

[61] Interview, Amman, September 3, 1994.

[62] Phyllis Bennis, "False Consensus: George Bush's United Nations," in Bennis and Moushabeck, eds., Beyond the Storm (1991), p. 122. I was able to obtain a copy of said transcript and verify Bennis' assessment. The office of the secretary-general refused to release the minutes of the meeting but did not dispute the authenticity of those privately made available by the Iraqi Mission to diplomats and journalists.

[63] Tariq 'Aziz, Press conference in Geneva, CNN, January 9, 1991.

[64] Interview, Rabat, September 15, 1994.

[65] "Minutes of the 'Aziz-Baker Meeting," p. 28.

[66] Chevènement, p.67.

[67] Ibid., p. 100.

[68] Tariq 'Aziz, interview with William Drozdiak, The Washington Post, May 8, 1991.

[69] The Baghdad Observer, March 9, 1992.

[70] "Minutes of the 'Aziz-Baker Meeting," pp. 41-42.

[71] The coalition was composed of the United States, Great Britain, Saudi Arabia, Kuwait, Egypt, France, Italy, Argentina, Bahrain, Bangladesh, Belgium, Canada, Denmark, the United Arab Emirates, Spain, Greece, Honduras, Morocco, Niger, Norway, Oman, Pakistan, Holland, Portugal, Senegal, Syria, Czechoslovakia, and Turkey.

[72] For a history of US-Iraqi relations, see Barry Rubin, "United States-Iraq Relations: A Spring Thaw," in Niblock, Iraq: The Contemporary State (1982), pp. 109-124; Nicholas G. Thacher, "Reflections on US Foreign Policy towards Iraq in the 1950s," in Fernea and Louis, eds., The Iraqi Revolution of 1958 - The Old Social Classes Revisited (1991), pp. 62-76; Axelgard, A New Iraq? The Gulf War and Implications for US Policy (1988); and Zachary Karabell, "Backfire: US Policy toward Iraq, 1988-2 August 1990," Middle East Journal 49, 1 (Winter 1995), pp. 28-47.

[73] Richard K. Herrmann, "US Policy in the Conflict," in Danchev and Keohane, eds., International Perspectives (1994), p. 127.

[74] "Minutes of the 'Aziz-Baker Meeting," p. 27.

[75] Of the US-USSR. relationship during the war, James Baker later wrote: "From the start, I had viewed the Soviets as key. In every strategic calculation, I considered their support a prerequisite to a credible coalition. They had to be courted, nurtured, and included to a degree once unthinkable by American policy makers. Indeed, Shevardnadze and I exchanged eleven phone calls and five letters in August alone – a level of consultation that would have been unimaginable just a year before" (Baker, 1995: 281).

[76] Interview with an Iraqi official, New York, July 1995.

[77] Nihad 'Abdallah, Baghdad resident, CNN, February 22, 1991, live interview by Peter Arnett.

[78] "The Hussayn-Glaspie Transcript," (Bennis and Moushabeck, 1991: 393).

[79] About the symbolism of the few hours of ground war, Baram (1994: 48) writes: "In hindsight this, too, became an epic, of one heroic army fighting the thirty-three strongest military machines of the advanced world and surviving to tell the tale."

[80] "Minutes of the 'Aziz-Baker Meeting," p. 29. About the last sentence of this statement, Secretary James Baker later wrote "In this, of course, Aziz was right" (Baker, 1995: 360). Keeping aside the issue of the army's rebellious potential itself, there was a further point in this connection: on January 13, 1990, the Iraqi authorities decided to provide all males over 16 years of age with a rifle weapon, thus demonstrating their apparent lack of concern about civilian uprisings.

[81] Ibid.

[82] John Lancaster, "Report: Allies Faced Only 183,000 Iraqis," *The Washington Post*, April 24, 1992; and Eric Schmitt, "Study Lists Lower Tally of Iraqi Troops in Gulf War," *The New York Times*, April 24, 1992.

[83] Tariq 'Aziz, interview with William Drozdiak, *The Washington Post*, May 8, 1991. Also see Faleh 'Abd al-Jabbar, "Why the Uprisings Failed," *Middle East Report* 176, 22, 3 (May-June 1992), pp. 2-14.

[84] Interview, New York, May 1994. For a discussion of the deceptive role France played in the release of the hostages and the mixed signals it sent to Baghdad as to the consequences of such a goodwill gesture, see Jolyon Howorth, "French Policy in the Conflict," in Danchev and Keohane, eds., *International Perspectives* (1994), pp. 175-200. As Howorth indicates: "It is important to stress the difference in approach to the hostage question of, on the one hand, the various missions to Baghdad on the part of leaders like Edward Heath and Willy Brandt, and, on the other hand, the French initiatives. The former were purely humanitarian missions with no political agenda and no hint of linkage either direct or indirect. This was not the case with the French initiatives, where the clear message to Saddam was: 'Without releasing the hostages, no discussions on a peace plan are possible. Once they are released, things can begin to happen.' It was this shortfall between the pre-release implications and the post-release reality that so angered the Iraqi President" (p. 183).

[85] Interview, Amman, September 1994.

[86] "Minutes of the 'Aziz-Baker Meeting," p. 45.

[87] The first Israeli nuclear alert took place in October 1973 when Egyptian and Syrian troops were gaining the upper hand during the Sinai war.

[88] Bernard Reich, "Israel and the Persian Gulf Crisis," in Ibrahim, ed., *The Gulf Crisis* (1992), p. 234. Also see Avi Shlaim, "Israel and the Conflict," in Danchev and Keohane, eds., *International Perspectives* (1994), pp. 59-79; and Avner Yaniv, "Israel Faces Iraq: The Politics of Confrontation," in Baram and Rubin, eds., *Iraq's Road to War* (1993), pp. 233-251.

[89] 'Aziz, "The Kuwait Question," p. 12.

[90] Jacob Goldberg, "Saudi Arabia: The Bank Vault Next Door," in Baram and Rubin, eds., *Iraq's Road to War* (1993), p. 118.

[91] Gordon and Trainor (1995: 268) remark: "In fact, despite the United States' best intelligence capabilities trained on Kuwait and with American planes flying over Iraq and the region at will, the Iraqis still managed to move their forces unnoticed through the open desert into attack positions near the Saudi border." Also see R. Jeffrey Smith, "Iraqi Tactics Surprise US Officials: Saddam's Army Demonstrates Ability to Maneuver in Darkness," *The Washington Post*, February 2, 1991. The sensitivity of the Khafji affair is attested to by Laura Flanders who reports that "Journalists who filmed the officially non-existent fighting in Khafji were forced at gunpoint to hand their videotape over to a US marine." See Laura Flanders, "Restricting Reality: Media Mind-Games and the War," in Bennis and Moushabeck, eds., *Beyond the Storm* (1991), pp. 160-170.

171

5

Evaluation of the Iraqi Foreign Policy Process

> In human affairs of danger and delicacy, successful conclusion is
> sharply limited by hurry. So often men trip by being in a rush. If one
> were properly to perform a difficult and subtle act, he should first
> inspect the end to be achieved and then, once he had accepted the
> end as desirable, he should forget it completely and concentrate
> solely on the means. By this method he would not be moved to false
> action by anxiety, or hurry, or fear. Very few people learn this.
> – *John Steinbeck*

This chapter focuses on the assessment of the foreign policy-making process that the
Iraqi leadership engaged in during the Second Gulf War. It evaluates the process first in
and of itself and then with regard to its consequences. Despite a major setback to both
state and regime at the cessation of hostilities, it is maintained that given the gigantic
nature and awesome power of the opposition to their designs and taking into
consideration the many decisional uncertainties that plagued their own policy-making
process all along the events, the Iraqi leaders' survival was a testimony that the
decisionmaking process was not totally unsuccessful – even though, again, it dealt a
very serious blow to both state and regime with long-term consequences. Some of the
larger consequences of the conflict in the Arab world are also examined.

The Dimensions of the Process

Just as the Iraqis thought of the First Gulf War as a way of executing a Six-Day War, it is fair to say that in 1990 they imagined that a quick operation in Kuwait would end up looking like a second Suez from which they would benefit politically and strategically. By reasoning analogically, the Iraqis also thought that the precedents were in their favor. Israel's occupation of the Palestinian territories in 1967, Turkey's take-over of Cyprus in 1974, and Syria's intervention in Lebanon in 1976 all remained Middle Eastern matters dealt with weakly by the international community. None, however, questioned the United States' strategic interests in the region as forcefully as Iraq's capture of the Kuwaiti Emirate.

In addition, if swift a successful operation on Kuwait would have concretized the Arab popular support that Iraq had been gathering since its defeat of Iran and which had reached new highs when, in April 1990, the Iraqi President warned Israel about chemical retaliation. As attested to by this remark made by Saddam Hussayn in 1975, consideration of the opinion of Arabs beyond Iraq has indeed long been a concern for the Iraqi leadership :

> It is not sufficient for the state of Iraq to make correct decisions according
> to our objective and scientific calculations. It is also necessary to maintain
> and develop the positive psychological links with the Arab people and the
> bridge of mutual trust between ourselves and some international circles
> whose opinions on the decisions adopted mean a great deal to us.[1]

In spite of their professed pan-Arabism, the Ba'thists had nonetheless been focusing on the erection of a modern Iraqi state since 1968 – concerned as they were about building a state that they felt had always been important. In effect, Iraqis often express the notion that they are consciously part of a state that has always existed but which needed to be given a modern identity.[2] In addition, they understand their regional environment as a predatory one. According to the Ba'thists, the most serious threats to the Iraqi state are Iran and oil. In their view, the fact that Iraq is oil-rich means that it will never be left alone and that its political independence will always be curbed by the dominant powers. The presence of Israel in the region has also had its own security implications for Iraq, but those always were secondary.[3]

The First Gulf War withheld a lot of progress from both Iraq and Iran. Bringing it to an end was important to Iraq. Yet the war also endowed the regime with a professional army, one that could now be used specifically as an apolitical specialized body within the state. In effect, the FGW put an end to the army's role as arbiter of domestic politics – a role established since Bakr al-Sidqi's 1936 coup – and forced it to focus on the defense of Iraq against external threats. The invasion of Kuwait provided the leadership with a chance to concretize this army's newfound foreign role by sending it out to fulfill another mission. In this sense, with regard to the SGW, one can speak of a process of war-induced state-building (see Tilly, 1975).

Finally, the Second Gulf War was a way for the Iraqi leadership to express its contestation of the status attributed to Arabs in general, and Iraqis in particular in the international order. Bertrand Badie (1992) explains this logic of contestation:

> [L]e coût des destructions subies par l'Irak l'emporte nettement sur les gains procurés par des mobilisations populaires, moins fortes que le président irakien ne l'espérait, mais pourtant beaucoup plus importantes que les diplomaties occidentales ne l'admettent. Néanmoins, ce conflit a marqué une étape, puisque, pour la première fois, la logique de la guerre contestataire a fonctionné dans son intégralité: un acteur a fait le pari de s'engager dans un conflit où il ne pouvait être que militairement et diplomatiquement battu et a ordonné son action et ses initiatives, en vue, non pas de vaincre, mais d'incarner une contestation. *Cet objectif a été en grande partie tenu.*[4] (Emphasis added.)

Regionally the contestation corresponded to Iraq's denouncement of the historical arrangements that had been imposed on it for the past seventy years. This aspect of the problem is supported by Tim Niblock who argues that, traditionally, the source of tension in Iraq's relation with the Gulf states is not the design of a "radical Iraq" but rather the gap between Iraqi perception of historical rights and changing international perspectives. In addition, Western interferences – in an attempt to structure a secure Gulf sub-region – can be seen as adding to the instability.[5]

To be certain, the process of state-building is open-ended at its inception. So whatever the intentions, the results of an action undertaken by a regime may be at odds with its objectives. Lentner (1984) notes that even the government which acts for the state may act inconsistently with the interests of that state. Along the same lines, Theda Skocpol (1985) pointed to the fact that:

> Not infrequently, states do pursue goals (whether their own or those pressed on them by powerful social groups) that are beyond their reach. Moreover, the implementation of state policies often leads to unintended consequences as well as intended consequences, both when states attempt tasks they cannot complete and when the means they use produce unforeseen structural changes and sociopolitical reactions.

Fundamentally, then, the Second Gulf War sprang from a regime's need to magnify its state's international position. By doing so, the Ba'thi regime hoped to fulfill a mission based on a shared Iraqi perception of Kuwait's appurtenance to Iraq. Success would have granted the regime a new, more legitimate lease on the conduct of the affairs of the Iraqi state. An accomplished enterprise in Kuwait would also have *a posteriori* justified the FGW. The interconnection between state-building and regime security parameters is apparent in this remark made by Saddam Hussayn to United Nations' secretary-general, Javier Pérez de Cuellar, on January 13, 1991:

> It is that we always take peace initiatives....because we want peace, and because we know that we can build our country in the right way only under the banner of peace. All this building activity which you see around you, including the thriving city of Baghdad, is the product of our own and no one else's efforts; and he who knows how to build and has a passion for building does not want war. But when our security, the opportunity for building and the free choice of our beliefs were threatened....we fought.[6]

176

Although it was the logical culmination of a two-year policy process, the invasion of Kuwait was hastily executed. In addition, all the available evidence points to the fact that the Iraqi leadership went into the Emirate with only a vague idea about how to terminate the crisis. Consequently, most of the policy-making process that followed – in particular the August 12, January 15, and February 23 decisions – bears the mark of improvisation. But, as we have seen, this improvised behavior remained largely true to the dual principle of state-building/regime security which pre-dated the invasion. Hence, we can speak of a process in which the leadership tried to remain focused on its initial reproduction (of state)/survival (of regime) goals while devising several ways to meet the particular challenges that arose with the UN and US oppositions.

In this sense, it can be said that the attempt to stay true to the initial objectives gradually rendered Iraq's position untenable until, in the mass confusion of the last part of February, the Iraqi government withdrew most of its forces, claiming a symbolic political victory. In hindsight, the detailed history of the immediate origins of the crisis, of the August 2 intervention, and of the days that followed would demonstrate that the Iraqi government did not think that it would have to resort to the extreme measures that it finally took (see De La Gorce, 1990). The constant reformulating of objectives was done within a very narrow decisional space. This process of incoming information processing and its potential effect on ongoing policies is explained by Michael Brecher (1972) , who noted the dynamic aspect of foreign policy-making:

> It is at the level of tactical decision-making that *strategic decisions undergo constant change and reformulation, in response to the myriad of competing demands* within the political system. Implementation of strategic policy acts through tactical decisions will affect the entire foreign policy system. (Emphasis added.)

One of the most consequential – and little known – dimensions of such improvised process is that the Iraqi leadership supervised a gradual withdrawal of its most valuable troops stationed in Kuwait while simultaneously vowing to leave the Emirate only when it would officially decide and announce so.[7] In other words, it would seem that the Iraqi troops secretly left Kuwait, and once the withdrawal was completed, Iraq started negotiating the withdrawal. This explains why the coalition offensive encountered only deserters and soldiers sacrificed by their headquarters, and why there were virtually no high-ranking officers among the 60,000 or so POWs.

The idea was the realistic understanding that the United States was poised to eliminate the Ba'thi regime and that, consequently, the conflict should be brought to an end under the first acceptable scenario. To that end, a mix of defeat and symbolic victory was immediately used domestically, first to stymie the revolts, then to rebuild the country under embargo. In that respect, one analyst spoke of the SGW's settlement as a surreal war in which victory and defeat had no corresponding coherence whatsoever (Baudrillard, 1991). Indeed, during the last hours of the conflict, a disorganized American army rendered the evacuation of remaining Iraqi soldiers easier. As Gordon and Trainor (1995) explain:

> The last hours had been a confusing series of stop and start orders that had left the field commanders wondering whether they were to make a maximum effort to protect their troops or an all-out effort to destroy as much of the Iraqi army as they could. Uncertain about its ultimate objective, the army had staggered to a halt....It was evident that the allies had not accomplished all of their goals.

Some, like former French Minister of Defense Jean-Pierre Chevènement, have suggested that the Americans chose to order a cease-fire because an offensive on Iraqi territory was not as easy as it seemed. Indeed, the American command was realistic enough to realize that pushing further into Iraq would have started a *real* war that the United States could have won but at a far greater human and political cost. Former US Secretary of State James Baker (1995) appears to confirm this analysis when he writes that

178

A longer war – even one lasting only a day or two more – could result in needless American casualties....More to the point, Iraqi soldiers and civilians could be expected to resist an enemy seizure of their country with a ferocity not previously demonstrated on the battlefield in Kuwait.

Hence, the dimensions of the Iraqi policy-making process were marked by an alternation of escalation and de-escalation phases. The dynamics of consideration were historical, regional, and domestically oriented. The result of the process can be summed up as follows. It is true that:

(i) Iraq had to withdraw its forces under the implied menace of an imminent invasion of its territory;

(ii) the uprisings that immediately followed brought the Ba'thi regime to its lowest point ever of internal legitimacy; and

(iii) the embargo was not lifted after the cease-fire, and demilitarization measures were forced on the country, thus setting back the Iraqi state's development and even encroaching upon its sovereignty.

It is no less true that:

(i) in spite of the many powerful and multiform internal and external threats, the regime did not collapse;

(ii) the Iraqi army was not vanquished for a genuine military confrontation in the classical sense never did occur (even the troops that were caught in Kuwait managed to retreat safely to Iraq)[8] – for its part, the Republican Guard was never really fully engaged and, in some little-reported cases, successfully battled US troops;[9]

179

(iii) the Iraqi government never asked for a cessation of hostilities, nor did it surrender; and

(iv) even though there was some brief penetration by the coalition, no invasion of Iraq took place, thus leaving the state intact in its territorial integrity and sovereignty.[10]

Of this *very* mixed record, the Ba'thi regime's survival is undeniably its biggest success. Facing actual military threats on five different fronts – (i) inside Kuwait, (ii) on the Saudi-Iraqi border, (iii) the Israeli front, (iv) the Iraq-Turkey border with Kurdish guerrillas, and (v) the Iran-Iraq border with Shiite rebels – not only did the regime survive the crisis and the war, but, for the past seven years, it has managed to devise an ambiguous policy of meeting the various demands of the UN resolutions while fiercely fighting every single one of them. Survival is the trump card of this regime.

Through a process of desperation and blaming of the United States and the United Nations, the Iraqi people slowly reinvested their hopes in a regime upon which they have come to depend on for daily rations – thus reestablishing the regime's legitimacy and economic viability in a most paradoxical manner. In addition, regular American efforts to bring the regime of Saddam Hussayn down[11] are dismissed with the same regularity by the Iraqi leader.[12] Hence, time seems to be on the Iraqi leadership's side.

The Consequences of the Process

Much has yet to be revealed about what really transpired during the Second Gulf War. Among the many myths that have so far been uncovered are: (i) the effectiveness of the Patriot missile[13] and of the Scud-launchers hunt by the US airforce,[14] (ii) the Iraqi "atrocities" in Kuwait,[15] (iii) the "100-hour war,"[16] (iv) the number of Iraqi casualties in the Kuwaiti Theater of Operations,[17] and (iv) the magnitude of the battle of Khafji. Amongst American officials, "bitter disagreements have ranged from the factual and technical....to semantic choices" about Gulf stories.[18] It is beyond the realm of this book to look at all the issues raised by the conflict. Suffice it to say that a full investigation and analysis of these and others matters is overdue. As Faleh 'Abd al-Jabar (1991) correctly remarked:

> There was (and perhaps there still is) a great oversimplification of the conflict. Any criticism of Saddam Hussein was considered pro-USA, and any criticism of the USA was conceived as pro-Saddam Hussein. No synthesis was attempted.[19]

The Gulf conflict has had disastrous consequences on the Iraqi population. The combined effect of 44 days of massive bombing and a stringent economic embargo in place since August 1990 – as well as the violence that erupted during the uprisings that followed the war – has greatly undermined the social tissue. It would not be amiss to say that the 1990-1997 period has been the most difficult one that Iraqi society has endured since the country's establishment in 1921. Even the eight years of the First Gulf War were less trying, for we have seen that there was a concerted and successful effort by the government to keep the war a distant matter. In contradistinction, the Second Gulf War was brought directly to virtually all Iraqi urban centers.

Keeping aside the March 1991 Shiite and Kurdish rebellions, which answered to long-term logics of religious and ethnic particularisms, paradoxically, Iraqi society never did rise against the Ba'thi regime at the end of the SGW. Exhausted by twelve consecutive years of war, dependent on the regime because of the current economic embargo, the Iraqi people have had no choice but to passively rally around the government and identify the continued US bombings in January 1992, June 1993, October 1994, and September 1996, as well as the UN embargo measures as their principal enemy – which they objectively were.

Despite a swift and impressive reconstruction – 133 of the 134 bridges destroyed during the war had been repaired by October 1992 – the country continued to suffer from socioeconomic crippling six years after the cease-fire.[20] Growing joblessness, an economy ravaged by inflation, and societal anomie are now rampant in Iraq. Crime is omnipresent, and most Iraqis express irritation at being poor (a situation new to a majority of them).[21] General health care and welfare of the country's children have been dramatically diminished. High levels of malnutrition are reported all over the country and water and wastewater systems suffered serious power outages and breaks in the water mains.[22] For the first time in its history, the field of education – which, as we saw in chapter three, has been given special attention since the mid-1920s – was declining. The number of students graduating from universities, colleges, and technical institutes went from a total of 43,685 for the 1989-1990 academic year to 38,054 in 1992-1993.[23] As of January 1994, approximately 400,000 deaths due to the embargo had been reported – for a population of 16,335,199 (1987 census).[24] By 1997, the figure had reached 500,000. In September 1995, the United Nations' World Food Programme reported that 4 million Iraqis, including 2.4 million children under five years of age, were at severe nutritional risk.[25] Clearly the post-SGW period was more lethal to the Iraqi population than the war itself.

But if the population hardly recovered from a traumatizing event, the regime was swift in recomposing its power internally. Isolated internationally, the Iraqi government launched massive reconstruction programs domestically. Thus doing, it acted in order to reestablish legitimacy through economic viability in spite of the embargo. Between 1994 and 1996, at least two oil refineries were active allowing some 200,000 barrels to be exported every day, mainly to Iran and Jordan. Then, on December 10, 1996, the UN Security Council authorized Iraq to start exporting oil for a $ 2.7 billion value during a renewable 90-day period.

Simultaneously, the government was also building new, firmer security pillars. Particular attention was paid to the military which was restructured. A more professional army of 400,000 replaced the 1,000,000-man all-encompassing machine that existed before the second Gulf conflict. Some units were disbanded and others regrouped to form the existing six corps. The Republican Guard itself was reformed and reduced from eight to seven divisions for a total of 120,000 men.[26] Two of these divisions are today deployed in the north, two in the south and the remaining form a wide circle around the Baghdad area positioned on the four main roads leading to the city. The Iraqi army is now equipped with approximately 2,700 tanks, 446 fighter planes (MiG-29s, MiG-23s, Mirage F-1s, SU-20s, and SU-25s), 520 helicopters, and 2,075 artillery pieces (see table 5.1).[27] There are serious indications that Iraq retains some 700 redesigned Scud B and C missiles. Even the nuclear program, that was supposedly terminated by UN inspectors in 1992, has not been totally abandoned.[28] Only three years after the conflict, an analyst had reported that

> Iraq remains a potential regional power and the foremost long-term threat to US interests into the Middle East. Iraq is still committed to acquiring nuclear weapons – it will continue to do so as long as President Saddam Hussein and his regime survive....Moreover, Iraq's armed forces are still the largest in the Gulf....Finally, Iraq has rebuilt much of its conventional military-industrial base since the war.[29]

Hence, in 1997, the Ba'thi regime in Iraq appears to be more in control of the country than it ever was. The defense reflexes of the nomenclature are in full swing.[30] In addition, although it enjoyed financial and logistical support by the United States and Syria, the Iraqi opposition abroad has proven to be unable to put forth a viable alternative societal project for the Iraqi population.[31] As for the longevity of Saddam Hussayn and the Ba'th party, it is attested to by the fact that most of their opponents during the conflict have disappeared while they still are firmly in control of their country. George Bush, Margaret Thatcher, John Major, Turgut Ozal, Brian Mulroney, Itzhak Shamir, Khalifa al-Thani, Mikhail Gorbatchev, and François Mitterand are no longer in office.[32] In fact, Saddam Hussayn's regime has surmounted the three challenges it was faced with: (i) war, (ii) internal troubles that followed the war, and

(iii) initiating an economic momentum – although this last challenge has not been fully met.

Bearing all of these reservations in mind, the regime is still very much vulnerable. For one thing, more clashes with the Kurds seem very likely. A pointer to future developments is that Turkey and Iran will assert more influence in northern Iraq and that, gradually, they will agree to some reassertion of Iraqi influence.[33] That was the case when, in late August 1996, the Iraqi army regained access to the northern part of the country that had been, up to that point, alternatively controlled by the Kurdish Democratic Party (KDP) of Massoud Barzani and the Patriotic Union of Kurdistan (PUK) of Jalal Talabani.

Nevertheless both state and regime have been seriously undermined. Since March 1991 and August 1992, two no-fly zones have been unilaterally imposed and enforced by the United States, France, and Britain on the northern and southern parts of Iraq. In September of 1996 the southern zone was extended from the 32nd to the 33rd parallel. These measures are nonetheless rejected by the Iraqis who sporadically violate the prohibited areas.[34] Further military clashes and tensions occurred anew between Iraq and the United States and its allies in January 1993, June 1993, October 1994, August 1995, and September 1996. These by-products of the 1991 war highlighted the fact that the original conflict remained unfinished primarily because of the survival of the regime of Saddam Hussayn. To be certain, the "Iraq problem," as President Bill Clinton called it in September of 1996, has become a conundrum for the United States. Still, since the fall of 1993, Iraq's opposition to UN inspections mellowed, and the government in Baghdad devised a policy of cooperation with the United Nations Special Commission and the monitoring missions of the International Atomic Energy Agency (IAEA).[35] Nevertheless, Iraq and the US will, in all likelihood, remain on a collision course for the time being.

Finally, publicized family quarrels in the entourage of Saddam Hussayn are a testimony to the frailty of the leadership's cohesiveness as well as a signal of internal divisions as to how to cope with the continuing question of the embargo. In that respect, the defection, on August 8, 1995, of the President's son-in-law, Lieutenant-General Hussayn Kamil Hassan al-Majid, was undoubtedly the heaviest blow dealt to the regime since the end of the conflict. Formerly in charge of the Ministry of Industry and Military Industrialization (MIMI), where he oversaw the development of the al-Hussayn and al-'Abbas missiles (redesigned Korean Scud B and C), Hussayn Kamil was in every aspect a true regime insider. If the consequences of the defection were not tremendous internally (at least on the surface), they were more significant regionally as King Hussayn – who granted asylum and protection to Kamil and his family (his brother, Colonel Saddam Kamil formerly in charge of security services, and their wives, President Saddam Hussayn's daughters, Raghad and Rana) – formally abandoned the Ba'thists to their plight. Publicly calling for a change of regime in Baghdad, the Hashemite ruler dramatically switched sides to join the United States, Saudi Arabia, and Kuwait. Saddam Hussayn was secure enough about his position inside Iraq to organize and win a national presidential referendum in a mere 65-day period after the defection.

Iraq is today enmeshed in an economic embargo that in many ways is a continuation of the war by other means. Seven years after its invasion of Kuwait, the Ba'th regime has come full circle, as was the case in 1990, its security is almost exclusively dependent upon the government's ability to get the Iraqi economy moving again. In a word, that means getting the embargo lifted. Yet paradoxically, the embargo has fueled anti-Western nationalism and Islamic radicalism in Iraq. Moreover, resentment against the regime, which was present immediately after the war, has gradually been transported onto the United States, the United Nations, and the West in general.

Hence, it could be said that the embargo is the last chapter of the unfinished Second Gulf War. As soon as it is fully lifted, the Ba'thi regime will be able to claim victory. (Opposition to a prolongation of the embargo has already been expressed in the UN Security Council by Russia, France, and China.)[36] The Iraqi leadership would then be able to convincingly argue that it has succeeded in surviving a formidable array

185

of challenges to its security while simultaneously acting to correct an Iraqi perception of spoiled historical rights over Kuwait. In effect, although national development at home and expansionism abroad have oftentimes been tied in Iraq's history since the monarchy, the Ba'thi Gulf wars represented an unprecedented level of foreign activism by any Iraqi regime.

The Second Gulf War is a traumatizing event in contemporary Arab political history whose effects will span several of the coming decades. According to the Arab Economic Report, a study of the Arab League, the Arab Monetary Fund, and the Organization of Arab Petroleum Exporting Countries, published in September 1992, the Gulf conflict cost the Arabs $620 billion, of which $190 billion were lost by Iraq and $160 billion by Kuwait.

Once the guns fell silent, analysts concluded that the conflict sounded the death knell of radicalism in the Middle East announcing a new political tide in favor of moderate/conservative Arab States. Noting the devastating character of the Gulf war, Barakat (1993) offered a more balanced picture. He emphasized the dynamic patterns of change that often emerge of conflict, and called for a new state-society dialogue in the Arab world.

It would be outside the scope of this study to examine the various repercussions of the war on the Arab world. However, mention should be made of the renewal of the debate on Arab nationalism – an ideology which was pronounced dead for the umpteenth time – and the reinvigoration of Orientalism.[37] In a seminal essay, Professor Samuel Huntington of Harvard University explained the rallying of a number of Arabs behind Iraq on the basis of civilizational commonalties and announced that the fundamental source of future conflicts will not be ideological or economic but, rather, caused by the fault line between civilizations.[38]

Table 5.1

Iraqi Armed Forces

	1990	1997
Active Forces	1,200,000	420,000
Reservists	650,000	92,000
Army		
Tanks (T-72s)	5,800	2,700
Personnel carriers	5,100	2,400
Artillery pieces	4,000	2,075
Navy		
Warships	5	2
Active forces	2,950	2,500
Airforce		
Bombers	17	6
Strike aircraft	300	130
Fighters	460	316
Attack helicopters	530	520
Missiles		
Scud launchers	22	22
SAM launchers	550	600

A number of issues have been brought to the fore by the Gulf conflict. According to Jordanian political scientist Kamel Abu Jaber, Iraq has won the conflict by bringing to the table the following issues: (i) the question of rich versus poor Arabs; (ii) the question of borders; (iii) the question of political legitimacy of Arab regimes; (iv) the relations between the United States and the Arabs; (v) the relationship between the Arabs and the West; and (vi) the place of the Arabs in the new international order.

187

To be certain, the conflict consolidated the various splits that had been developing between the Arab states.[39] The political and economic effect on poor Arab countries, such as Jordan and Mauritania, that had sided with Iraq were tremendous.[40] In addition to the haves/have-nots opposition, mention should be made of the differences that arose between the Maghreb and Mashreq. In effect, along with the Palestinians, Maghrebi countries had been Iraq's staunchest supporters, whereas Iraq's greatest criticism came from Mashreq countries (except Yemen, Sudan and Jordan). Finally, by revealing the struggle between state and civil society in the Arab world, the Gulf war made clearer the separation between democratizing and non-democratizing countries.[41] More importantly, the legitimacy of all these regimes was seriously undermined. Finally, according to Paul-Marie de La Gorce, these multiple Arab divisions were compounded during the conflict by three specific elements: (i) the economic and political weakness of Egypt, (ii) the need for a new Syrian foreign policy due mainly – but not exclusively – to the disappearance of the Soviet Union, and (iii) the decline in oil bargaining power.[42] In addition to post-Cold War rearrangements in the international environment, these particular agendas provided indeed the conjunctural structure for a configuration against Iraq.

The principal regional winner of the conflict was Iran: (i) its Iraqi rival was sidelined, (ii) the First Gulf War was settled in its favor; (iii) it gained a new strategic potential in Eurasia, and (iv) it was able to continue the build-up of its military potential. To be sure, Iran's newfound sure-footed attitude has been worrisome to Baghdad. Another victor was Israel which, despite having been the target of 39 unanswered Iraqi Scud attacks, saw its fiercest regional challenger and a radical Arab country internationally isolated.

For its part, Kuwait was liberated and restored but at a high strategic and financial price. The Sheikdom's dependence on the United States is today higher than ever. The resentment Kuwaitis fostered amongst this Iraqi generation will undoubtedly perpetuate the tension between the two countries. Certainly, the boundary matter still remains a loose end. By drawing a new border line awarding the Iraqi port of Umm

Qasr to Kuwait, the United Nations' Iraq-Kuwait Boundary Demarcation Border Commission (UNIKBDC) has complicated the problem more than it clarified it (see Schofield, 1991 and 1993). In fact, "if history is any guide, no foreseeable successor government is likely to abandon what Iraqis universally regard as Iraq's just historic claims to adequate access to the waters of the Gulf."[43] The pre-invasion attitude of the Kuwaiti leadership has also come under severe attack by Kuwaitis and non-Kuwaitis alike. With the benefit of hindsight, it seems evident that a more intelligent handling of the July 1990 crisis by the Kuwaiti government could have been far less expensive to all involved than the international conflict that took place.

Summary

The aim of the above discussion has been to place the consequences of the Second Gulf War in context. The policy-making process of the Iraqi leadership was assessed as initially being an attempt at betterment of the country's strategic and political position. Cashing in on post-First Gulf War recently acquired Arab support, the actions the Iraqi regime took in 1990 were of an inherently contestatory nature. That contestation was primarily of the prevailing international and regional orders. At the same time, it was also concerned with diffusing the general and particular threats that came to beset the Iraqi state and regime after the war with Iran. Ba'thi policy-making during the conflict was also characterized by a significant amount of improvisation in the face of unexpected reactions by the international community. Yet no matter how specific, the different improvised decisions were always highly determined by the general dimensions of the state-building/regime security rationale couple. Because of these self-imposed limitations, the Iraqi leadership enjoyed a narrow decisional space.

Notwithstanding, the regime's main accomplishments during the crisis were (i) its own survival and (ii) the de-escalation of the conflict while maintaining a facade of militarily "going all the way." Hence, the army was salvaged and territorial integrity

189

kept intact. But because it in fact had to back down in the face of a politically and militarily powerful coalition led by the United States, the result of the Ba'thi regime's policy-making process during the Second Gulf War is ultimately a fundamentally mixed one. The regime survived, but the state's development was tremendously slowed. The country rapidly reconstructed, but the embargo persisted. The population rallied around the government, but it remained resentful. Finally, the Gulf conflict revealed the various serious splits already existing inside the Arab world and launched new ones.

NOTES

[1] Saddam Hussayn, "The National Potential and International Politics," p. 66.

[2] Interviews, Baghdad, August 1994.

[3] Interview with a high-ranking Iraqi official, Baghdad, August 28, 1994.

[4] Translation: The cost of destruction suffered by Iraq is much more important than what it gained through popular mobilizations, although these were of a magnitude less than the Iraqi President had hoped for but yet much larger than the Western embassies say. Nevertheless, this conflict was a landmark since, for the first time, the logic of a contestatory war worked in its totality: an actor made the gamble of engaging himself in a conflict in which he could only be militarily and diplomatically beaten, and he organized his action and his initiatives with a view not to win but to incarnate a contestation. *This objective was largely met.*

[5] Tim Niblock, "Iraqi Policies Towards the Arab States of the Gulf, 1958-1981," in Tim Niblock, ed., *Iraq: The Contemporary State* (1982), pp. 125-149.

[6] Transcript of the meeting held on Sunday evening, January 13, 1991, between President Saddam Hussayn and Javier Pérez de Cuellar, secretary-general of the United Nations, New York: The Permanent Mission of Iraq to the United Nations, February 15, 1991, p. 7.

[7] The most important troops, the Republican Guard, were actually never positioned inside Kuwait. Immediately after conducting the invasion operation, they withdrew to positions in and around Basra. In the course of an address made on October 11, 1995, to the National Press Club, former US Secretary of State James Baker confirmed this assessment declaring that "some Republican Guard units were never sent to Kuwait."

[8] Michael R. Gordon and Eric Schmitt, "Much More Armor Than US Believed Fled Back to Iraq," *The New York Times*, March 25, 1991. Also of interest is Stephen Pelletiere's assessment that: "The Iraqi army is....professional and of a high caliber. Only a professional army could have stood up to one of the longest, most savage aerial bombings in history and then proceeded to restore order in the country. Our assessment that the army was loyal to Saddam also appears to have been proved by events" (1992: 153).

[9] US News and World Report Staff, *Triumph Without Victory: The Unreported History of the Persian Gulf War*, New York, New York: Random House, 1992, especially pp. 351-356 of chapter 20, "The

Republican Guard Fights Back." According to Gordon and Trainor (1995: 429), the Hammurabi division escaped largely intact and, of the few senior Iraqi officers captured during the war, only one was a Republican Guard officer. Although the intricacies of the conflict are still entangled to a large degree, these findings are supported by evidence that is still coming out.

[10] The Safwan airfield where cease-fire talks took place was in fact in possession of Iraqi units at the time of the cease-fire. Allied Joint Forces Commander, Khaled Bin Sultan, reports that General Norman Schwarzkopf and he had to request that the Iraqis withdraw their forces so that the meeting could be held in the small airstrip (1995: 427). The Iraqis refused to oblige for several hours, thus delaying the cease-fire ceremony until the next day.

[11] R. Jeffrey Smith and John M. Goshko, "US Considers More Aggressive Campaign to Topple Iraqi Leader," *The Washington Post*, November 25, 1991; Patrick E. Tyler, "Saudis Press US for Help in Ouster of Iraq's Leader," *The New York Times*, January 19, 1992; Patrick E. Tyler, "Gates, in Mideast, is Said to Discuss Ouster of Hussein," *The New York Times*, February 7, 1992; Patrick E. Tyler, "Congress Notified of Iraq Coup Plan," *The New York Times*, February 9, 1992; George Lardner Jr., "US Action Against Iraq Not Ruled Out," *The Washington Post*, April 13, 1992; Elaine Sciolino, "Greater US Effort Backed to Oust Iraqi," *The New York Times*, June 2, 1992; Don Oberdorfer, "US Had Covert Plan to Oust Iraq's Saddam, Bush Advisers Asserts," *The Washington Post*, January 20, 1993; and Elaine Sciolino, "Clinton to Scale Down Program to Oust Iraqi Leader," *The New York Times*, April 11, 1993.

[12] "Jovial Hussein, on TV, Mocks Talks of Coups," *The New York Times*, December 16, 1991.

[13] Initially, the US Army had claimed a 70% success rate for the missile. In 1992, that assessment was changed when army experts told the US Government Operations Committee that of the 82 Scuds fired on Israel and Saudi Arabia, only one may have been destroyed by the Patriot. A 1991 Israeli Air Force report concluded that "There is no evidence of even a single successful intercept." See Bob Davis, "Patriot Missile Shot Down Fewer Scuds Than Originally Thought, Army Says," *The Wall Street Journal*, April 8, 1992, p. A4; George Lardner Jr., "Army Cuts Claims of Patriot Success," *The Washington Post*, April 8, 1992, p. A8; ABC News' *Nightline*, "Patriot Missile Not What It Was Cracked Up to Be," April 6, 1992, transcript # 2836; and Tim Weiner, "Patriot Missile's Success a Myth, Israeli Aides Say," *The New York Times*, November 21, 1993. Also see Barton Gellman, "Study on Gulf War Points out Limits of Air Power," *The Washington Post*, May 13, 1991, p. A6.

[14] On January 18, 1991, General Schwarzkopf announced that at least 11 mobile erected Scud launchers had been destroyed and that others would be attacked. After the war, it was discovered that no Scud launcher was hunted down. See Mark Crispin Miller, "Desert Scam: Not One Mobile Scud Launcher Was Destroyed," *The International Herald Tribune*, January 25, 1992.

[15] The torture allegations were proved false when it was discovered that the young Kuwaiti "nurse" who had testified before the Congressional Human Rights Caucus on October 10, 1990, was in fact the daughter of the Kuwaiti Ambassador to the United States, Saud Nasir al-Sabah (later appointed Kuwait's Information Minister) and that the stories about Iraqi soldiers leaving babies on the cold floor to die had been fabricated. See John R. MacArthur, "Remember Nayirah, Witness for Kuwait?," *The New York Times*, January 6, 1992.

[16] Clashes between American and Iraqi ground forces continued after the February 28 cease-fire. On March 2, a serious engagement took place near the Rumaila oil field between the US 24th Infantry Division and the Mechanized Infantry of the Iraqi Hammurabi Division from the Republican Guard.

[17] Although Iraq and the United States never gave an official body count, the Pentagon estimated the number of dead Iraqis at 100,000. That number has been disputed and proved difficult to countenance. The US News and World Report staff (1992: 406-409) offer a well-researched demonstration "that yields a maximum number of killed ranging from 6,500 to 18,000." In a major article, "Gulf War: How Many Iraqis Died?," *Foreign Policy* 90 (Spring 1993), John G. Heidenrich argues convincingly that "the total death toll, from both the air and ground offensives, may have been only 1,500." Also see the reactions to Heidenrich's article and his response in *Foreign Policy* 91 (Summer 1993), pp. 182-192.

[18] Barton Gellman, "Disputes Delay Gulf War History," *The Washington Post*, January 28, 1992. Also see Anthony Cordsman, "Rushing to Judgment on the Gulf War," *Armed Forces International* (June 1991).

[19] For an illuminating discussion of the various post-hoc interpretations of the conflict, see Oliver Ramsbotham, "The Conflict in Comparative Perspective," in Danchev and Keohane, eds., *International Perspectives* (1994), pp. 295-324.

[20] Paul Lewis, "Effects of War Begin to Fade in Iraq," *The New York Times*, May 12, 1991; "As Life Improves in Iraq, Hussein Digs in," *The New York Times*, July 23, 1991; "Hussein Rebuilds Iraq's Economy Undeterred by the UN Sanctions," *The New York Times*, January 24, 1993; and Vincent Hugeux, "Le Retour de Saddam," *L'Express* 1722, 2145, August 13-19, 1992, pp. 24-34.

[21] Interview with a group of Iraqi women, Baghdad, August 30, 1994.

[22] See "Health and Welfare in Iraq after the Gulf War," report by the International Study Team of the Harvard University School of Public Health, Oxford University, and the London School of Economics, conducted after a visit in Iraq from August 23 to September 5, 1991.

[23] Republic of Iraq, Ministry of Planning, Central Statistical Organization, *Annual Abstract of Statistics 1993*, Baghdad: 1993.

[24] *The New York Times*, January 9, 1994. Also see *The Middle East Report* 193, 25, 2 (March-April 1995) special issue, "Intervention and Responsibility: The Iraq Sanctions Dilemma."

[25] *The Economist*, September 30, 1995, p. 6.

[26] The seven divisions are: Hammurabi, al-Madina al-Mounawara, al-Nida', al-'Abid, Baghdad, al-Fao, and 'Adnan.

[27] Michael Eisenstadt, *Like a Phoenix from the Ashes?: The Future of Iraqi Military Power*, Washington, D.C.: The Washington Institute for Near East Policy, 1993; Jacques Isnard, "Golfe: La Guerre Réévaluée," *Le Monde*, May 2, 1992; an interviews.

[28] See Kenneth R. Timmerman, "A Nuclear Iraq - Again," *The Asian Wall Street Journal*, November 15, 1993. Also see Timmerman's book *The Death Lobby: How the West Armed Iraq*, Boston, Massachusetts: Houghton Mifflin company, 1991. On the inception of the Iraqi nuclear program, see Jed C. Snyder, "The Road to Osiraq: Baghdad's Quest for the Bomb," *Middle East Journal* 37, 4 (Autumn 1983), pp. 565-593.

[29] Michael Eisenstadt, *Like a Phoenix From the Ashes*, p. xiv.

[30] See Pierre Luizard, "Baghdad: Une Métropole Moderne et Tribale, Siège de Gouvernements Asiégés," *Maghreb Machrek* 143 (1994), pp. 225-242.

[31] For an overview of the Iraqi opposition's views on the war and its aftermath see Fran Hazelton, ed., *Iraq Since the Gulf War: Prospects for Democracy*, London: Zed Books, 1994. Edited by the Committee against Repression and for Democratic Rights in Iraq (CARDRI), this volume discusses the situations of the Kurdish and Shiite populations and is critical of the West's "lack of resolve" towards Saddam Hussayn. Also see CARDRI's *Saddam's Iraq - Revolution or Reaction?* London: Zed Books, 1986; and, by the London-based Iraqi National Congress (INA), "Crimes Against Humanity and the Transition from Dictatorship to Democracy," report issued by the executive council of INA, May 25, 1993.

[32] On this point, James Baker (1995: 442) wrote: "To this day, [Saddam Hussayn] remains in control of his country....In occasionally reflecting on this perverse twist of history, I'm reminded of something Tariq 'Aziz said to me in Geneva: 'We will be here long after you're gone'."

[33] See Robert Olson, "The Kurdish Question and Geopolitic and Geostrategic Changes in the Middle East after the Gulf War," *Journal of South Asian and Middle Eastern Studies* 27, 4 (Summer 1994), pp. 44-67.

[34] Ministry of Foreign Affairs of Iraq, "Position Paper on the Two 'No-Fly Zones' Imposed on Iraq," Baghdad, January 30, 1993.

[35] See J. Keeley, "The IAEA and the Iraqi Challenge: Roots and Responses," *International Journal* 49, 1 (1993-1994), pp. 126-155; and B. Morel, "Nuclear Non-Proliferation and the International Inspection Experience in Iraq," *Disarmament* 16, 3 (1993), pp. 103-121.

[36] See Eric Rouleau, "The View from France: America's Unyielding Policy toward Iraq," *Foreign Affairs* 74, 1 (January-February 1995), pp. 59-72; D.C. Gladney. "Sino-Middle Eastern Perspectives and Relations Since the Gulf War: Views From Below," *International Journal of Middle Eastern Studies* 26, 4 (1994), pp. 677-691; and "China Supports Iraq's Endeavor to End Sanctions," *The Baghdad Observer*, August 28, 1994, p. 1.

[37] See, for instance, E. Evans, "Arab Nationalism and the Persian Gulf War," *Harvard Middle Eastern and Islamic Review* 1, 1 (1994), pp. 27-51; As'ad Abukhalil, "A New Arab Ideology?: The Rejuvenation of Arab Nationalism," *Middle East Journal* 46, 1 (Winter 1992), pp. 22-36; Bryan S. Turner, *Orientalism, Postmodernism, and Globalism*, New York, New York: Routledge, 1994; Jochen Hippler and Andrea Lueg, eds, *The Next Threat: Western Perceptions of Islam*, London: Pluto Press, 1995; and the special issue of *MARS (Le Monde Arabe dans la Recherche Scientifique)*, (Winter 1994), Paris: Institut du Monde Arabe (IMA).

[38] Samuel P. Huntington, "The Clash of Civilizations?," *Foreign Affairs* 72, 3 (Summer 1993), pp. 22-49. Also see the reactions of Fouad Ajami, Kishore Mahbubani, Robert L. Bartley, Liu Binyan, Jeane J. Kirkpatrick, Albert L. Weeks, and Gerard Piel, in *Foreign Affairs* 72, 4 (September/October 1993), pp. 2-26; and Huntington's response in *Foreign Affairs* 72, 5 (November/December 1993), pp. 186-194 as well as his book *The Clash of Civilizations and the Remaking of World Order*, New York, New York: Simon and Schuster, 1996. Other reactions include Adam Tarock, "Civilisational Conflict? Fighting the Enemy Under a New Banner," pp. 5-18; and Jacinta O'Hagan, "Civilisational Conflict? Looking for Cultural Enemies," pp. 19-38, *Third World Quarterly* 16, 1 (March 1995).

[39] See, for instance, Barbara Gregory Ebert, "The Gulf War and Its Aftermath: An Assessment of Evolving Arab Responses," *Middle East Policy* 4, 42 (1992), pp. 77-95.

[40] See Mustapha B. Hamarneh, "Jordan's Response to the Gulf Crisis," in Bennis and Moushabeck, eds., *Beyond the Storm* (1991), pp. 228-240; the Government of the Hashemite Kingdom of Jordan, *White Paper: Jordan and the Gulf Crisis, August 1990-March 1991*, Amman: Ministry of Foreign Affairs, 1991; John King, "Iraq's Growing Involvement in Mauritania," *Middle East International* (August 1990); and "Mauritania: Friends of Saddam," *Africa Confidential* 32, 3 (February 1991). On Iraq's testing of missiles in Mauritania, see "Washington Craint que l'Irak teste des Missiles en Mauritanie," *Le Monde*, April 26, 1990. On January 16, 1991, the Iraqis sent two Iraqi Airways Boeing 707s to the Mauritanian capital, Nouakchott, for safekeeping during the conflict. The episode gave rise to an erroneous report that Hussayn had sent his family into hiding in that North African country. See Paul Lewis, "Kuwait says Iraq Flew 10 Stolen Jets to Africa," *The New York Times*, January 19, 1991; and Ann V. Bollinger, "Saddam's Family Goes Into Hiding," *The New York Post*, January 19, 1991. On September 11, 1995, US News and World Report mistakenly reported that the Iraqi president was preparing an eventual exile in Mauritania.

[41] See Michael C. Hudson, "After the Gulf War: Prospects for Democratization in the Arab World," *Middle East Journal* 45, 3 (Summer 1991), pp. 407-426.

[42] Paul-Marie de La Gorce, "La Division du Monde Arabe," in *Crise du Golfe: Les Changements Stratégiques*, Paris: FEDN, 1990, pp. 90-91.

[43] David H. Finnie, "Review of Richard Schofield's Kuwait and Iraq: Historical Claims and Territorial Disputes," *The Middle East Journal* 49, 1 (Winter 1995), p. 159.

Summary and Conclusions

The history of the "Mother of All Battles" is full of secrets.
          – Saddam Hussayn

This study has examined the foreign policy-making process of the Iraqi leadership during the 1990-1991 Second Gulf War (SGW). The purpose of this work was to analyze and explain the sequence of decisions that the Ba'thi regime in Iraq enacted during the crisis and the conflict that followed its invasion and annexation of Kuwait on August 2, 1990. To that end, a state-centric framework for the analysis of foreign policy behavior was devised and an investigation was made of the events leading up to the SGW. An attempt has been made to place said policy-making process in a historical context.

Chapter One reviewed the history of foreign policy analysis (FPA) as a backdrop for the discussion. It was shown that the vast majority of FPA studies has overemphasized the importance of the decisionmaking process *per se* at the expense of the overarching and permanent role of the state. The few existing studies on Arab foreign policy-making were shown to have traditionally dealt more with the interaction between internal and external environments than statehood processes. It was suggested that a state-centric approach operating beyond the *ad hoc* level of decisionmaking instances was possible and applicable to Arab states. The argument offered was that short-term decisionmaking processes are more appropriately part of a general policy-making ensemble which is, in turn, influenced by the position of the state and the status of the regime at any given time.

In chapter Two, I argued that the state is an idea that is perpetually built by the different regimes of a country. Its reproduction over time is facilitated by the intrinsic abstractness of that idea of state. It was offered that this process of state-"building" is expressed in a country's foreign policy and that it can combine with a regime's effort to provide for its security. The conceptual couple of state-building/regime security can also be established through conflict and warfare. It constituted, I offered, the decisive influence on the policy-making process of Iraq during the Second Gulf War.

Chapter Three explained the contemporary Arab state in terms of five major characteristics: (i) its inherently modern nature due to recent decolonizations, (ii) the territorial problems that beset it, (iii) the existence of a difficult and complex state-society relationship, (iv) the presence of a one-man leadership system, and (v) the saliency of legitimacy issues. These five elements, along with the correlation between statehood and historical significance, were found to be particularly relevant in the case of the history of the Iraqi state, which was reviewed. It was demonstrated that this multi-layered situation is the background of policy-making in contemporary Iraq. In addition, we saw that efforts on the part of the successive Iraqi regimes to consolidate their power – in the face of chronic political restiveness – also characterized the history of the Iraqi state.

Using these theoretical tools, an examination was made in chapter Five of four decisions taken by the Ba'thi regime during the SGW. The four decisions isolated as being particularly consequential in the policy-making process were: (i) Iraq's invasion of Kuwait on August 2, 1990; (ii) President Saddam Hussayn's "linkage" proposal made on August 12; (iii) the rejection of the UN ultimatum to withdraw from Kuwait before January 15, 1991; and (iv) the refusal to abide by the second US ultimatum on February 23 to withdraw within the next 25 hours. The aspect that stands out as most significant from this examination is that the Iraqi policy-making process during the conflict, as exemplified by the four decisions studied, was generally largely determined by the state-building/regime security combination of concerns but that gradually, and specifically with the last major decision singled out in this regard, as the events turned more and more against Iraq, the regime's security concerns took precedence over the idea of state development – although never totally removing state-building elements.

Four other secondary decisions – the freeing of the Western hostages, the invasion of the Saudi city of Khafji, the launching of Scud missiles on Israel and Saudi Arabia, and the grounding of the Iraqi airforce – were also briefly discussed to explain the main aspects of their rationales. Again, it was found that these events were defined by a combination of short- and long-term political and strategic concerns, corresponding in most cases to the state-building/regime security framework.

Chapter Five assessed the policy-making process and outlined its domestic and regional consequences. I made the argument that initially the whole process was intrinsically an aborted attempt at repositioning the state of Iraq vis-à-vis its regional and international environments *at the same time* that it was a bid to reaffirm the Ba'thi regime's control over its society. As the crisis dramatically turned into an international event with the United States and its coalition allies resolved to defeat Iraq, the Iraqi authorities improvised a strategy of maximization of their regime's interests by closely associating them with the country's fate.

From a theoretical perspective, by integrating long-term statehood variables and short-term security concerns, this study has attempted to correct the shortcomings of analyses of a foreign policy-making situation based on the primacy of immediate concerns. By treating regime and state as key decisional sets whose interplay can be significant, this work has also shown that reliance on one man's psychological make-up, no matter how influential he may be (and the Iraqi President Saddam Hussayn is undoubtedly by far the primary decisiontaker in his country), is fundamentally reductionist. In spite of the importance of personality factors, this book avers the validity of a macro-level approach to foreign policy analysis.

If explored further, the combination of state-building and regime security might prove to be a valid analytical tool for understanding the multiple dimensions of the interaction between the domestic expression of the state's continuing needs by a regime and the latter's *ad hoc* policy behavior in foreign and national matters. In this study,

197

however, the level of correlation appeared particularly high due to Iraq's far-reaching history and its particular and explicit symbolism to the current regime in Iraq. For instance, the full configuration of the mechanisms of state-building and regime security can be further substantiated. Here, it was left loose on purpose because state-building and regime security appeared to be inherently parallel developments that met only conceptually in the formulation of the policy-making process of the different foreign policy decisions.

Roger Owen has correctly remarked that states have to be constructed in history, and that this is a process which is always contested and always incomplete. One potential problem in the dynamic of building of a state such as the Iraqi one is indeed the fact that ethnic homogeneity – which is lacking in Iraq – is, if not a requirement, at least a major condition for a successful build. In countries with a strong tradition of state, such as Germany and Austria, this was the case.

At a time when most policy-makers – especially those of the periphery – were not in a position to think in Clausewitzian categories, the Iraqi regime deliberately used war as an instrument of national policy. The Serbian effort initiated in the former Yugoslavia between 1992 and 1996 attested that, in a post-Cold War era, war can still be used successfully as a policy means. In such a context, it would be wrong to write off the Clausewitzian conception of war. What is changing today is the pattern of war, not its incidence or nature. War is simply *adapting* to the new environment. This is largely due to the fact that wars are essentially the reflection of *aspirations*. Ethnic (Bosnia-Herzegovina), religious (the Sudan), national (Somalia), or historical (Iraq), aspirations are furthered by the process of war. Consequently, changes in the environment can alter only that process of war, not its fundamentals. In a neo-Clausewitzian perspective, the Second Gulf War was then caused by a state pursuing domestic, regional, and international policies with specific objectives and using military means. In that sense, use of force was an important part of the development of the state because of the function of the state as monopoly of power (coercion). It was a rational instrument of national policy – albeit one that the international community condemned

– and it was facilitated by the anarchic nature of the international system.[1] If the action failed in its essential goals, it is because the *friction*, to use Clausewitzian parlance, inherent in a real war (in contradistinction to an abstract one) was such that idealized conditions were not realized. On the contrary, the Soviet Union's fall, George Bush's domestic difficulties, and Egypt's bankruptcy and regional competition with Iraq constituted an extraordinary combination of conjunctural factors that made it easy for various heterogeneous interests to join forces against Iraq for different reasons at that particular time. From that aspect, and although the invasion surprised most informed Middle East analysts, the Iraqi timing appears to have indeed been wrong. On the other hand, security pressures, financial troubles, the rapidly closing window of opportunity opened by the defeat of Iran, as well as Kuwaiti midsummer carelessness equally combined to precipitate an Iraqi invasion that had been in the makings for some time. By that reckoning, the invasion of Kuwait by Iraq was a rational action.

Table 6.1
The Iraqi State's Major Actions on the Kuwait Issue

LEADER	REGIME	ACTION	DATE
King Ghazi	Monarchy	troop movements	1938
Nouri al-Sa'id	Monarchy	federation proposal	1958
'Abdelkarim Qassem	Militaro-Communist	attempted invasion	1961
Saddam Hussayn	Ba'thist	invasion and annexation (reversed in 1991)	1990

The analysis of Iraq's foreign policy behavior during the Second Gulf War reveals that the many factors that entered into this configuration originated from a historically-determined reality. As can be seen from the four decisions studied, the Ba'thi regime systematically rationalized its behavior by referring to Iraq's historical rights over Kuwait. The coupling of security considerations with long-term statehood ones was the ultimate expression of the invasion's legitimacy.

Clearly, then, the issue of Kuwait antedated the 1990-1991 attempt at annexation. In the post-First Gulf War reconstruction period, the Ba'thi regime needed an issue that would give it occasion to act in the name of the Iraqi state; thus using statehood attributes to regenerate itself. It is exactly such a situation that materialized with Kuwait's refusal to yield to Iraq's financial demands. Guided by a dual set of motives and factors operating simultaneously at state and regime levels, the Ba'thists then set out to annex the Emirate and renew their lease on their own state. Ultimately, the need to consolidate the state's position and to ensure the regime's security passed by a renewal of hostilities towards Kuwait.

To all intents and purposes, the previous relation of Kuwait with the Ottoman *Vilayet* of Basra will certainly continue to create tensions with Iraq. Much like King Ghazi's troop movements, Prime Minister Nuri al-Sa'id's menaces, and President Qassem's failed annexation attempt, Saddam Hussayn's Second Gulf War will come to pass as an episode fitting in a general historical pattern (see table 6.1). As Christine Moss Helms (1984) aptly put it: "Geography and history produce similar and recurring challenges that confront all Iraqi governments regardless of their political coloration or the foundations of their support."

A harbinger of things to come is that the problem is particularly acute and emotionally charged.[2] Iraqi designs over Kuwait are still very much alive as can be seen in several declarations made by officials from that country after the war. In an interview with a Jordanian newspaper, *Sawt al-Sha'b*, published on May 27, 1991, a mere two months after the Safwan cease-fire, Iraqi Vice-President Taha Yassin Ramadan declared:

If history repeats itself, our position will remain unchanged. The statement that Kuwait is a part of Iraq is neither controversial nor fictitious, but factual. We are convinced of it....To date, we have had no choice but to yield....During the Mother of All Battles, we made immense sacrifices.... [W]e will reap the fruits of that battle during the next battle.

Similarly, in an interview with the Washington-based *Middle East Quarterly*, published in June of 1994, Deputy-Prime Minister Tariq 'Aziz candidly implied that the Kuwaiti matter may be reopened in the future:

> MEQ: Can we....assume that the Iraqi government is no longer interested in controlling Kuwait?
> 'Aziz: Well, as I said for the government of Iraq, when we were discussing this matter early in 1993, this chapter is closed.
> MEQ: It's closed permanently?
> 'Aziz: It's closed.
> MEQ: Permanently?
> 'Aziz: I don't know what future generations will do, you see.[3]

Finally, this assessment was echoed in October of 1996 by Kuwait's Deputy-Prime Minister Sabah al-Ahmad al-Sabah:

> Baghdad's designs towards our country constitute a reality that we will have to always take into account. Read history and you will see that Baghdad has never renounced its national objective, that is to put our country under its control even when it officially recognizes our independence and our borders. Even during the period of the pro-British regime of Nouri al-Sa'id, every Kuwaiti knew that the Iraqi menace was hanging over our heads....How could we forget the threats of General Qassem?....All Baghdad is waiting for is a favorable moment on the international or regional scene that would allow it to try to reconquer what it never ceases to consider as a province of its territory.[4]

The major conclusion that can be drawn from this study is that the Iraqi policy-making during the 1990-1991 Second Gulf War and subsequent related developments answered to two simultaneous logics, one pertaining to the Iraqi state, the other to the

Ba'thi regime. In essence, I have sought to demonstrate the duality of concerns and the synergistic relationship that lay at the bottom of the major decisions that were taken by the Iraqi leaders. The annexation of Kuwait by Iraq between August 2, 1990, and February 28, 1991, was but one episode in a long-running history of the Iraqi state. It is very likely that an another episode with the same themes will occur within the coming decades. The issue is beyond the territorial predicament. It encompasses the perception that Iraq has of itself.

NOTES

[1] See Mohammed Ayoob, *The Third World Security Predicament: State Making, Regional Conflict, and the International System*, Boulder, Colorado: Lynne Rienner Publishers, 1995. Offering an alternative to dependency and modernization perspectives, Ayoob makes the argument that the early stages of state-making are the underlying reasons of most Third World conflicts. The security problematic is, he offers, fundamentally tied to the issue of state development. For a more global discussion, see Joseph A. Camilleri, Anthony P. Jarvis, and Albert J. Paolini, eds. *The State in Transition: Reimagining Political Space*, Boulder, Colorado: Lynne Rienner, 1995.

[2] During my trip to Iraq, I asked ordinary citizens (a bus driver, a group of students, an artist....) about their feelings towards the aftermath of the conflict. Most of them related significant resentment towards the Kuwaiti rulers. One of them confided that, if somehow he didn't see the need for an invasion in 1990, he would support it wholeheartedly in the future.

[3] "Tariq 'Aziz, The View from Baghdad (with commentary by Amatzia Baram)," *Middle East Quarterly* 1, 2 (June 1994), pp. 59-71.

[4] Cited in Simon Malley, "Clinton: Les Dossiers Brûlants," *Le Nouvel Afrique-Asie* 86 (November 1996), pp. 8-9.

Chronology of Events

November 6, 1914: British troops land at Shatt-al-'Arab proceeding on to Basra.

March 11, 1917: Baghdad falls to the British.

October 30, 1918: The British take Mosul. The Ottomans sign the Mudros armistice.

April 3, 1920: At the San Remo Conference, the League of Nations awards Britain a mandate over Iraq.

June 1920-February 1921: A revolt takes place in Iraq against the mandate.

August 23, 1921: Faysal ibn Hussayn, son of the Hashemite Sharif of Mecca and Medina, becomes King of Iraq.

July 11, 1924: The first Iraqo-British treaty is ratified.

June 30, 1932: Iraq becomes formally independent from Britain.

October 3, 1932: Iraq is admitted to the League of Nations.

September 8, 1933: King Faysal dies in Berne, Switzerland. His son Ghazi becomes King.

October 29, 1936: Bakr al-Siddiq leads a military coup d'État in Baghdad. It is the first contemporary coup in the Middle East.

August 11, 1937: Al-Siddiq is assassinated.

April 3, 1939: King Ghazi dies in a car accident. His son Faysal being 3 year-old, his cousin and brother-in-law, Prince Abdul-Illah, takes up the regency.

April 1, 1941: A coup d'État by Rashid 'Ali al-Gaylani and leading army officers lasts 29 days. It is reversed by a British military intervention.

July 24, 1943: The Arab Ba'th movement is founded in Damascus.

1947: The Arab Ba'th Party is created in Damascus by Michel 'Aflaq, Salah al-Din al-Bitar, and Jallal Sa'id.

1951: Creation of the Iraqi section of the Arab Ba'th Socialist Party.

May 2, 1953: Faysal II comes of age and becomes King.

February 14, 1958: The Hashemite kingdoms of Iraq and Jordan join in a federation.

July 14, 1958: A military coup led by a coalition of Communists, nationalists, and Nasserites brings a bloody end to the Hashemite monarchy. Faysal II and the Regent are killed.

July 16, 1958: The United States dispatch 5,000 Marines to Lebanon.

September 1, 1958: Britain and the United States recognize the Republic of Iraq.

June 19, 1961: Kuwait becomes formally independent from Britain.

June 25, 1961: Iraqi President 'Abdelkarim Qassem claims Kuwait as Iraqi territory.

June 30, 1961: London announces that, at the request of the Kuwaiti Emir, a contingent has been dispatched to Kuwait.

June 31, 1961: A Saudi contingent arrives to protect Kuwait.

July 20, 1961: Kuwait is admitted to the League of Arab States by a vote of 8 against 2 (Iraq and the Yemen).

February 8, 1963: A coalition of militaro-nationalists and Ba'thists organize a bloody coup against the Communist regime of Qassem.

November 18, 1963: The Ba'thists are eased out of the new regime led by 'Abdelssalam 'Aref.

April 13, 1966: President 'Aref dies in an accidental helicopter crash in southern Iraq. He is succeeded by his brother, 'Abdelrahman 'Aref.

July 17, 1968: The Ba'thists organize a coup against the militaro-nationalist coalition. Ahmad Hassan al-Bakr becomes President. Saddam Hussayn is Assistant-Secretary General of the Ba'th party.

March 6, 1975: In Algiers, Iran and Iraq sign an agreement according to which Iraq grants Iran navigation rights in the Shatt-al-'Arab border waterway. In return, Iran agrees to discontinue its military aid to the Kurdish guerrilla groups rebelling in northern Iraq.

July 17, 1979: Saddam Hussayn replaces Ahmad Hassan al-Bakr as President, chairman of the Revolutionary Command Council, and secretary-general of the Ba'th party after al-Bakr resigns for health reasons.

September 4, 1980: Iran shells the Iraqi localities of Khanaqin and Mandali.

September 17, 1980: Iraq abrogates the Algiers Protocol of 1975.

September 22, 1980: Iraq invades Iran. The First Gulf War starts.

October 24, 1980: Iraqi forces occupy the Iranian city of Khorramshahr.

June 7, 1981: The Israeli airforce attacks and destroys Osiraq 1, a French-built nuclear reactor facility in northern Iraq.

May 24, 1982: Iran recaptures Khorramshahr.

March 1, 1984: Iraqi troops are driven out of the Majnoon marshes by advancing Iranians.

March 4, 1985: Iraq bombs the Iranian city of Ahwaz.

February 10, 1986: Iran captures the Iraqi al-Fao peninsula.

May 17, 1987: An Iraqi fighter jet mistakenly fires an Exocet missile at the American frigate USS Stark, killing 37 soldiers.

July 20, 1987: The UN Security Council adopts resolution 598 calling for a cease-fire between Iraq and Iran.

August 5, 1987: Iraq successfully test-fires its al-Hussayn ballistic missile, a redesigned version of the Scud B with an extended range of 650 kilometers.

February 29, 1988: For the first time in its conflict with Iran, Iraq fires 9 al-Hussayn missiles on Tehran. 189 missiles will be launched on the Iranian capital and five other cities by the end of the war.

April 18, 1988: Iraq recaptures the al-Fao peninsula.

May 25–June 25, 1988: Iraqi troops reconquer the Majnoon marshes and penetrate deep into Iranian territory.

July 18, 1988: Iran accepts UN Security Council resolution 598 calling for a cease-fire and withdrawal of troops to the internationally recognized border.

August 20, 1988: A cease-fire between Iraq and Iran is declared.

March 24, 1989: Iraq's Under-Secretary for Foreign Affairs, Nizar Hamdoon, meets with US Secretary of State James Baker in Washington. They talk of developing closer bilateral ties.

October 6, 1989: Iraq's Foreign Minister, Tariq 'Aziz, visits James Baker in Washington. Baker asks for Iraq's endorsement of Egyptian President Hosni Mubarak's "Ten Points" Middle East peace plan. 'Aziz offers unofficial support to the plan refraining from making a public statement on the matter. 'Aziz also conveys a message from his President seeking good relations with the United States "on the basis of mutual respect and understanding."

December 5, 1989: Iraq launches a space rocket named Tammuz 1.

January 17, 1990: US President George Bush signs a directive authorizing an export-import bank line of credit close to $200 million for Iraq's agricultural purchases.

February 12, 1990: US Assistant Secretary of State for Middle Eastern Affairs John Kelly visits Baghdad. Meeting with President Hussayn for ninety minutes, he offers that Iraq is a moderating factor in the region.

February 20, 1990: American reconnaissance planes discover that six Iraqi Scud missile launchers are stationed at an Iraqi base near Jordan.

February 23, 1990: At a Jordanian, Egyptian, Yemeni, and Iraqi summit in Amman, Iraq criticizes the new regional configuration and warns against American designs in the area in the wake of the end of the Cold War.

February 27, 1990: US National Security Adviser Brent Scowcroft informs the Iraqi Ambassador in Washington of the Bush administration's unhappiness with President Hussayn's recent criticism of the United States.

February 28, 1990: French Defense Minister Jean-Pierre Chevènement visits Baghdad. In his talks with the Iraqi President and members of the government, Chevènement discusses Iraq's request to manufacture French Alpha aircraft and AS-30L aerial missiles.

March 15, 1990: Farzad Bazoft, an Iranian-born journalist for the British newspaper *The Observer*, is hanged in the Abu Gharib prison in Baghdad after being found guilty of spying on Iraq by entering a prohibited military area. Daphne Parish, a British nurse at Baghdad's Ibn al Bitar Hospital, is sentenced to 15 years in jail as Bazoft's accomplice.

March 22, 1990: Dr. Gerald Bull, designer of the "supergun" and head of the Iraqi Project Babylon, is assassinated in Brussels.

March 28, 1990: US-made nuclear Krytron triggers destined to Iraq are seized by British Customs at Heathrow airport.

April 2, 1990: Iraq announces that if attacked by Israel, it will burn half of that country with chemical weapons.

April 5, 1990: Prince Bandar Bin Sultan, Saudi Arabia's Ambassador to the United States, meets with President Saddam Hussayn in Sarsank, Iraq. Hussayn asks the Ambassador to convey to President Bush and King Fahd that his country will not attack Israel and he requests that the United States obtain a similar commitment from Israel.

April 10, 1990: Giant steel tubes on their way to Iraq as part of Project Babylon are seized by British Customs at Teesport.

April 11, 1990: The US State Department transmits a démarche to the Iraqi government warning that "Iraq will be on a collision course with the US if it continues to engage in actions that threaten the stability of the region, undermine global arms efforts, and flout US laws."

April 12, 1990: A delegation of US Congressmen led by Robert Dole – and composed of James A. McClure, Howard M. Metzenbaum, Frank H. Murkowski, and Alan K. Simpson – meets with President Hussayn in Mosul. Upon returning to Washington, the delegation announces that Hussayn is a leader the US can work with.

May 25, 1990: President Bush sends a message to the Iraqi President reaffirming that Iraq is a factor of stability in the Middle East.

May 30, 1990: At an Arab League summit held in Baghdad, President Saddam Hussayn urges the Gulf states to abide by the quotas of the OPEC.

June 23, 1990: Iraqi Deputy-Prime Minister Sa'doun Hamadi visits Kuwait in an attempt to resolve the issues raised at the Baghdad summit.

June 26, 1990: Meeting with his Deputy-Prime Ministers, Sa'doun Hamadi and Taha Yassin Ramadhan, Foreign Minister Tariq 'Aziz, and Information Minister Latif Nasif Jassem, President Saddam Hussayn considers the possibility of a military action against Kuwait.

July 10-11, 1990: The oil ministers of Saudi Arabia, Kuwait, the United Arab Emirates, and Qatar meet in Jeddah and agree to resolve their disputes as regards production quotas.

July 12, 1990: Kuwait's Oil Minister, Rachid al 'Oumayri, declares that his country will only respect the new quota agreements of 1,350,000 barrels a day for a period of three months.

July 16, 1990: Iraqi Foreign Minister Tariq 'Aziz sends a letter (dated July 15) to the secretary-general of the Arab League in Tunis accusing Kuwait of direct aggression against Iraq, excessive oil extraction and territory usurpation of the Rumaila oil field. He complains that Kuwait has stolen $2.4 billion worth of oil from Iraq during the war with Iran. The British nurse, Daphne parish, is released from a Baghdad prison. President Saddam Hussayn meets with Hussayn Kamil, Minister of Local Collectivities, Hassan al Majid, and Iyad Fatih al-Rawi, head of the Republican Guard, to discuss plans for a partial or full invasion of Kuwait.

July 17, 1990: President Saddam Hussayn accuses Kuwait and the United Arab Emirates of exceeding their OPEC-allocated quotas.

July 18, 1990: President Hussayn reiterates his grievances against Kuwait and the UAE. King Fahd of Saudi Arabia calls Saddam Hussayn on the telephone to mediate. Kuwait convenes an emergency session of its National Council and sends emissaries to Arab states.

July 19, 1990: The Kuwaiti Minister for Foreign Affairs sends a letter to the secretary-general of the Arab League, Chadli Klibi, in response to 'Aziz's letter. Rejecting the Iraqi accusations, the Minister asks for the League's arbitration on the border matter.

The American Secretary of Defense, Richard Cheney, states that the United States is committed to the defense of Kuwait in case of attack. Later, his comments are repudiated by his spokesman, Pete Williams.

July 20, 1990: Kuwait upgrades its defense condition putting its forces on alert, while Iraqi forces mass on the border.

July 21, 1990: President Saddam Hussayn discusses Iraq's dispute with Kuwait with Egyptian President Hosni Mubarak and King Hussayn of Jordan. Chadli Klibi is in Kuwait to start a mediation. Tariq 'Aziz submits a memorandum to the Arab League Foreign Ministers Council.

July 22, 1990: At a meeting of the Arab Cooperation Council in Cairo, Foreign Minister Tariq 'Aziz delivers to Hosni Mubarak a message from President Hussayn about Iraq's situation with Kuwait. The foreign ministers of Jordan, Saudi Arabia, Kuwait, and the United Arab Emirates meet in Alexandria and decide to ask President Mubarak to fly to Baghdad on a mediation mission. US Ambassador to Iraq April Glaspie meets with the Kuwaiti Ambassador in Baghdad to discuss Kuwait's concern with Iraqi troop movements. Saudi Foreign Minister Saud al-Faysal meets with President Hussayn in Baghdad who agrees to an encounter between Iraq's Deputy Prime Minister, Ezzat Ibrahim, and Kuwait's Prime Minister, Sheikh Saad al-Sabah, to be held in Jeddah.

July 23, 1990: Mubarak and King Hussayn discuss the Iraq-Kuwait matter. President George Bush approves the holding of US-UAE joint military exercises as a show of solidarity against Iraq.

July 24, 1990: The maximum state of alert is decreed by the Kuwaiti army. Mubarak visits Baghdad. The Iraqi President tells him that Iraq will not attack Kuwait as long as negotiations endure. The State Department's spokesperson, Margaret Tutwiler, declares that the US have no defense treaties with Kuwait, and that there are no special defense or security commitments to Kuwait.

July 25, 1990: In Baghdad, the US Ambassador, April Glaspie, is summoned to a meeting with President Saddam Hussayn after meeting earlier in the same day with

Deputy Foreign Minister Nizar Hamdoun. She fails to signal to the Iraqi leader that her country will not tolerate a military action on Kuwait.

July 26, 1990: The Iraqi President meets with President Mubarak's special envoy Ossama al-Baz for two hours. He informs him that he is ready for dialogue with the Kuwaiti leaders.

July 27, 1990: Having been briefed by his envoy, President Mubarak calls King Fahd to arrange for a meeting between Saddam Hussayn and Kuwait's Emir Jaber.

July 28, 1990: Mubarak announces that Iraqis and Kuwaitis will meet in two days for direct talks. DIA analysts rate the invasion of Kuwait by Iraq scenario a 30% probability. President Bush is briefed by CIA Director William H. Webster and CIA Deputy-Director of Operations Richard Stolz who warn that an Iraqi invasion is imminent but that it will probably be limited to part of Kuwait.

July 29, 1990: Iraq announces that a planned meeting with the Kuwaitis in Saudi Arabia was not held as scheduled. A high-ranking Iranian official visits Kuwait-City and asks the Kuwaitis to make no concessions to the Iraqis.

July 30, 1990: King Hussayn travels to Baghdad and Kuwait-City to mediate.

July 31, 1990: The Iraqis and the Kuwaitis meet in Jeddah. The Kuwaiti delegation is headed by Crown Prince and Prime Minister Saad 'Abdallah al-Sabah, the Iraqi one by Deputy Prime Minister Ezzat Ibrahim al-Duri. After two hours, they fail to reach an agreement. The Kuwaitis decline to discuss the matter of the Warba and Bubyan islands. They also refuse to erase the $12 billion Iraqi debt of the First Gulf War. The Iraqis plea for a $10 billion loan in the form of a Marshall plan style reconstruction program is also rejected. In Washington, Assistant Secretary of State John H. Kelly tells the House Foreign Affairs Subcommittee on Europe and the Middle East that the US has no treaty obligation to defend Kuwait in the event of an invasion by Iraq.

August 1, 1990: The Iraqi Ambassador in Washington, Mohamed al-Mashat, is summoned by the US Department of State to inform him of the American desire to see the dispute with Kuwait resolved peacefully. The United States government approves the sale of $ 695,000-worth of advanced data transmission to Iraq. In Jeddah, the talks between Iraq and Kuwait break off early in the morning. Upon arrival in Baghdad at 11:30 a.m., Ezzat Ibrahim meets with President Saddam Hussayn in the presence of Deputy Prime Minister Taha Yassin Ramadan, Foreign Minister Tariq 'Aziz, Ba'th party Security Chief Ibrahim Sib'awi, Military Security Chief Watban Ibrahim, Military Industry Minister Hussayn Kamil, and Hussayn's sons Uday and Qusay. Late in the afternoon, an RCC meeting is held in with army leaders.

August 2, 1990: At 2:10 a.m. (Kuwait time), 100,000 Iraqi troops penetrate Kuwait with 350 tanks overrunning the Kuwaiti army. The Emir's palace is taken at 5:30 a.m.. The Kuwaiti ruling family and the government members flee to Saudi Arabia. The UN Security Council meets to adopt resolution 660 demanding an immediate Iraqi withdrawal. President George Bush orders economic sanctions against Iraq, including freezing of assets.

August 3, 1990: The Iraqis install a temporary government in Kuwait. In Cairo, a majority vote of the Ministerial Council of the Arab League, with 14 out of the 21 ministers for foreign affairs in attendance, calls for an immediate Iraqi withdrawal. Jordan, the PLO, the Yemen, and Sudan vote against; Mauritania abstains; Libya protests; and Iraq is excluded from the vote. In Moscow, in a joint statement with US Secretary of State James Baker, Soviet Foreign Minister Eduard Shevardnadze accepts to support the US condemnation and arms embargo against Iraq without clearing it with his President, Mikhail Gorbatchev.

August 4, 1990: Iraq moves some seized British servicemen from Kuwait-City to Baghdad. The European Community announces embargo measures against Iraq.

August 5, 1990: President Bush declares that the Iraqi aggression against Kuwait will not stand. US Secretary of State Baker calls Soviet Foreign Minister Shevardnadze to ask that Soviet forces join the coalition's military deployment in the Middle East. Shevardnaze declines to participate.

August 6, 1990: President Hussayn declares that Iraq has no intention of invading Saudi Arabia. The UN Security Council passes resolution 661 authorizing a trade and financial embargo on Iraq. The price of the oil barrel is at $28.

August 7, 1990: 4,000 American troops from the 82nd Airborne Division are sent to Saudi Arabia. Turkey announces that it will abide by the decisions of the UN Security Council regarding Iraq.

August 8, 1990: Iraq announces the annexation of Kuwait as its 19th province. Great Britain dispatches two fighter squadrons to the Gulf.

August 9, 1990: An extraordinary Arab summit is convened in Cairo. The UN Security Council passes resolution 662 judging the annexation of Kuwait null and void.

August 10, 1990: Iraq orders all foreign embassies in Kuwait City closed. In Cairo, at a summit attended by 12 of the 21 Arab heads of state, the Arab League votes to send a contingent to Saudi Arabia. Iraq, Libya, and the PLO vote against; Algeria and Yemen abstain; Mauritania and Sudan express reservations; and Tunisia does not attend. In Ankara, US Secretary of State Baker meets with Turkish President Turgut Ozal. In exchange for Turkey's logistical support to the coalition, the US give guarantees that the World Bank would increase its loans to Turkey from $400 million to $1.5 billion for each of the next two years. In addition, the US commits itself to pay the estimated $1 billion in annual revenues that Turkey would lose from closing the Iraqi pipeline.

August 11, 1990: Egyptian and Moroccan forces arrive in Saudi Arabia. Pro-Iraq demonstrations take place in Algeria, Mauritania, Tunisia, Jordan, Yemen, and Lebanon.

August 12, 1990: President Saddam Hussayn presents a proposal under which all the regional questions would be settled on the same basis and according to the same UN Security Council principles. President Bush rejects the offer.

August 13, 1990: King Hussayn warns the US about creating an explosive situation in the region.

August 14, 1990: Iraq offers a complete peace settlement to Iran with pre-First Gulf War conditions. The maritime blocus on Iraq becomes operational.

August 15, 1990: Some 3,000 foreigners, including Chinese, Indians, and Polish nationals are allowed to leave Iraq.

August 16, 1990: American and British nationals in Iraq are rounded up in hotels in Baghdad. Iran accepts the Iraqi peace offer but calls for an Iraqi withdrawal from Kuwait in order to create conditions for peace.

August 17, 1990: Israeli officials call for a massive and swift air attack on Iraq.

August 18, 1990: The UN Security Council adopts resolution 664 demanding that American and British citizens be released. In the Gulf of Oman, a US Marine vessel fires warning shots at an Iraqi tanker sailing towards Aden, Yemen. The ship ultimately reaches port.

August 19, 1990: Iraq offers to free the detained citizens if the UN and the US promise to lift the embargo. Washington rejects the offer calling it "unacceptable and ridiculous."

August 20, 1990: President Bush calls the Westerners held in Iraq "hostages."

August 21, 1990: Iraq's Foreign Minister, Tariq 'Aziz, calls for discussions with the United States. The Bush administration rejects the offer insisting on an immediate Iraqi withdrawal from Kuwait. Iraq demands that all embassies in Kuwait City be closed by August 25.

August 22, 1990: President Bush calls up army reservists.

August 23, 1990: President Saddam Hussayn appears on Iraqi television with a group of British hostages.

August 24, 1990: Soviet President Mikhail Gorbachev sends a message to President Saddam Hussayn warning him about the gravity of the situation. The price of the oil barrel is at $32.

August 25, 1990: After the US secure Soviet support to their proposal, the UN Security Council adopts resolution 665 authorizing a naval blockade to enforce the economic embargo on Iraq.

August 26, 1990: Iraq frees some 50 persons from the US embassy in Kuwait City, most of them women and children. Water, electricity, and telephone services are cut to the embassies still open in Kuwait.

August 27, 1990: Qatar invite coalition forces to be stationed in its territory. It is the fifth Gulf state to do so after Saudi Arabia, Bahrain, Oman, and the United Arab Emirates. Austrian President Kurt Waldheim arrives in Baghdad.

August 28, 1990: Iraq offers to free all the hostages against a promise of non-aggression and it announces that, as 19th Iraqi province, Kuwait is now subdivided into three counties as part of Iraq's administrative structure.

August 29, 1990: In Vienna, the OPEC decides to increase its production against the advises of Iraq, Iran, and Libya.

August 30, 1990: Iraqi Foreign Minister Tariq 'Aziz and UN secretary-general Javier Pérez de Cuellar meet in Amman to discuss the situation in the Gulf.

August 31, 1990: In Cairo, delegates from 13 Arab countries call for the liberation of the hostages held in Iraq.

September 1, 1990: 700 foreigners, mostly women and children, are allowed to leave Iraq.

September 2, 1990: Secretary-general Pérez de Cuellar leaves Amman without having achieved any progress in his talks with 'Aziz.

September 3, 1990: The secretary-general of the Arab League, Chadli Klibi, resigns from his office which he had held since 1979.

September 4, 1990: Egyptian, Syrian, and Moroccan forces are deployed in the United Arab Emirates.

September 5, 1990: Tariq 'Aziz meets with President Mikhail Gorbachev in Moscow.

September 6, 1990: The US Secretary of State meets with King Fahd who informs him that Saudi Arabia will finance Operation Desert Shield. The King agrees to a $15 billion envelope. Britain sends ground forces to the Gulf.

September 7, 1990: Saudi Arabia, Kuwait, and the United Arab Emirates pledge to donate a monthly contribution of $1 billion to the international coalition.

September 8, 1990: In Taif, Saudi Arabia, James Baker meets with the Emir of Kuwait who agrees to donate $15 billion to support US efforts. President Saddam Hussayn sends a message to the American and Soviet Presidents urging them to accept the reality of the new situation in Kuwait. The United States write off a $7.1 billion Egyptian debt.

September 9, 1990: Presidents Bush and Gorbachev meet in Helsinki. They agree to adopt a common policy towards Iraq. President Gorbatchev's proposal to hold a Middle East conference is strongly opposed and ultimately rejected by US State Department officials, in particular Dennis Ross. Subsequently, Moscow announces that it is in agreement with the UN resolutions about Iraq.

September 10, 1990: Iraq and Iran discuss resumption of diplomatic ties.

September 11, 1990: 6,000 British troops arrive in the Gulf with 120 tanks.

September 12, 1990: Syrian President Hafez al-Assad strongly condemns the Iraqi invasion of Kuwait and calls on Arab states to oppose it. In Moscow, Foreign Minister Shevardnadze asks Secretary of State Baker to help him obtain $5 billion line of credit from the Saudis. In Jeddah, the Muslim World League endorses the Saudi government's decision to invite non-Muslim forces to defend the kingdom.

September 13, 1990: 9 Iraqi divisions are deployed on the Saudi, Turkish, and Syrian borders. The UN Security Council adopts resolution 666 making provisions for humanitarian aid to Iraq if distributed through international aid agencies.

September 14, 1990: Iraqi troops occupy the French embassy in Kuwait City. Secretary of State Baker meets with Syrian President al-Assad in Damascus.

September 15, 1990: French President François Mitterand orders Operation Daguet sending 13,000 troops to the Gulf.

September 16, 1990: The UN Security Council adopts resolution 667 condemning Iraqi violation of diplomatic premises and personnel in Kuwait. US Airforce Chief of Staff General Michael J. Dugan is fired for revealing that the only effective way of ejecting the Iraqi army from Kuwait is a heavy and massive bombing of Baghdad and a targeting of Iraq's leadership.

September 17, 1990: Iraq offers to withdraw from Kuwait in exchange for a conference on Palestine. The price of oil is at $33.

215

September 18, 1990: The European Community decides to take additional measures to implement the embargo on Iraq.

September 19, 1990: King Hussayn, King Hassan of Morocco, and Algerian President Chadli Benjedid meet in Rabat to initiate an Arab mediation.

September 20, 1990: Saudi Arabia stops its oil delivery to Jordan.

September 21, 1990: The oil barrel is at $35.

September 22, 1990: Saudi Arabia orders out Yemeni and Jordanian diplomats.

September 23, 1990: The Iraqi government apologizes to France for its action against the French embassy in Kuwait City.

September 24, 1990: Speaking before the UN General Assembly, French President Mitterand offers a peace plan adhering to the linkage dynamic. The UN Security Council adopts resolution 669 making provisions for assisting member states who suffer economic costs as a result of implementing the sanctions on Iraq.

September 25, 1990: Iraq reacts favorably to Mitterand's speech commanding its "non-aggressive tone." UN Security Council adopts resolution 670 extending the embargo to aerial traffic.

September 26, 1990: President George Bush announces that the United States will sell 5 million barrels from their strategic petroleum reserve to curb oil prices.

September 27, 1990: The price of oil is at $40.

September 28, 1990: President Bush denounces the increase of the price of oil.

September 29, 1990: The United States ask Israel to keep out of the crisis.

September 30, 1990: Jordan requests international aid to cope with an influx of 620,000 refugees housed in 13 camps.

October 1, 1990: Speaking before the UN General Assembly, President Bush declares that an Iraqi withdrawal has to take place before any other regional question is considered.

October 2, 1990: President Saddam Hussayn visits Kuwait.

October 3, 1990: French President François Mitterand visits Saudi Arabia and the United Arab Emirates. Soviet Union's Foreign Minister Yevgeny Primakov meets with King Hussayn in Amman.

October 4, 1990: Japanese Prime Minister Tohishi Kaifu visits Baghdad.

October 5, 1990: Soviet envoy Yevgeni Primakov meets with President Hussayn in Baghdad.

October 6, 1990: Iranian President Ali Rafsanjani declares that the embargo should be fully enforced.

October 7, 1990: The commander of the Syrian forces in Saudi Arabia announces that his forces have a purely defensive role.

October 8, 1990: The commander of the Egyptian forces in Saudi Arabia says that his forces will not participate in an offensive on Iraqi land.

October 9, 1990: Italy closes its embassy in Kuwait. Germany, Belgium, and the Netherlands announce that they will soon close theirs.

October 10, 1990: The US army central command unveils its offensive military plan on Iraq to the White House.

October 11, 1990: 321 foreigners are allowed to leave Iraq.

October 12, 1990: Moroccan King Hassan calls for a peaceful settlement of the crisis.

October 13, 1990: Kuwaiti Crown Prince Saad al-Sabah promises the Popular Conference of the Kuwaitis meeting in Jeddah that a restored Kuwaiti government will be more democratic.

October 14, 1990: Diplomatic relations between Iraq and Iran are reinstated.

October 15, 1990: President Bush declares that he is in favor of a Nuremberg-like trial of Iraqi leaders once the crisis is over.

October 16, 1990: US Secretary of State Baker says he is confident about the effect of sanctions on Iraq.

October 17, 1990: James Baker rejects the idea of a partial Iraqi withdrawal.

October 18, 1990: The Iraqi Oil Minister announces that his country is disposed to sell oil at $21 to all interested, including the United States. Yevgeny Primakov, senior adviser to Soviet President Gorbachev, meets with US Secretary of State Baker and National Security Adviser Brent Scowcroft.

October 19, 1990: Details of a planned US military operation on Iraq dubbed Night Camel are published by the Paris-based magazine *L 'Express*.

October 20, 1990: Major anti-war demonstrations take place in the United States and in France.

October 21, 1990: In a press interview, Saudi Minister of Defense Sultan Bin 'Abdelaziz discusses the possibility of giving Iraq an access to the sea in exchange for its withdrawal.

October 22, 1990: President Bush rejects anything less than a full Iraqi withdrawal.

October 23, 1990: Distantiating himself from the declaration of the Defense Minister – his father –, the Saudi Ambassador to the US, Bandar ibn Sultan, declares that his country has not changed its positions with regard to Iraq.

October 24, 1990: 330 French hostages are freed by the Iraqi parliament.

October 25, 1990: US Secretary of Defense Richard Cheney announces that 100,000 more troops are being sent to the Gulf bringing US troops to a total of 210,000. The oil barrel sells at $35.

October 26, 1990: The US Department of State announces that terrorist attacks are to be expected in Europe and the Middle East.

October 27, 1990: The Soviet Union asks the UN Security Council to postpone a vote condemning Iraq.

October 28, 1990: Soviet President Gorbachev says that Iraq might become less intransigent in its position regarding Kuwait.

October 29, 1990: The UN Security Council adopts resolution 674 demanding that all hostages held in Iraq be freed and holding Iraq responsible for any breaches of the Geneva and Vienna conventions.

October 30, 1990: Iraq upgrades its defense condition to "extreme alert."

October 31, 1990: President Bush decides to double the number of US troops in the Gulf and to push for a "use of force" resolution by the UN Security Council.

November 1, 1990: The London-based human rights NGO Amnesty International reports that Saudi Arabia has arrested and tortured hundreds of Yemenis over their country's stand in the Gulf crisis.

November 2, 1990: Three French soldiers are captured by the Iraqis and delivered to the French Chargé d'Affaires in Baghdad.

November 3, 1990: Iraq announces a proposal for the resolution of the crisis echoing the August 12 offer and insisting on an Arab solution.

November 4, 1990: US Secretary of State James Baker initiates an eight-day visit to the Middle East and Europe to discuss a military option against Iraq.

November 5, 1990: Secretary Baker and King Fahd outline a logistical framework for the command and control of military forces in Saudi Arabia.

November 6, 1990: The Japanese government decides not to send the 2,000 men it had originally committed to the coalition against Iraq.

November 7, 1990: 305 Japanese hostages are freed in Baghdad. In Ankara, Secretary Baker meets for two hours with President Ozal who informs him of Iraq's domestic economic situation and agrees to permit an increase of US jets based at Incirlik from 48 to 130.

November 8, 1990: President Bush announces a 200,000 troops increase for Operation Desert Shield. In Moscow, Secretary Baker meets with President Gorbatchev and Minister Shevardnadze for thirteen hours of talk concerning a "use of force" resolution.

November 9, 1990: Former German Chancellor Willy Brandt secures the release of 206 Western hostages.

November 10, 1990: The US Congress asks President Bush to seek authorization before resorting to force in the Gulf.

November 11, 1990: King Hassan proposes an extraordinary Arab summit to search for a peaceful solution to the Gulf crisis.

November 12, 1990: China's Foreign Minister, Qian Qichen, meets with President Saddam Hussayn in Baghdad.

November 13, 1990: US Secretary of State Baker declares that the Iraqi invasion of Kuwait threatens the economic lifeline of the West.

November 14, 1990: King Hassan's summit proposal collapses after Saudi Arabia announces its opposition to Iraqi conditions.

November 15, 1990: Joint US-Saudi military exercises are held in the Gulf with 1,100 planes, 16 vessels, and 1,000 Marines. The operation is dubbed Imminent Thunder.

November 16, 1990: The US initiates diplomatic maneuvers to pass a "use of force" resolution at the UN Security Council.

November 17, 1990: In Geneva, President Bush meets with Syrian President al-Assad. Egyptian President Mubarak asks that the United States give Iraq three months to withdraw from Kuwait.

November 18, 1990: Iraq announces plans to gradually release the hostages.

November 19, 1990: 60,000 Iraqi reserves are recalled and 100,000 are conscripted. Baghdad announces that the remaining 3,500 foreign hostages will be allowed to depart before December 25.

November 20, 1990: 245 US Congressmen file a motion to force President Bush to seek authorization before launching a war on Iraq.

November 21, 1990: President Bush visits Saudi Arabia to spend Thanksgiving Day with the American troops.

November 22, 1990: The British government dispatches 14,000 additional men to the Gulf. In Sanaa, Secretary Baker meets with Yemeni President Ali 'Abdallah Saleh who refuses to join the coalition.

November 23, 1990: Syria promises to send 20,000 men to the Gulf. President Bush and President Mubarak meet in Geneva.

November 24, 1990: A group of British women meet with President Saddam Hussayn to plea for the release of the hostages.

November 25, 1990: A Labor member of the British Parliament arrives in Baghdad.

November 26, 1990: Soviet President Gorbachev and Iraqi Foreign Minister Tariq 'Aziz hold a tense and unproductive meeting in Moscow. Gorbachev warns 'Aziz that the Security Council will soon adopt a severe resolution against Iraq unless Kuwait is evacuated. 'Aziz protests against the Soviet stance.

November 27, 1990: Debates in the US Senate Armed Services Committee show a majority in favor of economic rather than military action on Iraq.

November 28, 1990: The UN Security Council adopts resolution 677 designed to protect the civilian affairs of Kuwait, in particular its register of population. Saudi Arabia, Kuwait, and the United Arab Emirates announce a $4 billion loan to the Soviet Union.

November 29, 1990: At its 2,963rd meeting, attended for the first time ever by the five foreign ministers of the permanent member countries, the UN Security Council adopts resolution 678 authorizing the use of force against Iraq if it does not withdraw totally and unconditionally from Kuwait before January 15, 1991. The US remits $186 million to the UN in partial payment of its debt to the organization.

November 30, 1990: President Bush calls for a dialogue with Iraq and proposes that Iraqi Foreign Minister Tariq 'Aziz comes to Washington and that US Secretary of State James Baker visits Baghdad.

December 1, 1990: President Saddam Hussayn accepts the American proposition for talks. He visits his front-line troops in Kuwait.

December 2, 1990: Iraq test-fires 2 Scud missiles. It is its first test since April of 1990.

December 3, 1990: A Saudi envoy, Sheik 'Ali ibn Muslim, visits Algerian President Chadli Benjedid who is trying to arrange a meeting between King Fahd and President Hussayn.

December 4, 1990: Baghdad authorizes 3,300 Soviet tanks stationed in Iraq to depart for the Soviet Union.

December 5, 1990: Iraq's Ambassador to Switzerland and half-brother of President Hussayn, Barzan al-Tikriti, secretly meets in Geneva with an advisor to President Mitterand, Edgar Pisani.

December 6, 1990: Iraq announces that it will free all the hostages indicating that this has been prompted by consultations with the Arab Maghreb Union countries, as well as Jordan, the Yemen, Palestine, and the Sudan.

December 7, 1990: President Bush rejects any possibility of linkage between the Palestinian issue and Iraq's withdrawal from Kuwait.

December 8, 1990: 'Aziz declares that Iraq is amenable to an agreement on the linkage issue providing the regional questions are recognized in any settlement.

December 9, 1990: The United States reject Iraq's proposed date for a Baker-Hussayn meeting in Baghdad as too late and counter-propose January 3.

December 10, 1990: French forces in the Gulf are increased.

December 11, 1990: Algerian President Chadli Benjedid starts a mediation tour in Arab capitals. King Fahd refuses to meet with him.

December 12, 1990: The Iraqi Minister of Defense, General Sa'di Touma al-'Abbas, veteran of the First Gulf War, is replaced by 'Abdeljabbar Khalil al-Shanshal. Algerian President Benjedid arrives in Baghdad.

December 13, 1990: The last non-diplomatic American citizen leaves Iraq.

December 14, 1990: President Bush says that the meeting with Foreign Minister 'Aziz is on hold. US Chairman of the Joint Chiefs of Staff General Colin Powell tells the House Armed Services Committee that his forces will only have full offensive capability after mid-February.

December 15, 1990: President Hussayn calls off 'Aziz's visit to Washington.

December 16, 1990: The Soviet Union evacuates all its personnel in Iraq. The British embassy in Kuwait – the last to be open – is closed.

December 17, 1990: The European Community announces that its acting President, Gianni De Micheli, will only meet with Tariq 'Aziz after the latter meets with James Baker.

December 18, 1990: President Saddam Hussayn asks for a complete solution to the Palestinian problem before an Iraqi withdrawal from Kuwait.

December 19, 1990: President Mitterand announces that France will seek direct talks with Iraq if a US-Iraq meeting does not materialize.

December 20, 1990: Following attacks on his Gulf policies by a Soviet parliamentary group, Soviet Foreign Minister Shevardnadze resigns.

December 21, 1990: Civil defense exercises, including evacuation of the city, are conducted in Baghdad. One third of the city's 3 million population participate in the exercises.

December 22, 1990: Meeting in Doha, Qatar, for its 11th annual summit, the Gulf Cooperation Council calls for an immediate Iraqi withdrawal from Kuwait.

December 23, 1990: 20 US soldiers accidentally perish on their way from Haifa in Israel to the USS Saratoga ship.

December 24, 1990: President Hussayn says that Israel would be the first Iraqi target if war erupts.

December 25, 1990: The Israeli army is put on full alert.

December 26, 1990: The US Chargé d'Affaires in Baghdad, Joe Wilson, announces that informal talks are being held between the United States and Iraq.

December 27, 1990: A meeting of the major Iraqi opposition groups is held in Damascus. It calls for the overthrow of the Ba'thi regime in Baghdad. 110 members of the Democratic party from the US House of Representatives ask President Bush to allow more time for sanctions to work.

December 28, 1990: A group of US senators meets with the Iraqi Ambassador in Washington and reports the possibility of Iraqi flexibility on an evacuation of Kuwait.

December 29, 1990: The United States and Britain take measures to protect their troops from possible bacteriological weapons attacks.

December 30, 1990: After meeting with President Hussayn in Baghdad, Yugoslav Foreign Minister, Budimir Loncar, carries a message to the US government about an Iraqi withdrawal from Kuwait.

December 31, 1990: Sudan asks Iraq to withdraw from Kuwait.

January 1, 1991: President Mubarak urges Iraq to leave Kuwait.

January 2, 1991: Iraq announces that it has posted 60 divisions facing Saudi Arabia. Iran conducts military maneuvers near its borders with Iraq.

January 3, 1991: President Bush proposes that 'Aziz and Baker meet in Geneva on January 7 or 9.

January 4, 1991: The EC invites 'Aziz to Luxembourg on January 10.

January 5, 1991: Iraq rejects the European offer but accepts to send 'Aziz to meet with Baker in Geneva on January 9.

January 6, 1991: In a speech to his armed forces, President Hussayn declares that if war erupts it will be known as *umm al-ma'arek* (the mother of all battles). The US Department of Defense announces that all journalists reporting on the Gulf situation will have to operate in pools under constant military supervision. They must also submit all reports to a security review.

January 7, 1991: Meeting in London, US and British Foreign Ministers reject the idea of extending the January 15 deadline.

January 8, 1991: President Bush sends a letter to the US Congress asking for a resolution of support to an action on Iraq. Baker and 'Aziz arrive in Geneva.

January 9, 1991: 'Aziz and Baker meet in Geneva for more than 6 hours. No progress is made.

January 10, 1991: Secretary Baker visits Saudi Arabia. He asks for $1.1 billion per month during hostilities, $800 million in economic aid to Turkey, $1 billion over five years for a Turkish defense fund, and $800 million for Eastern Europe. King Fahd accepts to pay the $3.7 billion price tag. Egypt announces that if Israel becomes involved in the conflict, it will have to reassess its position.

January 11, 1991: An Islamic conference, with delegates from various Arab countries attending, is held in Baghdad as a show of support to Iraq. Secretary Baker visits the Emir of Kuwait in Taif, Saudi Arabia. He requests $400 million a month during hostilities, $800 million for Turkey, and $400 million for Eastern Europe. Emir Jaber accepts to provide the total sum of $1.6 billion.

January 12, 1991: The US Congress votes narrowly to authorize the use of force against Iraq. Secretary Baker meets with President al-Assad in Damascus.

January 13, 1991: The UN Secretary General, Javier Pérez de Cuellar, meets with President Saddam Hussayn in Baghdad. No agreement is reached.

January 14, 1991: The French government announces a peace plan offering Iraq a non-aggression guarantee and the holding of an international conference on the regional issues if Iraqi troops withdraw from Kuwait. Hussayn invites the French to visit him with their plan. Advised not to do so by Pérez de Cuellar, the French decline.

January 15, 1991: The UN deadline passes without an Iraqi withdrawal. President Bush signs a national security directive formally authorizing an attack on Iraq the next night.

January 16, 1991: The French forego their peace plan and cancel a planned trip to Baghdad by Foreign Minister Roland Dumas and Élysée advisor Edgar Pisani.

January 17, 1991: At 2:38 a.m. (Iraqi time), 8 American Apache helicopters attack two radar centers in the southwestern part of Iraq. At 3:02 a.m., American F-117 Stealth planes bomb Baghdad destroying the International Telephone and Telegraph Building (ITTB) and the Tower for Wire and Wireless Communications (TWWC). Tomahawk cruise missiles are fired from US warships in the Gulf and the Red Sea. The Second Gulf War begins. It will last 44 days in its air phase, and 5 days in its ground phase.

January 18, 1991: The Iraqis launch 8 Scud missiles with conventional warheads on Israel of which 6 land in Tel Aviv and 2 in Haifa. 68 people are injured. 1 Iraqi Scud is fired at Saudi Arabia.

January 19, 1991: 5 Iraqi Scuds hit Israel injuring 47 people. 4,000 sorties are flown by coalition airplanes against various targets in Iraq. The bombing causes severe damage to Iraq's water, fuel, and electrical supplies.

January 20, 1991: 7 captured coalition pilots are shown on Iraqi television. Iraq fires 10 Scuds at Riyadh and Dhahran. US State Department senior officials Lawrence

Eagleburger and Paul Wolfowitz arrive in Tel Aviv to dissuade the Israeli authorities from retaliating against Iraq.

January 21, 1991: Iraq fires 6 Scud missiles at targets in Saudi Arabia. Iran protests that the allied attacks far exceed the UN mandate.

January 22, 1991: 3 Iraqi Scud missiles strike populated areas of Tel Aviv. There are 3 dead and 96 injured people. 5 Scuds are fired at Saudi Arabia.

January 23, 1991: 12,000 coalition sorties have been flown against and 216 cruise missiles launched on Iraq since January 17. The bombing of Iraqi aircraft shelters is intensified. An Iraqi Scud missile hits Tel Aviv killing 1 people and injuring 19.

January 24, 1991: Iraq closes off its border with Jordan. The UN Security Council privately debates a cease-fire proposal by Algeria, Libya, Mauritania, Morocco, and Tunisia. Japan increases its financial contribution to the coalition to $11 billion. French airforce starts bombing targets inside Iraq in a reversal of its decision to attack only Iraqi positions in Kuwait.

January 25, 1991: Iraq launches 7 Scud missiles at Tel Aviv, Haifa, and Riyadh. In Israel there are 42 injured, and in Saudi Arabia 1 dead and 30 wounded. US Marines and Iraqi artillery units exchange fire on the Saudi border.

January 26, 1991: Iraq sends 80 planes part of its fighter jet fleet to Iran. 135 planes will arrive in Iran by the end of the conflict. US marines in Oman rehearse an amphibious landing in Kuwait. 6 Scuds are fired by Iraq at Central Israel and Haifa. Widespread peace demonstrations take place with 200,000 protesters in Bonn; 100,000 in Washington; 100,000 in San Francisco; and 50,000 in Paris.

January 27, 1991: An oil slick 35 miles long and 10 miles wide is spilled in the Gulf. The US accuse Iraq of causing environmental damage to the region.

January 28, 1991: In an interview with CNN's correspondent Peter Arnett, President Hussayn declares that negotiations to end the conflict depend on President Bush. One Iraqi Scud missile hits Israel.

January 29, 1991: In the first major ground offensive of the war, Iraqi forces begin an incursion into Saudi Arabia with 1,500 troops capturing the coastal city of Khafji.

French Defense Minister Jean-Pierre Chevènement resigns in protest at the coalition's aims which, he says, are to overthrow President Hussayn's regime and decimate Iraq.

January 30, 1991: 11 US Marines and 12 Saudis are killed in ground fighting at Khafji. An American Delta force is established to hunt for Scuds.

January 31, 1991: One Scud is fired by Iraq at Israel.

February 1, 1991: Iran announces that it will fight alongside Iraq if Israel intervenes in the conflict. After three days of fierce fighting, coalition forces regain Khafji after it is evacuated by the main Iraqi elements who took it. Tomahawk missiles are launched on Baghdad.

February 2, 1991: Saudi Arabia and Syria declare that they will not take war aims beyond Kuwait. General Norman Schwarzkopf decides against the amphibious landing option. Iraq launches 2 Scuds at Israel.

February 3, 1991: Coalition air missions against Iraq reach 41,000. US Secretary of Defense Richard Cheney announces that the United States and its allies will not suspend economic sanctions on Iraq after Kuwait is evacuated. One Iraqi Scud lands in Israel.

February 4, 1991: Iran offers to organize a mediation between Iraq and the United States.

February 5, 1991: President Bush sends a letter to Iranian President Rafsanjani telling him that the US will leave the region as soon as the crisis is over.

February 6, 1991: Iraq severs its diplomatic ties with the United States, Britain, Canada, France, Italy, Egypt, and Saudi Arabia. An Iraqi Scud hits Israel injuring 17 people. A second wave of Iraqi planes flies to Iran.

February 7, 1991: The United States announce that the Amman-Baghdad highway is a legitimate target. 49,000 air sorties have been flown by the coalition against Iraq. The Central Intelligence Agency reports large discrepancies regarding figures concerning destruction of Iraqi armor by air attacks.

February 8, 1991: President Bush accuses Jordan of "moving way over to Saddam Hussayn's camp." Chairman Colin Powell and Secretary Richard Cheney visit their

Central Command in Riyadh to review ground war plans. Iraqi fires a Scud missile at Saudi Arabia.

February 9, 1991: A senior Iraqi official arrives in Tehran to discuss an Iranian peace plan. An Iraqi Scud missile hits the metropolitan area of Tel Aviv wounding 27.

February 10, 1991: President Gorbatchev announces that he is sending his special envoy, Yevgeni Primakov, to Baghdad to seek a solution to the war. Iraq says that it is prepared to negotiate an end to the conflict if the United States are excluded from the talks. A third wave of Iraqi jets flies to Iran.

February 11, 1991: The UN secretary-general says he is concerned about the loss of life in the Gulf conflict. In Washington, Israeli Defense Minister Moshe Arens complains about the ineffectiveness of Patriot missiles in hunting down Iraqi Scuds. Soviet envoy Yevgeni Primakov arrives in Baghdad to urge Iraq to withdraw. An Iraqi missile lands in central Israel.

February 12, 1991: In Belgrade, 15 Foreign Ministers of the Non-Aligned Movement consider a peace plan jointly sponsored by Iran and India. In Baghdad, Soviet envoy Primakov meets with President Hussayn. An Iraqi Scud attack wounds 7 in Tel Aviv.

February 13, 1991: 1,000-plus Iraqi civilians die when a US bomb hit a shelter in the al-'Amiriya district of Baghdad.

February 14, 1991: Union of the Arab Maghreb countries (Algeria, Libya, Mauritania, Morocco, and Tunisia), Sudan, Jordan, and Iran protest the bombing of al-'Amiriya shelter. Spain calls for an end of air attacks on Iraq. An Iraqi Scud attack is aimed at Hafr al-Batin in Saudi Arabia.

February 15, 1991: Iraq offers to leave Kuwait in exchange of an Israeli pull out from the occupied territories, a Syrian withdrawal from Lebanon, and the departure of coalition forces from the region. President Bush calls the offer a "cruel hoax."

February 16, 1991: The US VII Army Corps moves into positions in preparation for a ground assault on the Iraqis. Four Iraqi Scud are fired at the northern and southern regions of Israel.

228

February 17, 1991: UMA countries, Jordan, and Iran welcome the Iraqi statement as a positive step. The British Royal Airforce bombs a market in Fallujah.

February 18, 1991: Foreign Minister 'Aziz and President Gorbachev meet in Moscow. A Soviet plan to end the war is articulated. The USS Tripoli and the USS Princeton vessels are hit by Iraqi mines in the Gulf.

February 19, 1991: Italy endorses the Soviet plan. The French government announces a cease-fire plan which is rejected by the United States. Iraq launches a Scud missile on Israel.

February 20, 1991: King Fahd declares that there should be no agreement with Iraq unless it accepts to unconditionally withdraw and pay reparations. An engagement between an Iraqi division and the US 1st Cavalry Division occurs at Wadi al-Batin in Saudi Arabia. The Americans pull back with 3 dead and 9 wounded. Iraqi casualties are reported.

February 21, 1991: Iraq accepts the Soviet peace plan including an explicit statement of withdrawal. Three Iraqi missiles strike King Khalid Military City in Saudi Arabia.

February 22, 1991: President Bush rejects the Soviet plan and sets a noon (Washington time), February 23 deadline for Iraq to begin its withdrawal from Kuwait. In Moscow, the Kremlin announces a refined plan agreed to by Iraq including an immediate and unconditional withdrawal. US marines begin infiltrating into Kuwait at various locations. 580 oil wells are set on fire in Kuwait. Four Iraqi Scuds are aimed at US positions in Saudi Arabia.

February 23, 1991: The Iraqis announce that, in compliance with the Soviet plan, they agree to withdraw from Kuwait. In an 83-minute telephone conversation, Soviet President Gorbachev asks President Bush to delay the ground offensive since "an acceptable compromise" has been reached with Baghdad. Bush declines the Soviet plea. An Iraqi Scud missile hits the central part of Israel ten minutes before the ultimatum deadline.

February 24, 1991: At 4:08 a.m. (Dhahran time), US-led coalition divisions attack Iraqi positions in Kuwait advancing on two axes. Sixteen-inch guns of the USS

Wisconsin and USS Missouri fire at Iraqi positions inside Kuwait. The ground war codenamed Desert Sabre formally begins. The Soviet Union, Iran, and Jordan express their regret regarding the allied offensive.

February 25, 1991: 1,500 sorties are staged to provide air cover to the coalition ground advance. The Iraqis stage a counterattack on the US 1st Marine Division. The Soviet Union present a new peace plan. Iraq's Revolutionary Command Council announces that it is ordering its soldiers to withdraw from Kuwait as part of its acceptance of UN Security Council resolution 660. In a radio speech, President Hussayn declares that the withdrawal has already begun. He claims a "dignified" victory. An Iraqi Scud missile is fired at the southern part of Israel.

February 26, 1991: The United States reject the new Soviet peace initiative. At 8:23 p.m., an Iraqi Scud missile hits a warehouse at the al-Khobar barracks in eastern Saudi Arabia housing American troops. It kills 28 soldiers and wounds 100. Around 4:00 p.m., the US VII Corps fights the Tawakalna Division of the Iraqi Republican Guard at the "Battle of the 73rd Easting." The Soviet Union proposes a cease-fire.

February 27, 1991: In a letter to the UN Security Council, Iraq accepts the cease-fire and announces that it has completed its withdrawal from Kuwait. The US 1st Armored Division battles the al-Madina al-Mounawara Division of the Republican Guard.

February 28, 1991: A cease-fire taking effect at 8:00 a.m. (Kuwaiti time) is ordered by the United States.

March 1, 1991: Cease-fire proceedings between Iraqi and coalition military representatives are delayed.

March 2, 1991: A serious engagement takes place near the Rumaila oil field between the US 24th Mechanized Infantry Division and some 200 tanks from the Mechanized Infantry Division of the Republican Guard Hammurabi Division. The UN Security Council adopts resolution 686 noting the suspension of offensive combat operations by the coalition.

March 3, 1991: Iraqi military commanders, Lieutenant-General Salah Abu Mahmoud, III Corps commander, and Lieutenant-General Sultan Hashem Ahmad, Deputy-Chief of Staff at the Iraqi Ministry of Defense, meet with US General and coalition commander Norman Schwarzkopf and Khaled bin Sultan of Saudi Arabia at Safwan, three miles from the Iraq-Kuwait border to finalize cease-fire conditions.

March 4, 1991: In Iraq, Kurdish and Shiite rebellions start almost simultaneously in Ranya, Basra, Najaf, Karbala, and in northern districts.

March 5, 1991: The UN Security Council adopts resolution 788 demanding an end to the repression of Iraq's Kurdish and Shiite populations. Iraq releases the last 35 coalition POWs.

March 7, 1991: Iranian President Rafsanjani calls on Hussayn to share power with opposition groups.

March 8, 1991: Iraq releases 1,100 Kuwaiti prisoners.

March 9, 1991: The Iraqi army launches counterattacks on the Shiite insurgents.

March 11-12, 1991: Representatives of various exiled Iraqi opposition parties gather in Damascus to discuss ways to overthrow Saddam Hussayn's regime.

March 14, 1991: Iraqi governmental forces retake the city of Karbala. In the north, the Kurdish rebellion spreads to 12 cities including Irbil, Dohuk, Kirkuk, and Sulaymaniya. The Emir of Kuwait, Sheikh Jaber Ahmad al-Sabah, returns to Kuwait-City.

March 17, 1991: Iraqi governmental forces retake the city of Najaf. Allied and Iraqi military commanders meet in Safwan to discuss further cease-fire dispositions.

March 20, 1991: In the first aerial combat since the cease-fire, a US F-15 jet shoots down an Iraqi Sukhoi SU-20 fighter jet. The Iraqi Parliament Speaker, Saadi Mahdi Saleh, accuses Iran of supporting the Shiite and Kurdish revolts.

March 22, 1991: An Iraqi SU-22 is shot down by a US jet over northern Iraq.

March 28, 1991: The Iraqi army retakes Kirkuk.

March 30, 1991: The Kurds begin their exodus to the mountains bordering Iraq with Turkey.

April 3, 1991: The Iraqi army retakes the last city held by Kurd rebels, Sulaymaniya. The UN Security Council adopts resolution 687 which *inter alia* sets up a commission to demarcate the Iraq-Kuwait border and provides for a complete program of ballistic, chemical, biological, and nuclear demilitarization of Iraq.

April 5, 1991: The UN Security Council adopts resolution 688 demanding that Iraq allows humanitarian to the Kurdish refugees.

April 6, 1991: Iraq accepts UN resolution 687 formally ending the war. It agrees to pay war reparations to Kuwait and have its arsenal of weapons of mass destruction dismantled.

April 8, 1991: The US forces in Kuwait begin their withdrawal pulling back into Saudi Arabia. Secretary Baker visits Kurdish refugees in Turkish Kurdistan.

April 9, 1991: The UN Security Council adopts resolution 689 providing for the review of the sanctions on Iraq every 60 days.

April 11, 1991: 1,400 UN peacekeepers are positioned to monitor the cease-fire on the Iraq-Kuwait border.

April 16, 1991: The US announce that troops will be sent to set protection camps for the Kurds of northern Iraq. The operation is dubbed Provide Comfort.

April 19, 1991: Two Iraqi Generals meet with the US Commander in charge of operation Provide Comfort in Irbil to discuss arrangements for the establishment of safe heavens for the Kurdish refugees.

May 2, 1991: UN Secretary General Javier Pérez De Cuellar establishes the Iraq Kuwait Boundary Demarcation Commission (IKDBC) composed of five members including an Iraqi, Riyad al-Qaysi, and a Kuwaiti, Tariq al-Razzuqi.

May 9, 1991: Iraqi anti-aircraft artillery opens fire on a US A-6E Intruder attack plane northwest of Mosul.

May 15, 1991: 500,000 Kurdish refugees, who had fled to the border with Turkey, return home.

May 19, 1991: 628 Palestinians and Iraqis are tried in Kuwait for helping the Iraqi army during the Emirate's occupation.

May 20, 1991: The UN Security Council adopts resolution 692 establishing a damage fund for persons and entities to whom Iraq is to pay reparations.

July 15, 1991: US troops withdraw from northern Iraq after completing their operation of aid to Kurdish refugees.

June 17, 1991: UN Security Council adopts resolutions 699 and 700 specifying the authority of the UN Special Commission and the International Atomic Energy Agency (IAEA) for the destruction of Iraq's mass destruction weapons and requiring Iraq to pay the cost of eliminating the weapons.

June 28, 1991: Iraqi soldiers fire warning shots at a UN inspection team near a nuclear weapons facility.

August 5, 1991: Turkish army F-4 and F-104 bombers fly 92 sorties over northern Iraq to attack PKK rebels.

August 15, 1991: The UN Security Council adopts resolutions 705, establishing the level of Iraqi compensation; 706, authorizing Iraq to sell up to $1.6 billion worth of oil in a six-month period; and 707, demanding that Iraq fully cooperates with UN inspectors.

August 26, 1991: Iraqi authorities report that more than 14,000 children have died because of the lack of drugs since the United Nations imposed the trade embargo.

September 19, 1991: The UN Security Council adopts resolution 712 establishing conditions for the transfer of non-embargoed goods to Iraq.

September 23, 1991: Iraqi soldiers confiscate research documents from UN inspectors.

September 24, 1991: Iraqi soldiers detain UN inspectors after they refuse to surrender documents seized at the Iraqi Atomic Commission in Baghdad.

September 27, 1991: Iraq releases the inspectors after the UN agrees that a joint inventory of the documents be made.

October 4, 1991: The IAEA announces that it would have taken Iraq until 1995 to acquire the ability to produce a nuclear weapon.

October 11, 1991: The UN Security Council adopts resolution 715 demanding Iraq's full compliance to cease-fire conditions and ordering it to cooperate with the Special Commission and the IAEA.

233

October 26, 1991: The Turkish airforce conducts a retaliatory operation against PKK elements in northern Iraq.

January 19, 1992: *The New York Times* publishes information relating to a Saudi-sponsored coup attempt against Saddam Hussayn.

February 21-28, 1992: Iraq resists the destruction of equipment allegedly used in the construction of ballistic missiles.

March 20, 1992: Iraq accepts UN demands to destroy ballistic missile equipment and chemical data.

May 19, 1992: Elections are held in Kurdistan resulting in a virtual dead heat between Massoud Barzani's KDP (44.58%) and Jalal Talabani's PUK (44.33%).

July 5, 1992: In Baghdad, UN weapons inspectors are denied access to the Iraqi Agriculture Industry building. They begin a vigil outside the premises that lasts three weeks.

July 26, 1992: UN inspectors are allowed to enter and search unsuccessfully the Iraqi Agriculture Ministry.

August 9, 1992: The Iraqi government imposes a curfew in Najaf.

August 27, 1992: The United States, Britain, and France declare a no-fly zone below the 32nd parallel inside Iraq threatening to shoot down any plane that violates it. The operation is dubbed Southern Watch. Calling it a violation of international law, Iraq rejects the idea and vows to oppose it.

September 10, 1992: An Iraqi jet is shot down by a US aircraft inside the no-fly zone.

October 2, 1992: The UN Security Council adopts resolution 778 which provides for the seizure of frozen Iraqi accounts by UN member states and releasing them to the UN to pay for UN-related expenses in Iraq.

October 23, 1992: 5,000 Turkish troops penetrate inside Iraqi territory to conduct raids against PKK bases.

November 25, 1992: The UN Security Council rejects Iraq's demands for an end to the economic embargo.

December 27, 1992: At 10:20 a.m. (Iraqi time), a US Air Force F-16 shoots down an Iraqi MiG-25 fighter aircraft in southern Iraq. Iraq says it will respond "in a suitable manner at an appropriate time."

December 29, 1992: Iraqi jets fly into the southern no-fly zone.

December 30, 1992: Iraqi warplanes penetrate into the southern no-fly zone anew.

January 3, 1993: Iraq moves Soviet-made SA-2 and SA-3 surface-to-air missiles in the areas patrolled by US jets.

January 6, 1993: The United States and their allies set a 48-hour deadline for Iraq to dismantle its antiaircraft missiles threatening US planes patrolling southern Iraq.

January 7, 1993: Iraq rebuffs the ultimatum and pledges to assert its sovereignty throughout its territory.

January 9, 1993: The United States announce that the Iraqis have moved their missiles north of the 32nd parallel.

January 10, 1993: Iraq denies that it has moved the missiles and it bars a UN plane carrying weapons inspectors from landing into the country by refusing to give it clearance. 200 Iraqi troops penetrate in Kuwait and seize four Chinese-made Silkworm missiles and other weapons from a depot.

January 13, 1993: At 6:45 p.m. (Iraqi time), 114 US and allied planes bomb Iraqi missile sites at Tallil Air Base, al-Amara, Najaf, and Samawa during a 30-minute strike. There are 19 dead. 1,250 American ground troops are sent to Kuwait to deter further Iraqi incursions. Israel is on alert.

January 15, 1993: The Bush administration calls the attack a success and announces that one third of the targets were missed during the air raid and that an apartment building near Basra was hit by a stray 2,000-pound bomb. Iraq denounces the US action.

January 17, 1993: Two Iraqi MiG-23 are shot down in northern Iraq by US F-16s.

January 18, 1993: US warships in the Gulf and the Red Sea fire 45 Tomahawk cruise missiles at the Zaafaraniya industrial complex eight miles southeast of Baghdad. One of the missiles hits the Rashid Hotel in downtown Baghdad. 21 persons are killed. Near

Mosul, a US jet attacks a ground radar station and downs an Iraqi MiG-25 fighter plane. Kuwait is on alert. In Washington, Bill Clinton is sworn in as President.

January 19, 1993: US, British, and French jets fire on Iraqi missile batteries around Mosul, Najaf, Samawah, and Tallil. Allied and Iraqi fighter planes engage in hot pursuits above the 36th parallel. Iraq declares a unilateral cease-fire as a goodwill gesture to the incoming Clinton administration. Iraq also decides to allow UN observers to fly into Iraq.

January 21, 1993: 2 American warplanes attack a radar for an Iraqi surface-to-air missile battery. Baghdad calls it a provocation.

January 22, 1993: An American F-4G jet fires 2 missiles at an air-defense battery 15 miles east of Mosul.

January 23, 1993: A US Navy plane bombs an Iraqi position around Nasiriya in southern Iraq.

January 25, 1993: UN inspectors resume their work in Iraq.

February 1, 1993: Iraq announces that it is ordering all surveillance radars shut down to preserve the cease-fire it declared ten days earlier.

February 3, 1993: Iraqi anti-aircraft batteries hit French F-1 jets.

February 5, 1993: The UN Security Council adopts resolution 806 which calls for a phased deployment of additional UN troops into the demilitarized zone between Kuwait and Iraq.

February 24, 1993: Iraqi artillery aims its guns at the helicopters of two UN inspectors interrupting their search for Scud missiles.

April 9, 1993: Iraqi antiaircraft batteries fire on three US F-16 jets and one F-4G patrolling the no-fly zone who drop bombs in reply. One Iraqi soldier is wounded.

April 4-16, 1993: Former President Bush visits Kuwait.

April 18, 1993: An American F-4G fires on an Iraqi radar south of Mosul outside the northern no-fly zone.

May 7, 1993: Kuwait claims that it has uncovered an Iraqi assassination plot against President Bush that was supposed to take place during his April visit to the Emirate.

May 20, 1993: US jets patrolling the no-fly zones inside Iraq are fired upon by antiaircraft ground positions. Having held 82 meetings, the Iraq Kuwait Border Demarcation Commission (IKBDC) completes its work.

June 10, 1993: The Iraqi authorities impede UNSCOM efforts to install cameras and other monitoring equipment intended to supervise Iraq's weapons programs.

June 26, 1993: Alleging an Iraqi involvement in an assassination plot against President George Bush during his mid-April trip to Kuwait, President Clinton orders a cruise missile attack against the Iraqi intelligence headquarters in Baghdad. 23 Tomahawk missiles are launched from US Navy destroyers and cruisers in the Red Sea and the Gulf.

June 29, 1993: A US warplane fires a missile at an Iraqi artillery site near Basra.

July 19, 1993: Iraq agrees to allow the UN to monitor its military industries.

August 20, 1993: An Iraqi battery is bombed by two US F-15E planes after it fired two missiles at them.

September 1, 1993: Iraq reports that 300,000 Iraqis have died as a result of medical shortages caused by the UN blockade.

November 11, 1993: Iraqis and Kuwaitis exchange heavy fire at the 'Abdali observation post near the border.

November 16, 1993: 250 Iraqis penetrate into Kuwait with 60 vehicles.

November 20, 1993: 400 Iraqis enter Kuwait at the 103 and 104 boundary pillars. One Kuwaiti policeman is injured.

November 27, 1993: Iraq accepts UN Security Council resolution 715.

February 28, 1994: An UNSCOM investigation reports that, contrary to US Department of State allegations, there was no evidence that the Iraqi army has used chemical weapons against the southern Shiites.

March 26, 1994: Iraq informs UNSCOM that it is accepting long-term monitoring of its weapons of mass destruction under UN Security Council resolutions 618 and 715.

April 14, 1994: North of Irbil, two American F-15C fighter planes accidentally shoot down two US Black Hawk army helicopters carrying a team of US and allied officials. 26 persons are killed.

June 22, 1994: The UN Special Commission completes destruction of the Iraqi chemical weapons stock.

August 23, 1994: Turkish fighter planes bomb PKK bases inside Iraq.

August 28, 1994: In Amman, King Hussayn and Turkish President Suleyman Demirel ask that the embargo on Iraq be lifted.

October 6, 1994: Iraq issues an ultimatum to the international community, setting October 10 as a deadline for lifting sanctions and threatening to discontinue cooperation with UNSCOM.

October 7, 1994: Iraqi troops, including 14,000 men of the Hammurabi division, part of the Republican Guard, are deployed near the Kuwait border.

October 8, 1994: 4,000 US Marine and Navy forces along with Patriot missiles are dispatched to Kuwait. Dubbed Vigilant Warrior, the US operation is backed by 200 fighter planes and the potential deployment of 150,000 military personnel. Iraqi forces move to within 12 miles of the border.

October 10, 1994: Iraq announces that it is withdrawing its troops from threatening positions.

October 13, 1994: Iraq and Russia announce that they have reached an agreement that would lead to an Iraqi recognition of Kuwait. The announcement is made in Baghdad by Russian Foreign Minister, Andrei Kozyrev, and President Saddam Hussayn.

October 15, 1994: UN Security Council adopts resolution 949 demanding that Iraq withdraws its troops and, in the future, refrains from deploying them in the southern part of the country.

October 16, 1994: Iraqi Minister of Culture and Information Hamed Hamadi announces that the units have moved to rear positions.

November 6, 1994: Iran carries out a missile attack against an Iranian rebel base in Iraq.

November 8, 1994: Iraqi Deputy-Prime Minister Tariq 'Aziz delivers a letter to Russian President Boris Yeltsin concerning Iraqi recognition of Kuwait's borders and sovereignty.

November 9, 1994: Iran launches an air strike against Kurdish rebels in northern Iraq.

November 10, 1994: In the course of a visit to Baghdad by Russian Foreign Minister Kozyrev, the Iraqi Parliament votes to recognize the independence and territorial integrity of Kuwait.

January 6, 1995: Receiving the official visit of Deputy-Prime Minister Tariq 'Aziz, French Minister for Foreign Affairs Alain Juppé announces that France is resuming its relations with Iraq by opening an interest section at the Romanian embassy in Baghdad. Meanwhile, in Baghdad, President Saddam Hussayn declares that the Second Gulf War was not a success for the West.

March 13, 1995: William Barloon and David Daliberti, two American citizens working for the McDonnell Douglas Corporation, are detained as they stray in Iraq. Days later, they are sentenced to 8 years in prison on charges of spying.

March 20, 1995: A major military operation is conducted by the Turkish army in the north of Iraq to curb Kurdish guerrilla attacks. Penetrating some 40 kilometers inside Iraqi territory, the Turks kill around 200 members of the PKK. The operation lasts three weeks with a final death toll of 550.

April 10, 1995: UNSCOM reports to the UN Security Council that Iraq has not fully disclosed its biological weapons program. The special commission declares that 17 of 22 tons of biological weapons material have not been accounted for.

May 17, 1995: Following an uprising by the Doulaymi tribe in the al-Anbar province – sparked by the execution of one of its members, General Mohammad Madhloum al-Doulaymi accused of plotting a coup – a series of clashes occur between governmental forces and Doulaymi tribesmen. Some fifty persons are killed and 150 casualties are reported.

June 14, 1995: Led by General Turki Ismael al-Doulaymi, a member of the Doulaymi tribe, a rebellion is attempted by the July 14th Army Division in the Abu Ghrayb section of Baghdad. It is countered and put down by the troops of Saddam Hussayn's son, Qusay. There are 150 dead.

June 19, 1995: Rolf Ekeus, head of the UN Special Commission, releases a document indicating that the only stumbling block preventing the lifting of the embargo on Iraq is the missing information about the Iraqi biological program.

July 5, 1995: Rolf Ekeus reports to the UN Security Council that Iraq has acknowledged that it had developed an offensive biological weapons program but that the program had been dismantled in October of 1990. A spokesman for the US Department of State declares that 17 tons of biological material have not yet been accounted for.

July 7, 1995: Turkish forces launch a strike against Kurdish guerrillas in northern Iraq.

July 17, 1995: The two Americans detained in March and convicted to 8 years in prison are released after being granted a pardon by President Hussayn.

July 19, 1995: Iraq's Foreign Minister, Mohammad Sa'id al-Sahaf, declares that the embargo will be brought to an end the following September. He sets an August 31 deadline for UN inspectors to complete their mission and report to the UN Iraq's compliance with the Security Council's resolution. Iraq agrees to destroy its missile engine manufacturing equipment.

August 8, 1995: Former Iraqi Minister of Industry and Military Industrialization and son-in-law of President Hussayn, Lieutenant-General Hussayn Kamil Hassan al-Majid, defects to Jordan with his brother, Saddam Kamil, head of special security forces and also son-in-law of the Iraqi President. Upon arrival in Amman, the Kamil brothers and their wives, President Hussayn's daughters Raghad and Rana, ask for asylum which is granted by King Hussayn.

August 11, 1995: In Amman, US intelligence officers debrief Hussayn Kamil and his brother.

August 12, 1995: Hussayn Kamil holds an hour-long press conference in Amman. He calls for a military and civilian toppling of Saddam Hussayn and urges Iraqis to prepare for a major change.

August 15, 1995: The United States start building up its forces in the Gulf moving the USS Roosevelt aircraft carrier to the region. The operation is dubbed Infinite Moonlight. US Assistant Secretary of State Robert Pelletreau and Special Assistant to the President Mark Parris arrive in the Jordanian capital to meet with the Iraqi defector.

August 17, 1995: Iraq admits that it had produced a Nuclear Biological Chemical (NBC) program.

August 18, 1995: Joint Jordanian-American military maneuvers are held with 2,500 marines participating. Iraq denies the US allegations that it is moving troops in the direction of Kuwait. The United States dispatch 1,400 troops to Kuwait.

August 23, 1995: In a televised speech, Jordan's King Hussayn accuses Iraqi leader Saddam Hussayn of contemplating a new invasion of Kuwait and Saudi Arabia.

August 24, 1995: Former King Faysal II's cousin and heir to the Iraqi throne, 'Ali ibn al-Hussayn, calls for the restoration of the Hashemite monarchy in Baghdad.

October 1, 1995: Iraq is reported to have moved 100 tanks and armored personnel in the region near its border with Kuwait.

October 2, 1995: In Kuwait, 1600 marines conduct maneuvers 15 miles from the Iraqi border in response to rumored military movements by the Iraqi army.

October 15, 1995: A presidential referendum is held in Iraq with 7.5 million Iraqis voting. Saddam Hussayn is plebicited as President for a term of seven years with 99.96% of the vote.

October 16, 1995: President Sheikh Zaid Bin Sultan al-Nahayan of the United Arab Emirates calls for the lifting of UN sanctions on Iraq.

October 18, 1995: Qatar supports the UAE's call for the lifting of the UN embargo on Iraq.

December 14, 1995: The Iraqi Ministry for Foreign Affairs approves a US mission of 11 military officers and 4 Red Cross officials to search for the remains of Lieutenant Commander Michael Scott Speicher who was shot down by the Iraqis during the Gulf war.

January 6, 1996: The Iraqi government decrees economic austerity measures to cope with soaring inflation and shortages caused by sanctions.

January 19, 1996: Iraq agrees to meet with United Nations on proposal to sell $2 billion in oil for 180 days to buy food and medicine.

February 19, 1996: Hussayn Kamil announces his intention to return to Iraq with his family.

February 20, 1996: Hussayn Kamil and his family return to Iraq. They are met at Traybil, on the Iraq-Jordan border, by Saddam Hussayn's son, 'Uday.

February 23, 1996: Iraqi authorities announce that, during a family feud, Kamil and his brother were killed after being divorced of their wives. Also killed were Kamil's other brother Hakim and his cousins Tair ibn Abdelghafour and Ahmed ibn Abdelghafour, both of them high-ranking officers from the special security services of President Hussayn, the *jihaz al-khass* headed by Qusay Saddam Hussayn.

February 29, 1996: Iraqi troops conduct a series of raids on Kurdish localities near Irbil and Kirkuk..

March 8, 1996: In Baghdad, a UN weapons inspection team is barred from entering an Iraqi government building suspected of containing military records.

March 9, 1996: After an 18-hour stand-off, the UN inspectors are allowed into the site, but the materials have been removed.

March 11, 1996: Following a 12-hour stand-off, UN inspectors are granted access to a Republican Guard base in the southern part of the country.

March 20, 1996: UNSCOM Special Envoy Rolf Ekeus declares to the US Senate that Iraq is in possession of 16 mobile-launch biological missiles.

March 24, 1996: For the first time since April 1, 1989, legislative elections are held in Iraq. 689 candidates run for 250 seats.

May 13, 1996: 700 Kurds are arrested in Kirkuk.

May 20, 1996: After months of negotiations, the United Nations and Iraq agree on a plan allowing Iraq to sell $2 billion worth of oil in a renewable six-month period.

June 11, 1996: UN inspectors are prevented from entering a military site in the Baghdad area.

June 12, 1996: The UN inspectors are denied entry at three other military sites. The UN Security Council adopts resolution 1060 condemning Iraq's denial of access.

June 15, 1996: The inspectors leave without gaining access to the sites.

July 25, 1996: 2,000 soldiers suspected of plotting a coup, including 200 officers of the Republican Guard, are arrested by the Iraqi government.

August 17, 1996: Supported by 1,200 Iranian troops that crossed into Iraq to support him, Patriotic Union of Kurdistan (PUK) leader Jalal Talabani launches an attack against his rival Massoud Barzani, head of the Kurdistan Democratic Party (KDP).

August 22, 1996: Barzani sends a letter to President Saddam Hussayn requesting help in his fight against Talabani's PUK.

August 31, 1996: Fighting alongside KDP guerrillas, 35,000 Iraqi troops regain most of the northern part of the country capturing the cities of Irbil and Sulaymaniya.

September 1, 1996: UN secretary-general Boutros Boutros-Ghali announces a delay in implementing the oil-for-food deal.

September 3, 1996: US F-117s and B-52s attack Iraqi air-defense sites at Tallil airfield and around Nasiriyah in the southern part of the country. 27 Tomahawk and AGM-86 missiles are fired during a US raid dubbed as Desert Strike. For the first time since 1991, the Saudi government refuses to allow the United States to use their bases in the kingdom for launching the attacks on Iraq. The US extend the southern no-fly zone from the 32nd to the 33rd parallel, some 55 miles north. This measure and the attack on Iraq are criticized by the vast majority of the international community, except Kuwait, Great-Britain, Germany, and Canada.

September 4, 1996: At dawn, US airplanes conduct a second strike at Iraqi military sites in the south and around Baghdad. 17 Tomahawk are fired. At noon, 2 Iraqi Mig-21 defy the new extended no-fly zone. Later, an Iraqi S-8 mobile missile battery targets a US F-16 jet. Half of the 44 missiles launched on the two-day operation fail to reach their targets.

September 5-6, 1996: Iraq fires SA-6 surface-to-air missiles on US planes patrolling the southern no-fly zone.

September 13, 1996: Baghdad announces that it is suspending its firing of missiles at US planes.

October 13, 1996: The PUK launches a counter-offensive to recapture Sulaymanieh.

October 18, 1996: The KDP and the Iraqi army repulse the PUK offensive.

November 2, 1996: A US F-16 jet patrolling the southern no-fly zone fires a missile at an Iraqi radar site.

November 3, 1996: An American jet fires another missile at an Iraqi radar site.

November 25, 1996: Iraq and the United Nations announce that they have reached a final agreement on the oil-for-food deal which had originally been proposed in the spring of 1995. Most of the oil will flow from the Turkish pipeline, and another amount will be shipped from the Iraqi port of Mina al-Bakr.

December 9, 1996: UN secretary-general Boutros-Ghali allows Iraq to make limited oil sales under a closely monitored deal.

December 10, 1996: Iraq begins selling oil in accordance with UN Security Council resolution 986. The plan permits Iraq to sell up to $2 billion in oil over a six month renewable period of time, roughly 650,000 barrels a day.

December 13, 1996: President Saddam Hussayn's eldest son, 'Uday, is shot at and severely injured by unknown assailants in Baghdad.

December 18, 1997: UNSCOM leader Rolf Ekeus reports that Iraq prevented him from removing 130 Scud missile engines an that it is still hiding 25 operational missiles.

December 27, 1996: France announces that it will no longer take part in Operation Provide Comfort.

April 9, 1997: Iraq violates the US-imposed no-fly zone in the south by transporting citizens to Saudi Arabia for the annual pilgrimage to Mecca.

April 22, 1997: The Iraqis violate the flight restriction again by transporting the pilgrims back to Iraq via helicopters.

May 15-30, 1997: The Turkish army conducts a major offensive against PKK rebels based in northern Iraq.

June 4, 1997: The UN Security Council renews the oil-for-food deal for another six months.

June 21, 1997: The UN Security Council threatens to impose new sanctions on Iraq if it does not cooperate with UN inspectors by October 11, 1997.

Bibliography

For names starting with al, bin, de, van, or von, refer to the second component.

Articles

Abrams, Philip. "Notes on the Difficulty of Studying the State." *The Journal of Historical Sociology* 1, 1 (March 1988), pp. 58-89.

Abu Khalil, As'ad. "*Al-Jabriyyah* in the Political Discourse of Jamal 'Abd Al-Nasir and Saddam Husayn: The Rationalization of Defeat." *The Muslim World* 3-4 (July-October 1994), pp. 240-257.

Ahmad, Youssef Ahmad. "The Dialectics of Domestic Environment and Role Performance: The Foreign Policy of Iraq," in Bahgat Korany and A.E.H. Dessouki, eds. *The Foreign Policies of Arab States*. Boulder, Colorado: Westview Press, 1991, pp. 186-215.

Almond, Gabriel A. "The Return to the State." *American Political Science Review* 82 (1988), pp. 853-874.

Anderson, Lisa. "The State in the Middle East and North Africa." *Comparative Politics* 19 (October 1987), pp. 1-18.

Andriole, Stephen J., Jonathan Wilkenfeld, and Gerald W. Hopple. "A Framework for the Comparative Analysis of Foreign Policy Behavior." *International Studies Quarterly* 19, 2 (June 1975), pp. 160-198.

Anonymous. "La Nomenklatura Irakienne ou l'Organisation du Pouvoir en Irak." *Les Cahiers de l'Orient* 8-9, 4 (1987-1988), pp. 341-351.

Axelgard, Frederick W. "Iraq: The Postwar Political Setting." *American-Arab Affairs* 28, (Spring 1989), pp. 30-37.

Ball, George. "The Gulf Crisis." *The New York Review of Books* (December 6, 1990), pp. 14-17

Baram, Amatzia. "Saddam Hussein: A Political Profile." *The Jerusalem Quarterly* 17 (Fall 1980), pp. 115-144.

_____. "Qawmiyya and Wataniyya in Ba'thi Iraq: The Search for a New Balance." *Middle Eastern Studies* 19, 2 (1983), pp. 188-200.

_____. "The Ruling Elite in Ba'thi Iraq 1968-1986: The Changing Features of a Collective Profile." *International Journal of Middle Eastern Studies*, 24 (November 1988), pp. 447-493.

_____. "Saddam Hussein," in Bernard Reich, ed. *Political Leaders of the Contemporary Middle East and North Africa - A Biographical Dictionary.* New York, New York: Greenwood Press, 1990, pp. 240-249.

_____. "Baathi Iraq and Hashimite Jordan: From Hostility to Alignment." *Middle East Journal* 45, 1 (Winter 1991), pp. 51-70.

_____. "From Radicalism to Radical Pragmatism: The Shi'ite Fundamentalist Opposition Movements of Iraq," in James Piscatori, ed. *Islamic Fundamentalism and the Gulf Crisis.* Chicago, Illinois: American Academy of Arts and Sciences, 1991, pp. 28-51.

_____. "The Iraqi Invasion of Kuwait: Decision-Making in Baghdad," in Amatzia Baram and Barry Rubin, eds. *Iraq's Road to War*, New York, New York: St. Martin's Press, 1993, pp. 5-36.

_____. "The Future of Ba'thist Iraq: Power Structure, Challenges and Prospects," in Robert B. Satloff, ed. *The Politics of Change in the Middle East.* Boulder, Colorado: Westview Press, 1993, pp. 31-62.

_____. "Calculation and Miscalculation in Baghdad," in Alex Danchev and Dan Keohane, eds. *International Perspectives on the Gulf Conflict 1990-91*, New York, New York: St. Martin's Press, 1994, pp. 23-58.

_____. "Neo-Tribalism in Iraq: Saddam Hussein's Tribal Policies 1991-96." *International Journal of Middle East Studies* 29, 1 (February 1997), pp. 1-31.

Batatu, Hanna. "Political Power and Social Structure in Syria and Iraq," in Sami Farsoun, ed. *Arab Society*. London: Croom-Helm, 1985, pp. 34-47.

Bayart, Jean-François, ed. *La Greffe de l'État*. Paris: Karthala, 1997.

Bermudez, Joseph S. "Iraqi Missile Operations During Desert Storm." *Jane's Soviet Intelligence Review* 3, 3 (March 1991) and 3, 4 (May 1991).

Block, Fred. "Marxist Theories of the State in World System Analysis," in Barbara H. Kaplan, ed. *Social Change in the Capitalist World Economy*, Beverly Hills, California: Sage, 1978, pp. 395-403.

Boulding, Kenneth E. "National Images and International Systems." *Journal of Conflict Resolution* 3, 2 (June 1959), pp. 120-131.

Brzezinski, Zbigniew, Brent Scowcroft, and Richard Murphy. "Differentiated Containment." *Foreign Affairs* 76, 3 (May/June 1997), pp. 20-30.

Cainkar, Louise. "The Gulf War, Sanctions and the Lives of Iraqi Women." *Arab Studies Quarterly* 15, 2 (Spring 1993), pp. 15-51.

Chabry, A. and L. Chabry. "L'Irak et l'Émergence de Nouveaux Rapports Politiques Inter-Arabes." *Maghreb-Machrek* 88 (April-June 1980), pp. 5-24.

Conyers, John. "The Patriot Myth: Caveat Emptor." *Arms Control Today* (November 1992), pp. 3-10.

Dam, Nikolas Van. "Middle Eastern Political Clichés: 'Takriti' and 'Sunni Rule' in Iraq, 'Alawi Rule' in Syria: A Critical Appraisal." *Orient* 20, 1 (1980), pp. 42-57.

Dawisha, Adeed I. "Invoking the Spirit of Arabism: Islam in the Foreign Policy of Saddam's Iraq," in Adeed I. Dawisha, ed. *Islam in Foreign Policy*, Cambridge, Massachusetts: Cambridge University Press, 1983, pp. 112-128.

Dunn, Michael Collins. "A Formidable Opponent: Stereotypes and Iraq's Capabilities," in H.M. Amery and W.A. Madhoun, eds. *Shaping the Gulf: In Search of Order - Readings and Documents on the Iraq-Kuwait Crisis*, London, Canada: Canadian Institute for Policy Research and Analysis, 1992, pp. 465-467.

Errachidi, Ahmad. "Le Système Arabe de Sécurité Collective et la Crise du Golfe." *Annuaire de L'Afrique du Nord* 31 (1992), pp. 117-126.

Fahmi, Ali. "The Basic Sociological Features of Iraq: A Simplified Sociological Map." *National Review of Social Sciences* 18, 1-2 (1981), pp. 63-92.

Fandy, Mamoun. "Tribe vs. Islam: The Post-Colonial Arab State and the Democratic Imperative." *Middle East Policy* 3, 2 (August 1994), pp. 40-51.

Farouk-Sluglett, Marion. "'Socialist' Iraq 1963-1978: Towards a Reappraisal." *Orient* 23, 2, (1982), pp. 206-219.

_____. "Pouvoir et Responsabilité: Hégémonie Américaine et États Arabes au Moyen-Orient de l'Après Guerre du Golfe." *Stratégie II*, 64-65 (July-December 1993), pp. 155-181.

Freedman, Lawrence and Efraim Karsh. "How Kuwait Was Won: Strategy in the Gulf War." *International Security* 16, 2 (Fall 1991), pp. 5-41.

Ghadbian, Najib. "Some Remarks on the Distorting Literature about Saddam Hussein." *Political Psychology* 13, 4 (December 1992), pp. 783-789.

Good, Robert C. "State-Building as a determinant of Foreign Policy in the New States," in Lawrence W. Martin, ed. *Neutralism and Nonalignment*, New York, New York: Praeger, 1962, pp. 3-12.

Gunter, Michael M. "The Foreign Policy of the Iraqi Kurds." *Journal of South Asian and Middle Eastern Studies* 20, 3 (Spring 1997), pp. 1-19.

Hagan, Joe D. "Domestic Political Systems and War Proneness." *Mershon International Studies Review* 38 (1994), pp. 183-207.

Haj, Samira. *The Making of Iraq, 1900-1963*. Albany, New York: State University of New York Press, 1997.

Halliday, Fred. "The Gulf War 1990-1991 and the Study of International Relations." *Review of International Studies* 20, 2 (1994), pp. 109-130.

Heidenrich, John G. "How Many Iraqis Died?" *Foreign Policy* 90 (Spring 1993), pp. 108-125.

Hersh, Seymour. "Clinton and the FBI: How Real was Iraq's 'Plot' to Kill Bush?" *The New Yorker* (November 1, 1993), pp. 80-92.

Hovsepian, Nubar. "Competing Identities in the Arab World. *Journal of International Affairs* 49, 1 (Summer 1995), pp. 1-24.

Hudson, Michael. "The Middle East," in James N. Rosenau, Kenneth W. Thompson, and Gavin Boyd, eds. *World Politics - An Introduction*, New York, New York: The Free Press, 1976, pp. 466-500.

Isenberg, David. "Desert Storm Redux?" *The Middle East Journal* 47, 3 (Summer 1993), pp. 429-443.

Ishow, Habib. "Les Raisons du Conflit entre l'Irak et le Koweit." *Annuaire de l'Afrique du Nord* 31 (1992), pp. 127-136.

Ismael, Tareq Y. and Jacqueline Ismael. "Domestic Sources of Middle East Foreign Policy," in Tareq Y. Ismael, *International Relations of the Contemporary Middle East*, Syracuse, New York: Syracuse University Press, 1986, pp. 17-40.

_____ and Jacqueline S. Ismael. "Arab Politics and the Gulf War: Political Opinion and Political Culture." *Arab Studies Quarterly* 15, 1 (Winter 1993), pp. 1-11.

Jabar, Faleh Abd al-. "Roots of an Adventure: The Invasion of Kuwait, Iraqi Political Dynamics," in Victoria Brittain, ed. *The Gulf Between Us: The Gulf War and Beyond.* London: Virago, 1991, pp. 27-41.

Joffé, George. "Middle Eastern Views of the Gulf Conflict and its Aftermath." *Review of International Studies* 19, 2 (1993), pp. 177-199.

Karabell, Zachary. "Backfire: US Policy Toward Iraq, 1988-2 August 1990." *The Middle East Journal* 49, 1(Winter 1995), pp. 28-48.

Karsh, Efraim and Inari Rautsi. "Why Saddam Hussein Invaded Kuwait." *Survival* 33, 1 (January 1991), pp. 18-30.

Kelidar, Abbas. "Iraq: The Search for Stability." *Conflict Studies* 59 (July 1975), pp. 1-22.

_____. "The Wars of Saddam Hussein." *Middle Eastern Studies* 28, 4 (October 1992), pp. 778-798.

Khadduri, Majid. "Iraq's Claim to the Sovereignty of Kuwayt." *New York University Journal of International Law and Politics* 23, 1 (Fall 1990), pp. 5-34.

Kono, Tsutomu M. "Road to Invasion." *American Arab-Affairs* 34 (Fall 1990), pp. 29-45.

Krasner, Stephen. "Approaches to the State: Alternative Conceptions and Historical Dynamics." *Comparative Politics* 16, 2 (January 1984), pp. 223-246.

Lasswell, Harold D. "The Garrison State." *The American Journal of Sociology* XLVI (January 1941), pp. 455-468.

Lentner, Howard H. "The Concept of the State: A Response to Stephen Krasner." *Comparative Politics* 16, 3 (April 1984), pp. 367-377.

_____. "Rethinking Foreign Policy Analysis." Paper presented at the Annual Meeting of the International Studies Association, Washington, D.C. (March 30, 1994).

_____. "Foreign Policy and International Politics in the Post-Cold War Era." Paper presented at a Korean Political Science Association Workshop, Seoul, Korea (June 10, 1996).

Maddy-Weitzman, Bruce. "Jordan and Iraq: Efforts at Intra-Hashimite Unity." *Middle Eastern Studies* 26, 1 (January 1990), pp. 65-75.

Marr, Phoebe A. "Iraq's Leadership Dilemma: A Study in Leadership Trends 1948-1968." *The Middle East Journal* 24, 3 (Summer 1970), pp. 283-299.

_____. "The Political Elite in Iraq," in George Lenczowski, ed. *Political Elites in the Middle East*. Washington, D.C.: 1975, pp. 109-149.

Mastanduno, Michael, David A. Lake, and G. John Ikenberry. "Toward a Realist Theory of State Action." *International Studies Quarterly* 33 (1989), pp. 457-474.

Mejcher, Helmut. "Iraq's External Relations 1921-1936." *Middle Eastern Studies* 13 (1977), pp. 340-358.

Mitchell, Timothy. "The Limits of the State: Beyond Statist Approaches and Their Critics." *American Political Science Review* 85, 1 (March 1991), pp. 77-96.

_____ and Roger Owen. "Defining the State in the Middle East." *Middle East Studies Association Bulletin* 24, 2 (1990), pp. 179-183; 25, 1 (1991), pp. 25-29; and 26, 1 (1992), pp. 39-43.

Nettl, J.P. "The State as a Conceptual Variable." *World Politics* 20, 4 (July 1968), pp. 559-592.

Nonneman, Gerd. "The (Geo)Political Economy of Iraqi-Kuwait Relations." *Geopolitics and International Boundaries* 1, 2 (Autumn 1996), pp. 178-223.

Nordlinger, Eric. "Taking the State Seriously," in Myron Weiner and Samuel Huntington, eds. *Understanding Political Development*. Boston, Massachusetts: Little, Brown, & Co, 1987, pp. 353-390.

_____. "The Return to the State: Critique." *American Political Science Review* 82 (1988), pp. 875-885.

Ofuatey-Kodjoe, Wentworth. "Towards a Theoretical Framework for the Research and Analysis of Foreign Policy." The City University of New York Graduate School, Political Science Department, unpublished manuscript (1993).

Papadakis, Maria and Harvey Starr, "Opportunity, Willingness, and Small States: The Relationship Between Environment and Foreign Policy," in Charles F. Hermann, Charles W. Kegley Jr., and James N. Rosenau, eds. *New Directions in the Study of Foreign Policy*. London: HarperCollins, 1987, pp. 409-432.

Picard, Elizabeth. "Le Rapprochement Syro-Irakien: Vers Une Nouvelle Donne des Alliances au Proche-Orient," *Maghreb-Machrek* 83 (January-March), pp. 9-11.

Pipes, Daniel. "The View from Baghdad: Tariq 'Aziz." *Middle East Quarterly* 1, 2 (1994) pp. 59-70.

Post, Jerrold M. "Saddam Hussein of Iraq: A Political Psychology Profile." *Political Psychology* 12 (Spring 1991), pp. 279-287.

_____. "The Defining Moment of Saddam's Life: A Political Psychology Perspective on the Leadership and Decision Making of Saddam Hussein During the Gulf Crisis," in Stanley A. Renshon, ed. *The Political Psychology of the Gulf War: Leaders, Publics, and the Process of Conflict*, Pittsburgh, Pennsylvania: University of Pittsburgh Press, 1993, pp. 49-66.

Primakov, Yevgeni. "The Inside Story of Moscow's Quest for a Deal." *Time* (April 4, 1991).

_____. "My Final Visit with Saddam Hussein." *Time* (April 11, 1991).

Renshon, Stanley A. "The Psychology of Good Judgment: A Preliminary Model with Some Applications to the Gulf War." *Political Psychology* 13, 3 (September 1992), pp. 477-496.

_____. "Good Judgment, and the Lack Thereof, in the Gulf War: A Preliminary Psychological Model With Some Applications," in Stanley Renshon, ed. *The Political Psychology of the Gulf War: Leaders, Publics, and the Process of Conflict*, Pittsburgh, Pennsylvania: Pittsburgh University Press, 1993, pp. 67-105.

Rosenau, James N. "Pre-Theories and Theories of Foreign Policy," in R. Barry Farell, ed. *Approaches to Comparative and International Politics.* Evanston, Illinois: Northwestern University Press, 1966, pp. 27-92.

_____. "The Study of Foreign Policy," in James N. Rosenau, Kenneth W. Thompson, and Gavin Boyd, eds. *World Politics.* New York, New York: The Free Press, 1976, pp. 15-35.

_____. "Le Processus de Mondialisation: Retombées Significatives, Échanges Impalpables et Symbolique Subtile." *Études Internationales* 24, 3 (September 1993), pp. 497-512.

Ruggie, John Gerard. "Territoriality and Beyond: Problematizing Modernity in International Relations." *International Organization* 47, 1 (Winter 1993), pp. 139-174.

Sabine, George. "The State," in *Encyclopedia of the Social Sciences*. New York, New York: MacMillan, 1934.

Safran, Nadav. "Dimensions of the Middle East Problem," in Roy C. Macridis, ed. *Foreign Policy in World Politics.* Englewood Cliffs, New Jersey: Prentice-Hall, 1985, pp. 340-374.

Safronchuk, Vasili. "Diplomacy and Operation Desert Storm." *International Affairs* 5/6 (1996), pp. 69-91, and 1 (1997), pp. 64-78.

Shapiro, Michael J. and G. Matthew Bonham. "Cognitive Process and Foreign Policy Decision-Making." *International Studies Quarterly* 17, 2 (June 1973), pp. 147-174.

Sicherman, Harvey. "America's Alliance Anxieties: The Strange Death of Dual

Containment." *Orbis* 41, 2 (Spring 1997), pp. 223-240.

Simon, Reeva S. "The Hashemite 'Conspiracy': Hashemite Unity Attempts 1921-1958." *International Journal of Middle East Studies* 5 (1974), pp. 314-327.

_____. "The Teaching of History in Iraq before the Rashid Ali Coup of 1941." *Middle Eastern Studies* 22 (1986), pp. 37-51.

Skocpol, Theda. "Bringing the State Back In: Strategies of Analysis in Current Research," in Peter B. Evans, Dietrich Rueschemeyer, and Theda Skocpol, eds. *Bringing the State Back In*. Cambridge, Massachusetts: Cambridge University Press, 1985, pp. 3-37.

Sluglett, Peter. "Le Progrès Remis à Plus Tard: La Politique Pétrolière Irakienne: Passé, Présent, Avenir." *Peuples Méditerranéens* 64-65 (1993), pp 181-210.

Smith, Steve. "Describing and Explaining Foreign Policy Behavior." *Polity* 17, 3 (Spring 1985), pp. 595-607.

Smith, Steven B. "Hegel's View on War, the State, and International Relations." *The American Political Science Review* 77 (September 1983), pp. 624-632.

Snyder, Richard C. "The Nature of Foreign Policy." *Social Science* 27 (April 1952), pp. 61-69.

Springborg, Robert. "Pax Americana: De la Guerre Froide à la Guerre du Golfe et Au-Delà." *Peuples Méditerranéens* 64-65 (1993), pp. 119-130.

Stein, Janice Gross. "Deterrence and Compellence in the Gulf, 1990-91." *International Security* 17, 2 (Fall 1992), pp. 147-184.

Stork, Joe. "State Power and Economic Structure: Class Determination and State Formation in Contemporary Iraq," in Tim Niblock, ed. *Iraq: The Contemporary State*, New York, New York: St. Martin's Press, 1982, pp. 27-46.

Taminiaux, Pierre. "La Guerre du Golfe ou l'Histoire d'un Monde Sans Témoin." *Stratégie* II, 64-65 (July-December 1993), pp. 3-25.

Thoman, R. "Iraq under Baathist Rule." *Current History* 62, 1 (January 1972), pp. 31-37.

_____. "Iraq and the Persian Gulf Region." *Current History* 63, 1 (January 1973), pp. 21-25.

Vinogradov, Amal. "The 1920 Revolt in Iraq Reconsidered: The Role of the Tribes in National Politics." *International Journal of Middle East Studies* 3 (1972), pp. 123-139.

Waas, Murray and Craig Unger. "In the Loop: Bush's Secret Mission." *The New Yorker* (November 2, 1992), pp. 64-83

Waltzer, Michael. "On the Role of Symbolism in Political Thought." *Political Science Quarterly* 82 (June 1967), pp. 191-204.

Waterbury, John. "Iraq's Future: Is Democracy the Only Way Out?" *The Iranian Journal of International Affairs* 5, 3-4 (Fall/Winter 1993/94), pp. 775-780.

Watkins, Frederick. "The State," in *International Encyclopedia of the Social Sciences*. New York, New York: MacMillan, 1968.

Zureik, Elia. "Theoretical Considerations for a Sociological Study of the Arab State" *Arab Studies Quarterly* 3 (1981), pp. 229-257.

Books

Abu Jaber, Kamel S. *The Arab Ba'th Socialist Party: History, Ideology, and Organization*. New York, New York: Syracuse University Press, 1966.

Abu Laban, Baha and M. Ibrahim Alladin, eds. *Beyond the Gulf War: Muslims, Arabs, and the West*. Edmonton, Alberta, Canada: MRF Publishers, 1991.

Acosta Estévez, J.B. *La Crisis de Irak-Kuwait: Responsabilidad de Irak y Respuesta Internacional*. Barcelona: Promociones y Publicaciones Universitarias, 1994.

Aflaq, Michel. *Fi Sabil al Ba'th*. (On the Way to Renaissance). Beyrouth: Dar al-Kitab, 1972.

Algosaibi, Ghazi A. *The Gulf Crisis: An Attempt to Understand*. New York, New York: Routledge, Chapman, and Hall, 1993.

Ali, Omar. *Crisis in the Arabian Gulf - An Independent Iraqi View*. Westport, Connecticut: Praeger, 1993.

Alia, Josette and Christine Clerc. *La Guerre de Mitterand - La Dernière Grande Illusion*. Paris: Olivier Orban, 1991.

Allison, Graham. *Essence of Decision: Explaining the Cuban Missile Crisis* Boston, Massachusetts: Little Brown and Company, 1971.

Almos, Deborah. *Lines in the Sand: Desert Storm and the Remaking of the Arab World*. New York, New York: Simon & Schuster, 1992

Amery, H.M. and W.A. Madhoun, eds. *Shaping the Gulf: In Search of Order - Readings and Documents on the Iraq-Kuwait Crisis*. London, Canada: Canadian Institute for Policy Research and Analysis, 1992.

Amin, Samir. *Irak et Syrie: 1960-1982*. Paris: Éditions de Minuit, 1982.

Anderson, Evan W. *Iraq and the Triangle of Forces*. New York, New York: St. Martin's Press, 1991.

Angeli, Claude and Stéphanie Mesnier. *Notre Allié Saddam*. Paris: Olivier Orban, 1992.

Antonius, George. *The Arab Awakening*. London: Hamish Hamilton, 1945.

Ashford, Douglas. *British Dogmatism and French Pragmatism: Central-Local Policymaking in the Modern Welfare State* London: Allen and Unwin, 1983.

Assiri, Abdul-Reda. *Kuwait's Foreign Policy: City State in World Politics*. Boulder, Colorado: Westview Press, 1990

Atiyyah, Ghassan. *Iraq 1908-1921: A Political Study*. Beirut: Arab Institute for Research and Publishing, 1973.

Atkinson, Rick. *Crusade - The Untold Story of the Persian Gulf War*. New York, New York: Houghton Mifflin Company, 1993.

Avineri, Shlomo. *Hegel's Theory of the Modern State*. Cambridge, Massachusetts: Cambridge University Press, 1972.

Axelgard, Frederick W., ed. *Iraq in Transition: A Political, Economic, and Strategic Perspective.* Boulder, Colorado: Westview Press, 1986.

_____. *A New Iraq? The Gulf War and Implications for US Policy.* Westport, Connecticut: Praeger, 1988.

Ayubi, Nazih N. *Over-Stating the Arab State: Politics and Society in the Middle East.* London: I.B. Tauris, 1996.

'Aziz, Tariq. *Thawratu al-Tareeq al-Jadid* (The Revolution of the New Road). Baghdad: Dar al-Thawra, 1974.

Azmeh, Aziz al-. *Ibn Khaldun.* New York, New York: Routledge, 1982.

Badie, Bertrand. *L'État Importé - L'Occidentalisation de l'Ordre Politique.* Paris: Fayard, 1992.

_____ and Pierre Birnbaum. *The Sociology of the State.* Chicago, Illinois: Chicago University Press, 1983.

Baduel, Pierre Robert, ed. *Crise du Golfe - La Logique des Chercheurs.* Aix- en-Provence, France: Edisud, 1991.

Bailey, Kathleen C. *The UN Inspections in Iraq - Lessons for On-Site Verification* Boulder, Colorado: Westview Press, 1995.

Baker, James A. and Thomas M. DeFrank. *The Politics of Diplomacy - Revolution, War and Peace, 1989-1992.* New York, New York: G. P. Putnam's Sons, 1995.

Balta, Paul. *Iran-Irak - Une Guerre de Cinq Mille Ans.* Paris: Anthropos, 1987.

Banuazizi, Ali and Myron Weiner, eds. *The State, Religion, and Ethnic Politics - Afghanistan, Iran, and Pakistan.* Syracuse, New York: Syracuse University Press, 1986.

Barakat, Halim. *The Arab World - Society, Culture, and State* Berkeley, California: University of California Press, 1993.

Baram, Amatzia. *Culture, History, and Ideology in the Formation of Ba'thist Iraq.* New York, New York: St. Martin's Press, 1991.

_____ and Barry Rubin, eds. *Iraq's Road to War*. New York, New York: St Martin's Press, 1993.

Barzilai, Gad, Aharon Klieman and Gil Shidlo, eds. *The Gulf Crisis and its Global Aftermath*. New York, New York: Routledge, 1993.

Batatu, Hanna. *The Old Social Classes and the Revolutionary Movements of Iraq - A Study of Iraq's Old Landed and Commercial Classes and of its Ba'thists, and Free Officers*. Princeton, New Jersey: Princeton University Press, 1978.

Bazzaz, Sa'd al-. *Harb Tawlad Oukhra: Al-Tareekh al-Sirri li Harb al-Khalij* (A War Gives Birth to Another: The Secret History of the Gulf War). Amman: al-Ahliyya, 1992.

_____. *Ramad al-Hurub: Asrar Ma Ba'da Harb al Khalij* (Wars Sands. Post-Gulf War Secrets). Amman: al-Ahliyya, 1995.

Bellamy, Christopher. *Expert Witness - A Defence Correspondent's Gulf War 1990- 91*. London: Brassey's, 1993.

Ben-Dor, Gabriel. *State and Conflict in the Middle East: Emergence of the Post-Colonial State*. New York, New York: Praeger, 1983.

Bengio, Ofra. *Saddam Speaks on the Gulf Crisis: A Collection of Documents*. Syracuse, New York: Syracuse University Press, 1992.

Benjamin, Roger and Stephen L. Elkin, eds. *The Democratic State*. Lawrence, Kansas: The University Press of Kansas, 1985.

Bennis, Phyllis and Michel Moushabeck, eds. *Beyond the Storm: A Gulf Crisis Reader*. New York, New York: Olive Branch Press, 1991.

Bergot, Erwan and Alain Gandy. *Operation Daguet*. Paris. Presses de la Cité, 1991.

Bethlehem, D.L., ed. *The Kuwait Crisis: Sanctions and their Economic Consequences*. Cambridge, Massachusetts: Grotius Publications, 1991.

Biblawi, Hazem. *Azmat al-Khalij: Ba'ada an Yahda al-Ghubar* (The Gulf Crisis: After the Dust Storm Quiets). Cairo: Dar al-Shuruq, 1990.

Billière, Peter de la. *Storm Command: A Personal Account of the Gulf War*. London: HarperCollins, 1992.

Black, Ian. *Desert Fist: Allied Airpower for Desert Storm - A Pilot's View.*
Osceola, Wisconsin: Motorbrooks International, 1991.

Blackwell, James. *Thunder in the Desert: The Strategy and Tactics of the Persian
Gulf War.* New York, New York: Bantam Books, 1991.

Blumberg, Herbert H. and Christopher C. French, eds. *The Persian Gulf War -
Views From the Social and Behavioral Sciences.* Lanham, Maryland:
University Press of America, 1994.

Boutros-Auda, Auda. *Harb al-Khalij: Min al-Mas'ul?* (The Gulf War· Who is
Responsible?). Amman: Wakalat al-Tawzi' al-Urduniya, 1992.

Bresheeth, Haim and Nira Yuval-Davis, eds. *The Gulf War and the New World
Order.* Atlantic Highlands, New Jersey: Zed Books Ltd, 1991.

Brittain, Victoria. *The Gulf Between Us: The Gulf War and Beyond.* London: Virago
Press Ltd, 1991.

Brown, Ben and David Shukman. *All Necessary Means: Inside the Gulf War*
London: BBC Books, 1991.

Brune, Lester H. *America and the Iraqi Crisis, 1990-1992: Origins and Aftermath*
Claremont, California: Regina Books, 1993.

Bull, Gerald and Charles Murphy. *Paris Kanonen - The Paris Gun and Project
Harp.* Bonn: Mittler, 1988.

Bulloch, John and Harvey Morris. *The Gulf War: The Origins, History, and
Consequences.* London: Methuen, 1989.

_____. *Saddam's War: The Origins of the Kuwait
Conflict and the International Response* London: Faber and Faber, 1991

Burdeau, Georges. *L'État.* Paris: Éditions du Seuil, 1970

Cadiot, Jean-Michel. *Quand l'Irak entre en Guerre: La Qadissiyah de Saddam.*
Paris: L'Harmattan, 1989.

Campbell, David. *Politics Without Principle: Sovereignty, Ethics, and the
Narratives of the Gulf War.* Boulder, Colorado. Lynne Reinner Publishers,
1993.

Caractacus (pseudonym of Frederick John Snell). *Revolution in Iraq - An Essay in Comparative Public Opinion.* London: Victor Gollancz Ltd, 1959

Carpenter, Ted Galen, ed. *America Entangled - The Persian Gulf and Its Consequences.* Washington, D.C.: Cato, 1991.

Chevènement, Jean-Pierre. *Le Vert et le Noir - Intégrisme, Pétrole, Dollar.* Paris: Grasset, 1995.

Chrisco, Carrie. *Reactions to the Persian Gulf War - Editorials in the Conflict Zone.* Lanham, Maryland: University Press of America, 1995.

Cipkowski, Peter. *Understanding the Crisis in the Persian Gulf.* New York, New York: John Wiley and Sons, 1992.

Clancy, Tom and Fred Franks, Jr. *Into the Storm - A Study in Command.* New York, New York: G.P. Putnam's Sons, 1997.

Clausewitz, Carl Von. *On War [Vom Kriege].* New York, New York: Penguin Classics, 1968.

Committee Against Repression and for Democratic Rights in Iraq (CARDRI). *Saddam's Iraq Revolution or Reaction?* London: Zed Books, 1986.

Cooke, James T. *100 Miles From Baghdad - With the French in Desert Storm.* Westport, Connecticut: 1993.

Cordesman, Anthony H. *Iran and Iraq - The Threat from the Northern Gulf.* Boulder, Colorado: Westview Press, 1994.

_____ and Abraham R. Wagner. *The Lessons of Modern War, vol. IV: The Gulf War.* Boulder, Colorado: Westview Press, 1996.

_____ and Ahmed S. Hashim. *Iraq: Sanctions and Beyond.* Boulder, CO: Westview Press, 1997.

Coulon, Jocelyn. *La Dernière Croisade et le Rôle Caché du Canada.* Québec: Éditions du Méridien, 1992.

Cox, Richard H., ed. *The State in International Relations.* San Francisco, California: Chandler Publishing Company, 1965.

D'Athis, Thierry and Jean-Paul Croizé. *Golfe: La Guerre Cachée.* Paris: Jean Picollec, 1991.

Dabezies, Pierre, *et al. Crise du Golfe: Les Changements Stratégiques.* Paris: Fondation pour les Études de Défense Nationale, 1990.

Dahl, Robert. *Who Governs: Democracy and Power in an American City.* New Haven, Connecticut: Yale University Press, 1961.

Danchev, Alex and Dan Keohane, eds. *International Perspectives on the Gulf Conflict, 1990-91.* New York, New York: St. Martin's Press, 1994.

Dann, Uriel. *Iraq Under Qassem: A Political History 1958-1963.* New York, New York: Praeger, 1969.

Danspeckgruber, Wolfgang F. and Charles R. H. Tripp, eds. *The Iraqi Aggression against Kuwait - Strategic Lessons and Implications for Europe.* Boulder, Colorado: Westview Press, 1996.

Darwish, Adel and Gregory Alexander. *The Secret History of Saddam's War: Unholy Babylon.* London: Victor Gollany, 1991.

Dauphin, Jacques. *Incertain Irak: Tableau d'un Royaume avant la Tempête 1914-1953.* Paris: Paul Geuthner, 1991

David, Charles-Phillipe. *La Guerre du Golfe - l'Illusion de la Victoire.* Montréal: Art Global, 1991.

Davis, Eric and Nicolas Gavrielides, eds. *Statecraft in the Middle East - Oil, Historical Memory, and Popular Culture.* Miami, Florida: Florida International University Press, 1991.

Dawisha, Adeed and I. William Zartman. *Beyond Coercion: The Durability of the Arab State.* New York, New York: Croom-Helm, 1988.

Decosse, David E. *But Was it Just? Reflection on the Morality of the Persian Gulf War.* New York, New York: Doubleday, 1992.

Deen, Irfan Nizam al-. *The Gulf War and the Roots of the Arabs' Dilemma.* London: Dar al-Saqi, 1991.

Delcorde, Raoul. *La Sécurité et la Stratégie dans le Golfe Arabo-Persique 1968-1982.* Paris: Le Sycomore, 1983.

Denton, Jr., Robert E. *The Media and the Persian Gulf War*. Wesport, Connecticut: Praeger, 1993.

Devlin, John F. *The Ba'th Party: A History from its Origins to 1966*. Standford, California: Hoover Institution Press, 1976.

Dickson, H.R.P. *Kuwait and Her Neighbors*. London: Allen & Unwin, 1963.

Dorr, Robert E. *The Desert Shield - The Build-Up: The Complete Story*. Osceola, Wisconsin: Motorbrooks International, 1991.

Dunnigan, James F. and Austin Bay. *From Shield to Storm: High-Tech Weapons, Military Strategy, and Coalition Warfare in the Persian Gulf* New York, New York: Morrow, 1991.

Dupuy, Trevor N., Curt Johnson, David L. Bongard, and Arnold C. Dupuy. *How to Defeat Saddam Hussein: Scenarios and Strategies for the Gulf War* New York, New York: Warner Books, 1991.

Dyson, Kenneth, and Stephen Wilkes, eds. *Industrial Crisis: A Comparative Study of the State and Industry*. New York, New York: St. Martin's Press, 1983.

Echeverri-Gent, John. *The State and the Poor: Public Policy and Political Development in India and the United States* Berkeley, California: University of California Press, 1993.

Ehteshami, Anoushiravan, Gerd Nonneman and Charles C. Tripp. *War and Peace in the Gulf, Domestic Politics and Regional Relations into the 1990s*. London: Ithaca Press, 1991.

Evans, Peter. *Dependent Development: The Alliance of Multinational, State, and Local Capital in Brazil*. Princeton, New Jersey: Princeton University Press, 1979.

_____, Dietrich Rueschemeyer, and Theda Skocpol, eds. *Bringing the State Back In*. Cambridge, Massachusetts: Cambridge University Press, 1985.

Eyd, Khadim A. al-. *Oil Revenues and Accelerated Growth: Absorptive Capacity in Iraq*. New York, New York: Praeger, 1979.

Farouk-Sluggett, Marion and Peter Sluggett. *Iraq Since 1958*. London: I.B. Tauris, 1990.

Faour, Muhammad. *The Arab World After Desert Storm*. Washington, D.C.: United States Institute of Peace Press, 1993.

Fernea, Robert A. and WM. Roger Louis, eds. *The Iraqi Revolution of 1958 - The Old Social Classes Revisited*. London: I.B. Tauris, 1991.

Fialka, John J. *Hotel Warriors: Covering the Gulf War*. Baltimore: The John Hopkins University Press, 1992.

Finnie, David H. *Shifting Lines in the Sand - Kuwait's Elusive Frontier with Iraq*. Cambridge, Massachusetts: Harvard University Press, 1992.

Fleury-Villette, Béatrice. *Les Médias et la Guerre du Golfe*. Nancy, France: Presses Universitaires de France, 1992.

Foster, Henry A. *The Making of Modern Iraq - A Product of World Forces*. Norman, Oklahoma: University of Oklahoma Press, 1935.

Fox, Thomas C. *Iraq - Military Victory, Moral Defeat*. Kansas City, Missouri: Sheed and Ward, 1991.

Freedman, Lawrence and Efraim Karsh. *The Gulf Conflict 1990-1991: Diplomacy and War in the New World Order*. Princeton, New Jersey Princeton University Press, 1993.

Freedman, Robert O., ed. *The Middle East after Iraq's Invasion of Kuwait*. Gainesville, Florida: University of Florida Press, 1993.

French, Christopher C. *Psychological Aspects of the Gulf War*. London: Scientists Against Nuclear Arms, 1991.

Friedman, Alan. *Spider's Web: Bush, Saddam, Thatcher and the Decade of Deceit*. London: Faber and Faber, 1993.

Friedman, Norman. *Desert Victory: The War for Kuwait*. Annapolis, Maryland: Naval Institute Press, 1991.

Friedrich, Otto, ed. *Desert Storm: The War in the Persian Gulf*. Boston, Massachusetts: Times Books, 1991.

Fuller, Graham E. *Iraq in the Next Decade: Will Iraq Survive Until 2002*. Santa Monica, California: Rand, 1993.

264

Geertz, Clifford. *Negara: The Theatre State in Nineteenth Century Bali*. Princeton, New Jersey: Princeton University Press, 1981.

Ghalioun, Burhan. *Le Malaise Arabe: L'État contre la Nation*. Paris: La Découverte, 1991

Ghareeb, Edmund. *The Kurdish Question in Iraq*. Syracuse, New York: Syracuse University Press, 1981.

Gilbert, Felix. *The Historical Essays of Otto Hintze*. New York, New York: Oxford University Press, 1975.

Gilpin, Robert. *War and Change in World Politics*. Cambridge, Massachusetts: Cambridge University Press, 1981.

Gittings, John, ed. *Beyond the Gulf War: The Middle East and the New World Order*. London: Catholic Institute for International Relations, 1991.

Godden, John, ed. *Shield and Storm - Personal Recollections of the Air War in the Gulf*. London: Brassey's, 1994.

Gordon, Michael R. and Bernard E. Trainor. *The Generals' War - The Inside Story of the Conflict in the Gulf*. Boston, Massachusetts: Little, Brown, and Company, 1995.

Gow, James, ed. *Iraq, the Gulf Conflict, and the World Community*. London. Brassey's, 1993.

Graubard, Stephen R. *Mr. Bush's War - Adventures in the Politics of Illusion*. New York, New York: Hill and Wang, 1992.

Graz, Liesl. *Le Golfe des Turbulences*. Paris: L'Harmattan, 1990.

Greenberg, Bradley S. and Walter Gantz, eds. *Desert Storm and the Mass Media*. Cresskill, New Jersey: Hampton Press, Inc., 1993.

Gresh, Alain and Dominique Vidal. *Golfe - Clefs pour une Guerre Annoncée*. Paris: Le Monde Éditions, 1991.

Haas, Richard N. *The Reluctant Sheriff - The United States After the Cold War*. Washington, D.C.: Brookings Institution Press, 1997.

Hadithi, Naji al-, ed. *Iraq 1990*. Baghdad: Dar al-Ma'mun, 1990.

Haghighat, Chapour. *Histoire de la Crise du Golfe - Des Origines aux Conséquences.* Brussels: Éditions Complexes, 1992.

Hallion, Richard P. *Storm Over Iraq: Air Power and the Gulf War.* Washington, D.C.: Smithsonian Institution Press, 1992.

Handel, Michael. *War, Strategy, and Intelligence.* London: Frank Cass, 1989.

Hassani, Abdelrazzaq al-. *Tareekh al-'Iraq al-Siyasi al-Hadeth* (The Modern Political History of Iraq). Seda, Lebanon: Irfan Printing Office, 1958.

Hazelton, Fran, ed. *Iraq Since the Gulf War.* London: Zed Books, 1994.

Heclo, Hugh. *Modern Social Politics in Britain and Sweden.* New Haven, Connecticut: Yale University Press, 1974.

Hegel, Georg Wilhelm Friedrich. *The Philosophy of Right* Chicago, Illinois: The University of Chicago, 1971 [1821].

Helms, Christine Moss. *Iraq: Eastern Flank of the Arab World.* Washington, D.C.: The Brookings Institution, 1984.

Henderson, Simon. *Instant Empire: Saddam Hussein's Ambition for Iraq.* San Francisco, California: Mercury House, 1991.

Heikal, Mohammad. *Illusions of Triumph - An Arab View of the Gulf War.* London: Harper Collins, 1992.

Hilsman, Roger. *George Bush vs. Saddam Hussein: Military Success! Political Failure?* Novato, California: Lyford Books, 1992.

Hiro, Dilip. *The Longest War - The Iran-Iraq Military Conflict.* London: Paladin, 1990.

Hiro, Dilip. *Desert Shield to Desert Storm - The Second Gulf War.* New York, New York: Routledge, 1992.

Hirszowicz, Lukasz. *The Third Reich and the Arab East.* London: Routledge and Kegan Paul, 1966.

Hopwood, Derek *et al.*, ed. *Iraq: Power and Society.* London: Ithaca Press, 1993.

Hume, Cameron R. *The United Nations, Iran and Iraq: How Peacemaking Changed.* Bloomington, Indiana: Indiana University Press, 1994.

Hussein, Saddam. *Saddam Hussein On Current Events in Iraq.* London: Longman, 1977.

_____. *Nadhra fi 'l Din wa al-Turath* (Reflection on Religion and Heritage). Baghdad: Dar al-Huriya, 1978.

_____. *Al-Milkiyya al-Khassa wa Mas 'uliyat al-Dawla* (Private Propriety and the Responsibility of the State). Baghdad: Dar al-Thawra, 1978.

_____. *Nidhaluna wa 'l Siyassa al-Kharijiya* (Our Struggle and Foreign Policy). Baghdad: Dar al-Tali'a, 1978.

_____. *Social and Foreign Affairs in Iraq.* London. Croom-Helm, 1979.

Hybel, Alex Roberto. *Power Over Rationality -- The Bush Administration and the Gulf Crisis.* Albany, New York: State University of New York Press, 1993.

Ibn Khaldun. *The Muqaddimah: An Introduction to History* (Translated by Franz Rosenthal). Princeton, New Jersey: Princeton University Press, 1967.

Ibrahim, Ibrahim, ed. *The Gulf Crisis: Background and Consequences.* Washington, D.C.: Center for Contemporary Arab Studies, 1992.

Ismael, Tareq Y. *International Relations of the Contemporary Middle East - A Study in World Politics.* Syracuse, New York. Syracuse University Press, 1986.

Jabar, Abdelrahman abd al-. *A Bibliography of Iraq: A Classified List of Printed Materials on the Land and People.* Baghdad: al-Irshad Press, 1977.

Jackson, Robert H and Alan James, eds. *States in a Changing World - A Contemporary Analysis.* New York, New York· Oxford University Press, 1993.

Jalal, Ferhang. *The Role of Government in the Industrialization of Iraq, 1950-1965.* London: 1972.

Janis, Irving L. *Victims of Groupthink - A Psychological Study of Foreign Policy Decisions and Fiascoes.* Boston, Massachusetts: Houghton Mifflin Company, 1972.

Jawad, Saad. *Iraq and the Kurdish Question: 1958-1970*. London: Ithaca Press, 1981.

Jeffords, Susan and Lauren Rabinovitz. *Seeing Through the Media - The Persian Gulf War*. New Brunswick, New Jersey: Rutgers University Press, 1994.

Jentleson, Bruce W. *With Friends Like These: Reagan, Bush and Saddam: 1982-1990*. New York, New York: W.W. Norton and Company, 1994.

Jervis, Robert. *The Logic of Images in International Relations*. Princeton, New Jersey: Princeton University Press, 1970.

_____. *Perception and Misperception in International Relations*. Princeton, New Jersey: Princeton University Press, 1976.

Johnstone, Ian. *Aftermath of the Gulf War: An Assessment of UN Action*. Boulder, Colorado: Lynne Rienner Publishers, 1994.

Jones, Gregory S. *The Iraqi Ballistic Missile Program*. Marina Del Rey, California. American Institute for Strategic Cooperation, 1992.

Joyner, Christopher C. *The Persian Gulf War: Lessons for Strategy, Law, and Diplomacy*. New York, New York: Greenwood Press, 1990.

July, Serge. *La Diagonale du Golfe*. Paris: Grasset, 1991.

Kabadaya, Salah. *Tempête du Désert - Point de Vue Arabe*. Rabat: The Moroccan Printing and Publishing Company, 1991.

Karsh, Efraim and Inari Rautsi. *Saddam Hussein: A Political Biography*. New York, New York: The Free Press, 1991.

Katzenstein, Peter J., ed. *Between Power and Plenty: Foreign Economic Policies of Advanced Industrial States*. Madison, Wisconsin: University of Wisconsin Press, 1978.

Kelidar Abbas, ed. *The Integration of Modern Iraq*. New York, New York: St. Martin's Press, 1979.

Kelly, Michael. *Martyr's Day - Chronicle of a Small War*. New York, New York: Vintage Books, 1991.

Kerr, Malcolm H. *The Arab Cold War - Gamal 'Abd al-Nasir and His Rivals, 1958-1970.* New York, New York: Oxford University Press, 1971.

Khadduri, Majid. *Independent Iraq: A Study in Iraqi Politics from 1932 to 1958.* London: Oxford University Press, 1960.

_____. *Republican Iraq: A Study in Iraqi Politics Since the Revolution of 1958.* London: Oxford University Press, 1969.

_____. *Socialist Iraq: A Study in Iraqi Politics Since 1968* Los Angeles and Berkeley, California: University of California Press, 1978.

_____ and Edmund Ghareeb. *War in the Gulf 1990-91 - The Iraq-Kuwait Conflict and its Implications.* New York, New York: Oxford University Press, 1997.

Khalil, Samir al- (pseudonym of Kanan Makiya). *Republic of Fear: The Politics of Modern Iraq.* Berkeley, California: University of California Press, 1989

Kienle, Eberhard. *Ba'th vs Ba'th: The Conflict between Syria and Iraq* London: I.B.Tauris, 1990.

Kimball, Lorenzo Kent. *The Changing Pattern of Political Power in Iraq: 1958 to 1971.* New York, New York: Robert Speller and Sons, 1972.

Klare, Michael. *Rogue States and Nuclear Outlaws: America's Search for a New Foreign Policy.* New York, New York: Hill and Wang, 1995.

Kodmani-Darwish, Bassma and May Charouni-Dubarry. *Golfe et Moyen-Orient: Les Conflits.* Paris: Institut Français des Relations Internationales, 1991.

Korany, Bahgat and A.E.H. Dessouki, eds. *The Foreign Policies of Arab States.* Boulder, Colorado: Westview Press, 1991.

_____, Paul Noble and Rex Brynen, eds. *The Many Faces of Faces of National Security in the Arab World.* New York, New York: St. Martin's Press, 1993.

Laizer, Sheri. *Martyrs, Traitors and Patriots - Kurdistan after the Gulf War.* London: Zed Books, 1996.

Laurent, Eric. *Tempête du Désert - Les Secrets de la Maison Blanche.* Paris: Olivier Orban, 1991.

Lauterpacht E., C.J. Greenwood, Marc Weller, and Daniel Bethlehem, eds *Kuwait Crisis: Basic Documents*. Cambridge, Massachusetts: Grotius Publications, 1991.

Lekfir-Laffitte, Naïma and Roland Laffitte. *L'Irak Sous le Déluge*. Paris: Éditions Hermé, 1992.

Lentner, Howard H. *Foreign Policy Analysis: A Comparative and Conceptual Approach*. Columbus, Ohio: Charles E. Merrill Publishing Company, 1974.

_____. *International Politics - Theory and Practice*. St. Paul, Minneapolis: West Publishing Company, 1997.

Leslie, Paul. *The Gulf War as Popular Entertainment - An Analysis of the Military-Industrial Complex*. Lewiston, New York: The Edwin Mellen Press, 1997.

Leyden, Andrew. *Gulf War Debriefing Book - An After Action Report*. Grants Pass, Oregon: Hellgate Press, 1997.

Longrigg, Stephen Helmsley. *Iraq, 1900 to 1950 - A Political, Social, and Economic History*. Beirut: Lebanon Bookshop, 1953.

Lubasz, Heinz. *The Development of the Modern State*. New York, New York: MacMillan, 1974.

_____. *The Reason of States: A Study in International Political Theory*. London: George Allen & Unwin, 1978.

Luciani, Giacomo. *The Arab State*. Berkeley, California: The University of California Press, 1990.

Lustick, Ian. *State Building Failure in British Ireland and French Algeria*. Berkeley, California: Institute of International Studies, 1985.

Lyons, Gene and Michael Mastanduno, eds. *Beyond Westphalia: National Sovereignty and International Intervention*. Baltimore, Maryland: The John Hopkins University Press, 1991.

MacAthur, Brian, ed. *Despatches from the Gulf War*. London: Bloomsbury, 1991.

MacArthur, John R. *Second Front - Censorship and Propaganda in The Gulf War*. New York, New York: Hill and Wang, 1992.

Machiavelli, Niccólo. *The Prince*. Chicago, Illinois: The University of Chicago Press, 1985.

Marayati, Abid A. al-. *A Diplomatic History of Modern Iraq*. New York, New York: Robert Speller & Sons, 1961.

Marr, Phoebe. *The Modern History of Iraq*. Boulder, Colorado: Westview Press, 1985.

Matar, Fouad. *Saddam Hussein - A Biography*. London. Highlight Productions, 1990.

Matthews, Ken. *The Gulf Conflict and International Relations*. New York, New York: Routledge, 1993.

Mazar, Michael J., Don M. Snider, and James A. Blackwell, Jr. *Desert Storm - The Gulf War and What We Learned*. Boulder, Colorado: Westview Press, 1992.

Mazidi, Feisal al-. *The Future of the Gulf - The Legacy of the War and the Challenges of the 1990s.* London: I.B. Tauris, 1994.

McCain, Thomas A. and Leonard Shyles, eds. *The 1,000 Hour War - Communication in the Gulf*. Westport, Connecticut: Greenwood Press, 1994.

McLaurin, R.D., Mohammed Mughisuddin, and Abraham R. Wagner. *Foreign Policy Making in the Middle East*. New York, New York: Praeger Publishers, 1977.

_____, Don Peretz, and Lewis W. Snider. *Middle East Foreign Policy - Issues and Processes*. New York, New York: Praeger Publishers, 1982.

Meinecke, Friederich. *Machiavellism: The Doctrine of Raison d'État and its Place in Modern History*. New Haven, Connecticut: Yale University Press, 1957.

Merle, Marcel. *La Crise du Golfe et le Nouvel Ordre International*. Paris: Economica, 1991.

Mezerik, A.G. *Kuwait-Iraq Dispute, 1961*. New York, New York: International Review Service, 1961.

Miller, Judith and Laurie Mylroie. *Saddam Hussein and the Crisis in the Gulf.* New York, New York: Random House, 1990.

Modelski, George. *A Theory of Foreign Policy*. New York, New York: Praeger, 1962.

Morse, Stan, ed. *Gulf Air War Debrief*. Westport, Connecticut: Airtime Publishing, 1991.

Mowlana, Hamid, George Gerbner, and Herbert I. Schiller, eds. *Triumph of the Image - The Media's War in the Persian Gulf: A Global Perspective*. Boulder, Colorado: Westview Press, 1992.

Mufti, Malik. *Sovereign Creations: Pan-Arabism and Political Order in Syria and Iraq*. Ithaca, New York: Cornell University Press, 1996.

Mueller, John. *Policy and Opinion in the Gulf War*. Chicago, Illinois: University of Chicago Press, 1994.

Mughisudin Muhammad, R.D. Mc Laurin, and A.R. Wagner. *Foreign Policy Making in the Middle East: Domestic Influences on Policy in Egypt, Iraq, Israel, and Syria*. New York, New York: Praeger, 1977.

Munro, Alan. *An Arabian Affair - Politics and Diplomacy Behind the Gulf War*. London: Brassey's, 1996.

Musallam, Ali Musallam. *The Iraqi Invasion of Kuwait: Saddam Hussein, His State and International Power Politics*. New York, New York: I.B. Tauris and Company, 1996.

Najjar, Mustapha Abdelqader al- and Mohammad Abd-al-Motaleb al-Baka'. *Al-Kuwayt 'Iraqiya: Dirasssat Wathaqqiya, Tarikhiya, wa Siyassiya*. (Iraqi Kuwait: Evidenciary, Historical, and Political Studies) Baghdad: Dar al-Shu'un al-Thaqafiya al-'Ama, 1990.

Namiq, Abdelfattah Fikrat. *Siyasat 'Iraq al-Kharijiyya fil-Mantiqa al-'Arabiyya: 1932-1958*. (The Foreign Policy of Iraq in the Arab Region: 1932-1958). Baghdad: Dar al-Rashid lil Nashr, 1981.

Naqeeb, Khaldoun Hasan al-. *Society and State in the Gulf and Arab Peninsula: A Different Perspective*. New York, New York: Routledge, 1990.

Nefzaoui, Ali. *Trait d'Union sur le Koweit: La Crise*. Paris: De Facto, 1991.

Niblock, Tim, ed. *Iraq: The Contemporary State*. New York, New York: St. Martin's Press 1982.

Nordlinger, Eric. *On the Autonomy of the Democratic State* Cambridge, Massachusetts: Harvard University Press, 1981.

Nye, Joseph S., Jr. and Roger K. Smith, eds. *After the Storm - Lessons from the Gulf War.* Lanham, Maryland: Madison Books, 1992.

Nyrop, Richard F., ed. *Iraq, A Country Study.* Washington, D.C.: The American University, 1979.

Owen, Roger. *State, Power and Politics in the Making of the Modern Middle East* New York, New York: Routledge, 1992.

Pagonis, William G. *Moving Mountains - Lessons in Leadership and Logistics from the Gulf War.* Boston, Massachusetts. Harvard Business School Press, 1992

Panitch, Leo, ed. *The Canadian State: Political Economy and Political Power.* Toronto: University of Toronto Press, 1977.

Pelletiere, Stephen C. *The Iran-Iraq War - Chaos in a Vacuum.* New York, New York: Praeger, 1992.

_____, Douglas V. Johnson II, and Leif R. Rosenberg. *Iraqi Power and US Security in the Middle East.* Carlisle Barracks, Pennsylvania: US Army War College, 1990.

Penrose, Edith and E.F. Penrose. *Iraq: International Relations and National Development.* London: Ernest Benn Limited, 1978.

Pimlott, John and Stephen Badsey, eds. *The Gulf War Assessed.* London: Arms & Armour, 1992.

Poggi, Gianfranco. *The State: Its Nature, Development, and Prospects.* Standford, California: Standford University Press, 1990.

Powell, Colin and Joseph E. Persico. *My American Journey.* New York, New York: Ballantine Books, 1996.

Primakov, Evgueni. *Missions à Bagdad - Histoire d'une Négociation Secrète.* Paris: Éditions Le Seuil, 1991.

Rajab, Jehan S. *Invasion Kuwait - An English Woman's Tale.* London: The Radcliffe Press, 1993.

Raouf, Wafik. *Nouveau Regard Sur le Nationalisme Arabe - Ba'th et Nassérisme*. Paris: L'Harmattan, 1984.

_____. *Irak: 70 ans de Séismes*. Paris: Éditions Alcuin, 1992

Record, Jeffrey. *Hollow Victory: A Contrary View of the Gulf War*. New York, New York: Brassey's Inc, 1993.

Renshon, Stanley, ed. *The Political Psychology of the Gulf War: Leadership, Publics, and the Process of Conflict*. Pittsburgh, Pennsylvania: Pittsburgh University Press, 1993.

Reporters Sans Frontières. *Les Mensonges du Golfe*. Paris: Arléa, 1992.

Rezun, Miron. *Saddam Hussein's Gulf Wars - Ambivalent Stakes in the Middle East*. Westport, Connecticut: Praeger, 1992.

Rosati, Jerel A., Joe D. Hagan, and Martin W. Sampson III, eds. *Foreign Policy Restructuring - How Governments Respond to Change*. Columbia, South Carolina: University of South Carolina Press, 1994.

Rosenau, James N., ed. *Linkage Politics: Essays on the Convergence of National and International Systems*. New York, New York: The Free Press, 1969.

_____. *The Scientific Study of Foreign Policy*. New York, New York: The Free Press, 1971.

_____. *Turbulence in World Politics: A Theory of Change and Continuity*. Princeton, New Jersey: Princeton University Press, 1990.

Sackur, Stephen. *On the Basra Road*. London: London Review of Books, 1991.

Saint-Prot, Charles. *Saddam Hussein: Un Gaullisme Arabe?* Paris: Albin Michel, 1987.

Saleh, Youssef A. *Les Réfugiés Irakiens en Arabie Saoudite*. London: The Kensal Press, 1993.

Salinger, Pierre and Eric Laurent. *Guerre du Golfe - Le Dossier Secret*. Paris: Olivier Orban, 1990.

_____. *Secret Dossier: The Hidden Agenda Behind the Gulf War*. New York, New York: Penguin Books, 1991.

Samaan, Samaan B. and Abdullah H. Muhareb, eds. *An Aggression on the Mind - A Critical Study of Sa'd al-Bazzaz's Book 'A War Gives Birth to Another '* Kuwait: Center for Research and Studies on Kuwait, 1995.

Scales, Jr. Robert H. *Certain Victory: The U.S. Army in the Gulf War.* Washington, D.C.: Brassey's, 1994.

Schofield, Richard. *Kuwait and Iraq: Historical Claims and Territorial Disputes,* second edition. London: Royal Institute of International Affairs, 1993

Schwarzkopf, Norman H. and Peter Petre. *It Doesn't take a Hero.* New York, New York: Bantam, 1992.

Sciolino, Elaine. *The Outlaw State: Saddam Hussein's Quest for Power and the Gulf Crisis.* New York, New York: Wiley, 1991.

Serrano, Andrew Smith. *Las Claves de la Guerra del Golfo.* Barcelona: Asesa, 1991.

Shikara, Ahmed A.R. *Iraqi Politics, 1921-1941: The Interaction between Domestic Politics and Foreign Policy.* London: LAAM Ltd, 1987.

Sifry, Micah and Christopher Cerf, eds. *The Gulf Reader: History, Documents, and Opinions.* New York, New York: Random House, 1991.

Simon, Bob. *Forty Days.* New York, New York: Putnam, 1992.

Simon, Reeva S. *Iraq between the two World Wars: The Creation and Implementation of a Nationalist Ideology.* New York, New York: Columbia University Press, 1986.

Simons, Geoff. *Iraq - From Sumer to Saddam.* New York, New York: St. Martin's Press, 1996.

_____. *The Scourging of Iraq: Sanctions, Law and Natural Justice.* New York, New York: St. Martin's Press, 1996.

Simpson, John. *From the House of War.* London: Arrow Books, 1991.

Sklar, Richard. *Corporate Power in an African State: The Political Impact of Multinational Mining Companies in Zambia.* Berkeley, California: University of California Press, 1975.

Skowronek, Stephen. *Building a New American State: The Expansion of National Administrative Capacities*. New York, New York Cambridge University Press, 1982.

Slugett, Peter and Marion Farouk-Slugett. *Iraq Since 1958 - From Revolution to Dictatorship*. London: Kegan Paul, 1988.

Smith, Jean Edward. *George Bush's War*. New York, New York: Holt, 1992.

Smith, Perry M. *The Gulf War, Day by Day: An Illustrated History of the Political and Military Events of Desert Storm*. New York, New York: Avery Publications, 1991.

Smock, David R. *Religious Perspectives on War: Christian, Muslim, and Jewish Attitudes Toward Force After the Gulf War* Washington, D.C.: United States Institute of Peace Press, 1992.

Snyder, Richard C., H. W. Bruck, and Burton Sapin, eds. *Foreign Policy Decision-Making: An Approach to the Study of International Politics*. New York, New York: The Free Press, 1962.

Solh, Raghid El-. *Britain's Two Wars with Iraq: 1941-1991*. Berkshire, England: Ithaca Press, 1996.

Solingen, Etel, ed. *Scientists and the State: Domestic Structures and the International Context*. Ann Arbor, Michigan: University of Michigan Press, 1994.

Steinbrunner, John. *The Cybernetic Theory of Decision - New Dimensions of Political Analysis*. Princeton, New Jersey: Princeton University Press, 1974

Stepan, Alfred. *The State and Society: Peru in Comparative Perspective*. Princeton, New Jersey: Princeton University Press, 1978.

Stern, Brigitte, Habib Gherari, and Olivier Delorme. *Guerre du Golfe: Le Dossier d'une Crise Internationale 1990-1992* Paris: La Documentation Française, 1993.

Sultan, Khaled Bin and Patrick Seale. *Desert Warrior - A Personal View of the Gulf War by the Joint Forces Commander*. New York, New York: HarperCollins, 1995.

Sumaida Hussein and Carole Jerome. *Circle of Fear - A Renegade's Journey From the Mossad To the Iraqi Secret Service.* Toronto, Canada: Stoddart Publishing Co., 1991.

Summers, Harry G. Jr. *On Strategy II: A Critical Analysis of the Gulf War.* New York, New York: Dell, 1992.

_____. *Persian Gulf War Almanac.* New York, New York: Facts On File, 1995.

Tarbush, Mohammad A. *The Role of the Military in Politics: A Case Study of Iraq to 1941.* London: Kegan Paul, 1982.

Taylor, Philip M. *War and the Media - Propaganda and Persuasion in the Gulf War.* New York, New York: St. Martin's Press, 1992.

Timmerman, Kenneth R. *The Death Lobby: How the West Armed Iraq.* London. Fourth Estate, 1992.

Treitschke, Heinrich Von. *Politics.* New York, New York: The MacMillan Company, 1916, two volumes.

Trimberger, Ellen Kay. *Revolution From Above: Military Bureaucrats and Development in Japan, Turkey, Egypt, and Peru.* New Brunswick, New Jersey: Transaction Books, 1978.

US News and World Report Staff. *Triumph Without Victory - The Unreported History of the Persian Gulf War.* New York, New York: Times Books/Random House, 1992.

Vabres, Jacques Donnedieu De. *L'État.* Paris: Presses Universitaires de France, 1992.

Vaux, Kenneth L. *Ethics and the Gulf War - Religion, Rhetoric, and Righteousness.* Boulder, Colorado: Westview Press, 1992.

Walsh, Jeffrey, ed. *The Gulf War Did Not Happen - Politics, Culture, and Warfare Post-Vietnam.* Brookfield, Vermont: Ashgate, 1995.

Waltz, Kenneth N. *Man, the State and War - A Theoretical Analysis.* New York, New York: Columbia University Press, 1959

Watkins, Frederick M. *The State as a Concept in Political Science.* New York, New York: Harper & Brothers Publishers, 1934.

Watson, Bruce W., ed. *Military Lessons of the Gulf War.* London: Greenhill Books, 1991.

Weller, Marc and Philip Hatfield, eds. *The Control and Monitoring of Iraqi Weaponry of Mass Destruction.* New York, New York. Cambridge University Press, 1995.

Whicker, Marcia Lynn, James P. Pfiffner, and Raymond A. Moore, eds. *The Presidency and the Persian Gulf War.* Westport, Connecticut: Praeger, 1993.

Wiener, Robert. *Live From Baghdad.* New York, New York: Doubleday, 1992.

Woodward, Bob. *Veil - The Secret Wars of the CIA 1981-1987.* New York, New York: Simon and Schuster, 1987.

_____. *The Commanders.* New York, New York: Simon and Schuster, 1991.

Wright, Erik Olin. *Class, Crisis, and the State.* London: New Left Books, 1978.

Yant, Martin. *Desert Mirage - The True Story of the Gulf War.* Buffalo, New York: Prometheus Books, 1991.

Doctoral Dissertations

Crawford, Neta Carol. "Force-Prone States: Sources of Highly Militarized Foreign Policy." Massachusetts Institute of Technology, 1992.

Khadduri, Walid Yusif. "The Social Background of Modern Iraqi Politics." The John Hopkins University, 1970.

Mufti, Malik. "Pan-Arabism and State Formation in Syria and Iraq: 1920-1992." Harvard University, 1993.

Musallam, Musallam. "The Iraqi Invasion of Kuwait: A Theoretical Explanation." Georgetown University, 1994.

Index

ABOUT THE AUTHOR

Mohammad-Mahmoud Mohamedou is Research Associate for the Middle East and North Africa at the Ralph Bunche Institute on the United Nations in New York In 1997, he was a Visiting Scholar at the Center for Middle Eastern Studies of Harvard University. He has published essays on Arab politics in such journals as *Civil Society*, *The Journal of Maghrebi Studies*, *Le Monde*, *Le Monde Diplomatique*, and *Défense Nationale*. A 29-year old native of Mauritania, he studied in Paris, Madrid, and New York where he earned a Master's in International Relations and a Ph.D. in Political Science at the City University of New York Graduate School. His present project is *The Rise and Demise of Democracy in the North Africa*.